Others
Like
Me

Others
Like
Me

**The Lives of Women
without Children**

Others
Like
Me

Nicole Louie

dialogue
books

DIALOGUE BOOKS

First published in Great Britain in 2024 by Dialogue Books

10 9 8 7 6 5 4 3 2 1

A CIP catalogue record for this book
is available from the British Library.

Hardback ISBN 978-1-408-74833-6

Typeset in Berling by M Rules
Printed and bound in Great Britain by
Clays Ltd, Elcograf S.p.A

Papers used by Dialogue Books are from well-managed forests
and other responsible sources.

Dialogue Books
An imprint of Dialogue
Carmelite House
50 Victoria Embankment
London EC4Y 0DZ

www.dialoguebooks.co.uk

Dialogue, part of Little, Brown Book Group Limited,
an Hachette UK company.

To all the women who told me their stories.

And to Molly, who showed me how to tell mine.

Contents

Part II: Looking at Others

Introduction

Since the 1950s, the global average fertility rate has fallen from 5 children per woman to 2.5, and is projected to fall to 2.1 in 2050.[1]

The average birth rate has dropped below 1 child per woman in South Korea and Puerto Rico.[2]

1 in 5 women in their late forties in England, Wales,[3] Germany, and the Netherlands[4] do not have children.

1 in 4 women in their late forties in Italy and Switzerland do not have children.[5]

3 in 10 women in Japan, Hong Kong, and Singapore do not have children.[6]

44 per cent of Americans surveyed, aged eighteen to forty-nine, say it is not likely they will have children someday.[7]

I'm one of them – the people without children. And I remember exactly when I decided to forgo motherhood. It wasn't a conscious decision then, but it happened all the same. I was six years old and had just been given a new doll. It was a doll with an appendage in the form of a belly – if pressed in, then pulled out, the piece would detach. One side was a full moon, the other was flat. Inside the cavity above the doll's pelvis was a tiny baby. I traded the baby for a pencil and the doll for butterfly stationery. On one of the sheets, I wrote what I wanted to be when I grew up: banjo player, pony trainer, story maker. Mother was not one of them.

Sister Betina, my seventh-grade teacher in an all-girls school in Brazil, started her class by inspecting our scrunchies, socks and shoes to ensure they were black or navy blue to match our uniforms. Once she was satisfied there were no dress-code violations, she'd instruct us to sit down and listen to the story of the day. Most of them were biblical. The school's name started with 'Madre', Betina was also known as 'Mother Superior' and not a day went by without a prayer for or a mention of 'the mother of Jesus'. Mary's story made zero sense to me, so I was the annoying kid playing detective. 'But was the Holy Spirit her husband too? And did she want to have a baby?' No satisfactory answers ever came my way.

At home, my mother would tell me I had to respect what the nuns said but didn't have to believe them – I could decide what I wanted to believe when I was older. And so, at twelve, I focused instead on imagining alternative endings for the female characters Sister Betina brought to class.

I didn't know I'd write an alternative ending for myself too one day.

Only in my mid-twenties and already married did I realise I had always thought of childlessness as a destination. I knew I wanted to go there, but I had never asked myself what would happen once I arrived. Now that the future of some-one I loved would also be shaped by my intent not to have a child, it suddenly felt urgent to understand what it would be like not just to pass through but to live in that childfree place for the rest of my life. Back then, no woman I knew had lived or wanted to live without being a mother, so I inched closer to this life without motherhood in total darkness, relying solely on my intuition. Whenever I considered increasing my pace, waves of fear, suspicion and isolation followed in quick succession. I feared what I couldn't see; I suspected the journey ahead would be miserable, and I imagined dying alone in a decrepit house without anyone noticing for days.

The bleakness of my imagined future eclipsed what I knew about myself and eroded my confidence, making me doubt I knew what was best for me. Soon, I was not advancing but regressing, wondering if I should be on that path at all. How much of what I imagined was true? And what had made me believe a life without children of my own would be a horrible one?

I thought about it and realised it was all due to having no role models to tell me otherwise. Not just in my family or circle of friends or acquaintances, but anywhere. And that's because a woman's life without children is rarely told in literature, cinema or media. When told, it is presented as a counter-example of what brings contentment to humans or is distorted into stereotypes. You know the ones: the crazy cat lady, the sorrowful barren woman, the selfish childfree woman, the overambitious career woman, the child hater, the pitiful spinster, the immature woman, the incomplete woman, the cold-hearted woman, the unnatural woman, and so on. It's no wonder that such a set of pejorative terms for childlessness repeated across various cultural channels had led my brain to present me with doomed scenarios that did nothing but cause panic and paralysis.

Other questions kept emerging from the darkness:

Are there others like me?
Where are they?
Why can't I see them?

Had I started looking at statistics then (in the late 2000s), maybe I'd have felt slightly less alone, at least quantitatively. But I suspect the feeling would not have lasted because I wanted to know the stories, the people behind those numbers. As I couldn't find them in my own life, I looked for them else-where. First, in books, magazines and movies. Then online: in blogs and social media. Until I finally found them in meetup groups, at work and on holidays; I found them on buses, trains and planes; I started getting to know them. I spoke with them on the phone, by email, in video calls; during lunch, coffee breaks, road trips and short stays. We met at my house, their house, a new country, a neutral ground. It didn't matter where or how, I had to know what they knew. And so we talked – for hours. And in those hours, I got to ask them all the questions burning in my brain:

Who are you? What does your life look like? Did you choose this, or did it happen to you? How do you spend your time? And your energy? And your money? Are you happy? Are you scared? Are you lonely? Are you preparing for the future in any way? Do you care about what people say? And what do they say? Do you feel you are treated differently by your relatives, partners, friends or colleagues? Do you regret not having kids? If yes, why? If not, why not?

The answers were varied and nuanced; the people were complex and captivating. Their backgrounds, circumstances, personalities and reasons for not having children were never the same, nor were the ways they lived their lives or derived purpose and meaning. Nothing I read, saw or heard matched what had populated my mind about the paths in life that didn't include motherhood.

If, initially, I had sought out women without children to find comfort and validation of my own experience, then, over time, it became about sharing their stories with others like me so that they too could find comfort. Later on, the conversations evolved into a sense of responsibility to share them even more broadly, outside an echo chamber. It was a question of universal nurturing. As the statistics above show, millions worldwide don't have children. Whatever their reasons, they are part of a global community that struggles to feel socially valued, treated equitably in workplaces, supported by public policy and accurately represented in media and cultural narratives,[8] causing many of them to feel invisible, misunderstood and even vilified. It was also a question of offering multiple and more positive examples of rewarding lives *outside* of parenthood, allowing younger generations to make an informed decision about whether or not they wish to become parents and enabling them to connect without stigma those who are not parents.

With this in mind and with the consent of the women who

wished their stories to be known, I listened to and recorded every word entrusted to me. When I had reflected upon the importance of these encounters and their impact on my own decision regarding motherhood, I wrote this book.

Others Like Me: The Lives of Women without Children is the story of fourteen women who don't have children. Well, fifteen. It's their story and mine. It's the story of why I had to find these women and what they taught me. Part memoir, part exploration of childlessness through candid conversations, this book showcases the many ways in which women find fulfilment and how their womanhood can manifest and bloom outside of motherhood.[9]

Aiming to offer a global perspective, I interviewed women aged between twenty-five and sixty-five from fourteen countries, different social classes, marital statuses and religious beliefs. Among them is a professor who became the first Turkish woman to climb Everest, an asexual international development professional and trumpet player from Ghana who grew up in Tokyo, a visually impaired Canadian writer who loves to travel the world, an autistic Peruvian anthropologist who fought for her right to have a tubal ligation and an Icelandic singer and actor who is passionate about folk music and theatre productions for children.

In addition to exploring different cultural backgrounds, this book portrays childlessness not as a condition but as a rich spectrum of experiences by bringing together women who have no children by choice, infertility or other impeding circumstances, as well as women still in the process of deciding whether or not they wish to become mothers. As they recount their past, present and envisioned future, the women featured here highlight values, emotions and challenges in distinct stages of their journeys.

Ten years ago, when I started collecting these stories, each of them was a panel on their own. My aim was to stitch them together to create a patchwork quilt that celebrates how diverse and gratifying a life without bearing or raising children can be. The quilt is this book that you hold in your hands.

PART I

Looking Back

2009

A War with Myself That Started in My Womb

Some cultures believe that evil spirits emerge on the winter solstice. Mine didn't – in Brazil, where I come from, there are no winters. Not really. Not counted in blizzards – but home was a long way away.

On the winter solstice of our second year living together, my husband and I were both in our flat in Lund, and I was alone on the windowsill, just inches from our bed, watching the snowfall. Eyes swollen almost shut, arms wrapped around legs and head buried into knees, I sat, my mind stuck in one endless loop, as I asked myself the same question again and again:

Do I want to become a mother?

I must have been there for a few hours because an ominous line of icicles had formed on the roof edge of the building directly opposite mine, and the sun had started making its way through the clouds, tinting the balcony gold. The cobwebs at the bottom of my second-floor window impeded my view of the amount of snow we had got this time – but a neighbour crossing the garden in slow motion while carrying a chihuahua in her arms was as good an indication as any that it had been a lot. It certainly had felt like it – my disorientation amid the whiteouts in southern Sweden and my husband's newfound wish, both revealing themselves in full force that night – *was* a lot to take in.

He wanted to become a father.

What about what *I* wanted? I kept prodding the emptiness in my womb.

To become a mother
Do I want to?
Do I?

Bit by bit, this ice-cold question ringing in my ears began to deplete my sense of self – of certainty. I started doubting what had brought me to that frozen archipelago in the first place. Whatever it was, it seemed to be melting away.

Staring at the fork in the road ahead, I couldn't help but wonder: how was it that, at twenty-six, I knew no other woman who intended to circumvent motherhood? Not a single one. How was it that, even without knowing anything about being a woman who would not become a mother, I felt scared, yet compelled, to follow that dimly lit path?

When I could no longer feel the cushion beneath me, I got up, opened our bedroom door and returned to the living room. There, I found him still sitting on the red sofa. His eyes were swollen too. He reached for my hand as I sat beside him, gazing at our pictures on the wall. We interlocked fingers.

Feeling his openness, I then rested my head on his chest.

'This caught me by surprise,' I said.

'Same here.'

'Have you been wishing for a baby for long?'

'No. Not for long.'

'I don't know if I want a child.'

He said nothing but tilted his head slightly to meet mine, so I continued.

'Right now, it feels like ...' I stopped, worrying I'd hurt him if I said it.

'Like what? I can take it, Nic,' he insisted.

'Like trying to grow a third arm.'

The sharp edges of my words shut us both into silence for a while.

'We should go to bed,' he muttered.

'We will. It's just that ...' Scrapping my last trace of energy, I tried to finish the thought. 'I need time to figure this out.'

'We have time.'

'Yes, but this could take a while ...'

'I know.'

'You don't have to stay.'

'I'm not going anywhere, *amor,*' he said, bringing me back to his chest.

There and then, I remembered why I had crossed to his side of the world: I felt the most loved I ever had held within the curve of his arms.

2007–2008

Highlands

I was at the height of my discontent at being a twenty-three-year-old who still lived with their mother when I met Erik – a charming, introverted and erudite Swedish cellist. I'd just started a postgraduate course in translation, and I wanted out of that house. The plan was to eventually move in with Gabriela, who had been my best friend since I was ten (who also lived with her mother). However, what I earned working as a freelance copywriter, plus what she earned in her first year as a child psychologist, didn't amount to what we needed to rent even the tiniest studio in Brasília, so we stayed put, if restless, at our family homes and hung out on weekends to iterate the plan for our grand escape.

The free time I had left, I spent on Orkut, the first social network to gain traction in Latin America. Despite the enormous improbability of it all, on a Sunday evening in April 2007, my online activity collided with Erik's in a community about movie soundtracks. From the open fields of a public forum, we slid into each other's DMs.

Two weeks into our ping-ponging and there was no denying how attracted I was to him – or the version of him in that small picture next to his messages: sitting on a wooden chair in what looked like a church, feet flat on the floor, knees slightly lower than his hips, the cello between his legs, resting on his chest, left fingertips pressing on the strings changing the notes, right hand holding the bow, two leather bands adorning his wrist, white long-sleeved shirt with contrasting cuffs, short and thick dark brown hair gently messed at the top ... I had clicked, maximised and stared at that picture for longer than I was ready to admit, my body always reacting the same way: I wanted to be that cello. But considering how far we were from each other, I thought it best to keep that feeling to myself.

From that point onwards, we met on MSN almost every evening. I'd sit in front of the shared computer in my step-father's home office in Brasília, Erik would sit in front of a sleek MacBook in his living room in Lund, and we'd start video calls that lasted for hours.

Three months passed before the day my mother answered the doorbell and came into my room carrying an exquisite bouquet of red roses. She handed it to me and said she'd help me find something to put the flowers in. I walked to the kitchen, placed the roses carefully in the sink, and started cutting the ends of their stems. She brought a tall, delicate vase inlaid with mother-of-pearl from her bedroom and placed it next to me. Then, seeing his name on the little card taped to the cellophane, she said:

'Erik with a K. Is he a foreigner?'

'Yes. Swedish.'

'I didn't know you were seeing someone,' she said, opening the packet of flower food and emptying its contents into the vase.

'I'm not. Unless you count the webcam.'

'So that's what's keeping you in that room.'

'That and my weekly assignments,' I said, trying to play it down.

'When am I going to meet him?'

'When are you ... Mom, I haven't met him myself! I don't know if this will ever happen.'

'Why wouldn't this happen?'

'He's in Sweden,' I replied.

'In Sweden?!'

'Yes, Mom, that's where Swedes are from.'

'I know where Swedes are from, Nicole. But what if he's lying?'

'What do you mean? Why are you angry?'

'I'm not angry. I'm worried. What if he's a weird guy living in his parents' basement and lying to you?'

'Lying to me about what? Living in Sweden?' I sped up the flower arranging.

'I don't know. This whole "meeting people on the internet" sounds strange to me.' She folded the cellophane sheet into a small rectangle and smoothed it with her fingers.

'We're just talking. He's a musician who also writes and he's proofreading poems I wrote in English. That's it. He doesn't need to come to Brazil to do that. He's just being nice.'

'Just being nice? Erik is clearly a romantic. He sent you

flowers. What's the point of all of this if he won't come?' Her hands were on her hips.

'Look, this is all very new. It could be something, or it could be nothing. I don't know yet.'

Losing my patience, I grabbed the rest of the roses and shoved them into the vase at once.

'Fine. I just want him to know that you are not alone in the world. That you have a family.'

'He knows that, Mom.'

'Once you have children, you'll understand how I feel.'

I walked back to my room with my flowers trapped in her favourite vase – a perfect metaphor for how I felt in her house. I didn't know then, but being told about all that I could not understand because I had no children would become a refrain in my life.

What I did know was that the bouquet Erik sent me on my twenty-fourth birthday made me believe that he too wished to reduce the gap between our hemispheres.

Fifteen months after the day we met online, we married in the ruins of a castle in the Scottish Highlands. Just the two of us by a lake, reciting the vows we had written the night before, blessed by the mountains of a country we had both dreamed of visiting one day.

2009

Candle Path

It was Christmas week. The traditional Swedish seven-arm candle holder and the little Santa Claus were on display by the window of our flat in Lund. A fragrant cloud of clove, nutmeg, and cinnamon wafted from our mugs of mulled wine as I pressed *Play* on the remote control.

Erik and I were watching a movie about a grief-stricken man who had to learn to care for his daughter after his wife died, and I noticed him crying. I knew which scene had hit a nerve: the one where the man consoles his little girl and realises that his bond with his child is stronger than the bond with his wife. Comforting Erik in my arms, I stayed silent. So did he. No words were needed.

There had been other signs before, subtler ones. But I had brushed them off, certain that the case was closed. We had talked about it from day one. And by day one, I mean the first time we heard each other's voices on an MSN call and talked about all the big things in life, including families – the ones we came from and the one I didn't plan to have, at least not in the traditional sense of the word. He asked me why. I told him I just didn't wish for it. That I wanted a different way of life. I then asked how he felt about parenting, and he said he had never felt strongly about it and that his previous relationship had ended, due in part to his ex-girlfriend's pressure to get married and have children. They had been together for eight years and they each wanted different things. At the time, I had interpreted this as a confirmation that he didn't want to have children either.

In the two-and-a-half years since that first call, we had spoken a lot more about parenthood, but rarely had we discussed it as a real possibility, and more as if confirming the agreement not to become parents. 'Oh, they look so tired,' we'd say after spending time with our friends with kids. 'If we had children, there's no way we'd be flying overnight to Helsinki for a Bruce Springsteen concert,' we'd say on our way to the airport. Or maybe I was the one saying it, and he was the one listening? I was no longer sure.

There was never any paper agreeing to this, but it was an agreement in my head from the start. I told him I didn't understand what was happening. Why had he gone to such lengths, literally across the world several times, to be with me when he knew I wanted no children? Did he conceal his true wish thinking I'd change my mind? Did he believe back then that he would never want a child so we'd be fine?

Life, of course, is in no way that simple. I had changed a great deal in those three years. Wouldn't it be only fair to accept that he had changed too? Maybe getting married and building a home together had sowed the seeds for new yearnings to grow. What was I to do? I couldn't ignore the fact that the person I loved the most was in pain. He sobbed when he finally disclosed that the desire to become a father, though not there when we met, had since crept into his mind and grown bigger and bigger until he no longer knew how to expurgate it. It wasn't his fault. It was nobody's fault. But realising that we now wanted such different things was devastating for both of us. He felt guilty and conflicted, and I felt forced to reconsider something I had thought was already settled.

I held him close until the movie was over. Was our marriage over too?

That was the night my mind started spiralling as I watched the snowfall from our bedroom window while he sat alone on the red sofa in our living room.

The snowfall would stop by springtime; the spiralling wouldn't.

2010

Beyond Motherhood

When we arrived in Stockholm on Mother's Day, I looked forward to seeing Joanne again.

My mother-in-law and I were two birds of a feather: she had left the United States after meeting Erik's father and lived in Sweden for forty years; she was a bookworm and an aspiring author. And so our conversations revolved around our favourite books, what we were working on and ways to keep our identities while living abroad. No matter how long the visits were, there never seemed to be enough time to talk about all we had in common.

That Sunday, she told me about her mother, who had never forgiven her for leaving the country and who now lived in a care home in New Orleans. She wished to see her again. I knew the feeling well. Together, we flicked through her many family albums – her sitting on her green polka dot armchair and me sitting on an embroidered ottoman next to her. Then it was my turn, and I turned on an iPod Touch that stored pictures from my past life in Brazil.

'What's your mother's name again?' Joanne asked.

'Yara.'

'Yara. She reminds me of Salma Hayek.'

'She does?'

'Yes. Petite, curvy, lush dark hair, big smile. I see you've got her hair, eyes and eyebrows.'

'I guess I do.'

'Most definitely. Very Salma. Is your father tall?'

'Not much, but quite a bit taller than her.'

'That's why. You have more of an elongated figure.' She swiped right across the screen. 'Tell me about this picture.'

'Let me see ... ' I said, leaning on her arm. 'This is my brother trying to blow out the candles on his birthday cake. Mom held the back of the chair to be sure it wouldn't tumble.'

'Such a sweet face.'

'He was adorable, yes. Next is the only picture I have of my parents together. Mom said I was less than a year old when my grandfather took this picture.'

'They look quite happy there, don't they?'

'They do. Though I haven't heard happy stories about that time. What else is there?' I asked.

'This! Look at those flowers! And her hat. I looove the hat!'

'Right? That's a special one: Mom celebrating her graduation in the Hydrangeas Path.'

'The Hydrangeas Path?'

'Yeah, it's one of the most beautiful roads in Brazil. It connects several cities in the south of the country, so when you drive through them, you see large patches of purple, white and blue hydrangeas. It's one of my mother's favourite places on earth.'

'I'd love to go there, but it's too far away for old me. I'd also love to meet your mom.'

'That would be lovely, but I don't know if she will ever come.' I stared down at the black and red Persian rug. She ran her fingers through my hair.

'I don't see pictures of you when you were little.'

'There aren't many. Dad has some, but Mom doesn't, so I scanned what I could find.'

'Do you know why?'

'She was always working. I don't think she had time to think about photos.' My voice cracked.

'Are you okay?' Joanne asked, putting her head on my right shoulder.

'Yeah. Sorry, I haven't seen these pictures in a long time. I wasn't prepared for their effect on me. The thing about my mother is ...' I started rambling about how she had put on a smile even when things were precarious for us after my parents got divorced but I could always see anguish and exhaustion under the veneer, how I loved her, missed her and was grateful for everything she had done for me, and how I wished I'd be able to pay it all back somehow.

When I finished my ode, Joanne held my hand, and with the softest voice, she said, 'This is what mothers do, dear. You don't have to pay her back.' It took me a minute to process her words. To understand what they meant. First, I watched my tears fall into the peppermint tea she'd poured me earlier. Then came the pain in my chest, and I couldn't breathe.

What was I feeling this time? I knew it was fear, but which kind? Fear of never seeing my mother again? Fear of seeing her again and realising she was still unhappy? Fear of being the reason my mother was not happy? Fear of becoming a mother? Fear of losing Erik if I didn't? Fear of losing myself if I did?

Yes. Yes. Yes. To all of these questions. But who to talk to about them? There are boundaries, even for love. And while I loved Joanne and we confided in each other, talking to her about the conflicting feelings between her son and me didn't seem right.

Who then? There was nobody.

In lieu of people, I looked for books. Every other day, I'd bike to the Lund library and head to the quiet booth with a view of a pond filled with green-headed ducks, where I'd read my emails and manage the workload sent by clients. Once I was done translating the text of websites, apps and marketing campaigns from English into Portuguese, I'd choose a new spot with a different view. Sometimes, it would be the children's books section, where I'd attempt to learn Swedish by reading *Pippi Longstocking* or *The Wonderful Adventure of Nils*. Other times, it would be the international news section, where I'd keep in touch with what was happening in Brazil. Then, I'd reserve the last hour before closing time for my newfound mission: discovering books about childlessness.

Watching the senior librarian go out of her way to help people, I thought I'd try my luck and ask her if she knew any books about women without children. She asked if I meant books about infertility. I clarified that I meant books about women who chose not to have children. Ten minutes later, she returned to the front desk with a book.

Beyond Motherhood: Choosing a Life Without Children was the first book I ever read on motherhood ambivalence. In it,

Jeanne Safer advises the reader: 'Reflect on your childhood. Would you be a good mother? Which maternal qualities do you have? Which ones do you lack, and how important are they? How much of your past do you think you'd have to overcome to become a good mother, and are you ready for this confrontation? The time to look deeply into these questions is before getting pregnant.'

So I did.

1988–1993

Colourful Cocoon

Everything about my childhood was incomplete.

What I remember the most is how unfinished my bedroom was. How intruded-upon it felt. It had no door. To its right was a kitchen, often occupied by people I didn't know. To its left, a small bathroom with a white ceramic toilet and a marble sink, but no soap or toilet paper holder. There was also a pipe protruding from the tiled walls, but no showerhead. The window had cracks; the floor, cockroaches; and the air was thick with mosquitoes training to become vampires. It was a bedroom with no bed, so I'd swing myself to sleep in a rainbow-striped hammock with my toes tangled up in its crochet fringe – my mouldy, low-hanging, colourful cocoon.

A few months earlier, Yara had decided to leave São Paulo – the most populous, cosmopolitan and wealthy of Brazilian cities – and return to her hometown, Fortaleza, taking only a couple of boxes and my five-year-old self with her, which is how we ended up in this house that I was yet to recognise as mine.

With the divorce finalised, my father, Afonso, moved to a city called Natal. 'Natal' means Christmas, but I never got to spend Christmas there. While Fortaleza and Natal are much smaller than São Paulo, in 1988, they still had more than two million and close to half a million inhabitants, respectively – a lot of people fighting for opportunities in a time that is known as the 'Lost Decade' thanks to the stagnation, hyperinflation and socio-economic crisis. Although both cities sit under the equator and on the north-east coast of Brazil, my country is so vast that they are still a few hundred miles apart. My parents could afford one plane ticket a year, so I'd only see Dad during the school recess in July.

Racing to conquer the tallest dune in Ponta Negra beach, resting and drinking coconut water under palm trees, buying barbecued fish from the straw kiosks and riding our bikes along the waterfront looking for ice cream, these month-long visits quickly became the highlights of my early years. The moment I anticipated most of all was the morning of my birthday, at the end of the month, when Simone, my father's new wife, would hand me a card with a rhyme she had written for me, and they would take me to the children's toys section of the biggest department store in town so that I could choose a birthday gift.

Year after year, no matter what the shop had on display, I'd always pick a doll. Never too big or expensive – the notion of financial boundaries was firmly inbuilt in me; I don't even know how or by whom. But it was always there, and I'd run up and down the aisles, scanning the price tags until I found the perfect affordable addition to my family of dolls.

By the time I was nine, that collection comprised six ladies: one that could clap, one that could crawl, one that would giggle cutely if I pressed her belly, one that would laugh creepily if I touched her lips, one that would pee if I gave her a bottle and a ragged one with bright yellow braided hair. She did nothing. She was my favourite.

But that was the end of that tradition. On my tenth birthday, I asked for a small, round watch with a thin brown leather band instead. I also wanted to watch a movie on the big screen. My wishes were granted. I got my pretty watch and I was taken to the movies. I happily shared a bag of jelly beans with my father, my stepmother, her daughter, Beatriz, and her five nieces and nephews as we watched *Jurassic Park*. It was a special day. With them, most days were.

An accomplished secondary school teacher, kids' party planner and mother of a girl almost my age, Simone was heaven-sent and even looked like it. Her long golden locks, serene amber eyes and ever-tanned skin gave her a mono-chromatic quality: a radiant appearance that was impossible to miss. She had grown up in a stunning mansion in the Portuguese colonial style smack in the middle of half an acre of land, which the government had awarded her father, a prominent general during the two-decades-long military dictatorship in Brazil. There, he lived with his wife and seven children. Then the children had children, and the house became the main venue for their many family gatherings.

It was in this lively, dream-like place that I got to spend my vacations, and I cherished every second there. I'd wake up around 7 a.m. with the sound of Chico, the family's hyper-active parrot, shouting 'You're late again!' at Rita as she closed the main gate. Then I would go downstairs to meet her. Rita was their maid for fifteen years. She was in her early forties, always wore her hair in a simple bun with a headscarf to keep it in place, and had four children, who were raised mainly by her mother so that she could work. On Saturdays (she only had Sundays off), she would bring in her two youngest children to allow her mother some rest. Rita's relentless pace reminded me of my mother's, so I'd play with her children, hoping she would get some rest. When they were not around, she would send me to the backyard to pick mangoes, and I'd help her blend the fruits and fill the jars with fresh juice for breakfast. Then we'd set the large table in the dining room but would eat corn pudding or tapioca crêpes sitting on stools in the kitchen. Rita didn't talk much, so our early mornings together were mostly spent in silence – a comfortable and intimate silence I grew to appreciate.

Waiting for the rest of the house to wake up, I'd feed sugar water to the hummingbirds on the patio or try to save the *calangos* from Tantor, the doofus Rottweiler who didn't notice the burglars when the house was broken into, but who wouldn't cut any slack for the lizards that claimed the garden as their habitat. I'd soon hear Simone's voice calling me and we'd head out to the beach, or I'd help her decorate the cake tables for children's parties.

If, for the most part, this was my Neverland, it also re-minded me of how different everything was back home in Fortaleza. The other children in Simone's life had bedrooms filled with comic books, video games, Disney-character bedding and green alien ceiling stickers that would glow in the dark. Meanwhile, I had a hammock strung across a bedroom that would get flooded when it rained and a three-drawer chest for all my clothes and toys. They had brand-new shoes and shiny hair while I walked around in mismatched flip-flops and had to soak my hair in vinegar and get it chopped to my chin to stop the lice from eating my scalp.

There was no money for a doll's house in my kingdom, so Barbie lived in the barn with the pony. There was no money for a Ken, so Barbie dated the pony. They never had children.

1994

Tiny Cuts

Once, after I returned from Natal, there was only one egg on the table to be shared between us. My mother didn't eat her half. She gave it to me. More than once, she had to beg the Mother Superior not to expel me from school for lack of payments. Wearing a khaki blazer with her black hair fixed half-up, she'd walk into Sister Betina's office:

'My daughter is an excellent student.'

'Yes, she is.'

'I need her to continue studying.'

'I understand.'

'I just need more time. I can pay a couple of months now and the rest soon.'

By handing over a crumpled envelope with however much money she had gathered up to that point and signing papers committing to pay the remaining debt in instalments with interest, she'd secure my seat in a classroom for another semester.

The money my father sent helped, but it wasn't enough to cover the bills. So Yara raised me single-handedly by waxing women in beauty salons, frying pastries to sell in bars and taking on contracts to cook at political conferences. I helped on weekends. Our days would start at 5 a.m. by buying ingredients in the outdoor markets and would end late in the evenings in a mint green Volkswagen Bus, with our clothes smelling like fried garlic and our hands full of tiny cuts from peeling and chopping kilos of potatoes, onions and cabbage. From an early age, I was painfully aware of how hard her life was – and how much harder mine *wasn't* because of her. I idolised her but also felt overwhelmingly indebted to her for the sacrifices she made for me. At that time, I thought the best way to express gratitude was to be quiet, mostly silent, almost invisible.

As we walked down the unpaved street that separated our house from the neighbourhood's well, Lia, my mother's closest friend, remarked, as if I wasn't there: 'Your girl looks sadder than usual.' To which my mother replied, 'That's just the way she is,' without turning back to look at me. If I looked sad before, I certainly looked sadder after that.

Another time, upon entering the political-party dining hall with a big tray of lasagne, Mom found me sitting at one of the tables filled with politicians and observed them laughing at a story I had just told. I wanted to help keep them entertained as she had to deal with an empty cooking-gas cylinder that had delayed the serving of the lunch meals. Upon seeing her approach his table, a very tall and slender man exclaimed, 'That's a funny kid you have there, Yara!' Her response was, 'I had no idea she had a sense of humour.' They laughed even more. She looked at me. I wasn't laughing. Until that moment, I too had no idea that, driven by my desire not to become a burden to her, I had become a shadow. No distinctive traits, no depth. Only a silhouette under the same roof.

The very tall and slender man became her second husband. His name was Tácio, and Tácio was a renowned judge and recently elected senator. As a senator, he lived in the country's capital and regularly travelled to his home state. That meant Mom and I had to relocate to Brasília, where we drove around in a car that smelled like air freshener and moved into a four-bedroom flat in the north 'wing' of the city designed like an aeroplane. I was elated by everything this new city offered. Brasília was modern, green, safe and clean, starkly contrasting the vibrant but poverty-stricken Fortaleza and the picturesque but exceedingly touristy Natal.

With a lot of space came a lot of company and a home that felt even less like mine. Suddenly, we had a maid, a driver and a cook; two fluffy white poodles; an open-door policy; and a landline that wouldn't stop ringing. I was not used to having company except for when I was in Natal, so I'd sneak into Tácio's office, grab one of his books about slavery, labour unions, land reform or human rights, and insulate myself from the crowds and chaos behind those pages in the safety of my new bedroom that had curtains and a door – lock and all.

It was about that time that I noticed I could hear my thoughts when I opened a book. A revelation and relief in equal measure. A soothing ritual to which I kept returning. From his side of the home library, I moved to the shelf where Yara had started stacking books with names such as Cleopatra, Hypatia, Joan of Arc, Elizabeth I, Maria I of Portugal and Isabel, Princess Imperial of Brazil, on their covers. I was too young to know then, but I realised decades later that my mother mostly read historical fiction and biographies about some of the most powerful women in the world. Many of whom never had children.

I didn't always understand what I was reading, but I read it anyway. The books became dog-eared as time passed, and I started dragging pen on paper to muffle the human sounds inside and the cricket sounds outside. Still, reading and writing only comforted me up to a point. The loneliness I felt diminished only when I met Gabriela. We were both in the fourth grade at a private Catholic all-girls school. One day, a girl with a light-brown ponytail and freckles on her cheeks sat next to me.

That was just the beginning. Gabriela wanted to know where I was born, how long since I had moved to Brasília, what it was like to live close to the beach ... I didn't mind her curiosity. On the contrary, I liked it when people asked me things. It made me think of Simone. I answered Gabriela's questions as we swapped lunchboxes: mine had a pack of chocolate wafers and a small plastic bottle of Fanta. Gabriela's had orange juice and the cheese puffs her mother sold in their bakery. Her food didn't get as stuck in my braces, so she let me have it. Every day. We decided we should spend more time together after school. And boy, did we! We went biking and rollerblading. Then we had sleepovers over and over. Soon we were sharing fruit-shaped lip balm, wearing matching fake tattoos and swapping mix tapes. We spent hours watching MTV, imitating Mariah Carey and Gwen Stefani. Gabriela

was the perfect Robin to my gloomy Batman, and my pre-
teenage years were ten times more fun because of her.

At school, Gabi and I spent our mornings learning to 'share
faith, serve others, study wisdom, worship together' and at no
time were we taught any sex education. At home, we shared
the space with overworked mothers who didn't know how
to talk to us about our prepubescent bodies. Back in 1994,
eleven-year-old girls didn't have access to the internet, so the
day I got hold of a hand mirror and looked at my vagina, I ran
to my mother's bedroom to tell her about a brown piece of
wobbly skin growing down there. She checked between my
legs, told me everything was fine, and asked me to stop looking at it. I called Gabriela and asked her if she had a brown
piece of wobbly skin growing down there too.

'So weird,' I said, holding the telephone with my chin and
the hand mirror between my legs.

'And gross . . . '

'You think it's gross?'

'I'll call you back,' she said abruptly. The phone rang again
after a few minutes.

'Labia minora,' she said.

'Come again?'

'The wobbly skin. I found a drawing with a bunch of
stuff in the encyclopedia. There's a part that says: "The labia
minora are two small folds of skin that extend on each side
of the opening into the vagina." The next page shows a baby
upside down inside the woman's belly.'

'Why would it be upside down?' I asked.

'No clue. It says: "The cerrr-vix is the lower part of the
uterus that opens into the vagina. During childbirth, it

expands so the baby can travel through the vagina and into the world."'

'So the baby comes out of the pee hole?'

'Maybe?'

'But that's such a tiny hole. How does the baby come out? That makes no sense!'

'My aunt said women get pregnant by swallowing water-melon seeds. I know she was lying, but I don't know how babies are made or how they come out without the women dying.'

Then she joked that she'd eat lots of watermelon seeds to have a baby one day. I didn't know how to react. Imagining myself eating watermelon seeds made me afraid of choking to death. And, up to that moment, I had never thought about what would happen if my best friend had a baby and I didn't. Would we still be best friends? I made her promise that there would be no babies until we stuck to our plan: to grow up, move in together and go to a non-nun university. She agreed. And that was that. No more baby talk for a while.

That was until Mom announced I was going to have a little brother.

1997

Glass Bones

A sudden scream coming from our new house in suburbia propelled me out of the garden and back inside. I found Davi lying flat in his crib. I called Mom, and we took him to the doctor. 'His foot is broken,' the doctor said. That meant my two-year-old half-brother would have to be immobilised in a plaster cast for weeks and use corrective boots for even longer. Months later, we heard a similarly distressed groaning after he fell from a swing. His kneecap was broken. 'Osteogenesis imperfecta,' the doctor said. A genetic disorder that affects the bones causing them to break easily, often from mild trauma. Davi's was type I – the least severe of many. Still, I heard Mom sob as she shared the news with Tácio on the phone.

Eleven years older than Davi, I spent much time and energy weaving a protective net around him. I picked him up from daycare, took him to swimming classes and physiotherapy, helped him deliver a Valentine's Day card he made for a girl in his class when he was five; I was called by his teacher when he failed a maths test at six, and when he hit back at a bully and got suspended at seven. I was also called when he went missing for hours, only to be found playing *Mortal Kombat* at an arcade near our house. I felt like I was his mother, except that I wasn't. I wanted to be mothered myself, not just provided for, but my mother was busy mothering her husband, and I was busy mothering her son.

I think my brother wanted to be mothered by his mother too, because the once well-behaved Davi became notoriously troublesome from his seventh birthday onwards. The problem was that our mother didn't know how to raise someone who demanded attention. There didn't seem to be much attention left in her to give. Now that her children lived comfortably and had access to premium education and health care, she focused on Tácio. She was his right hand inside and outside of the National Congress. It was all her, from deciding who would be his chief of staff to editing his speeches to choosing the decor for his office and the colour of his tie. She became his devoted sidekick, and together they would build an empire that would rise and fall over the next thirty years. As their babysitter, I was one of the many who helped this empire run.

Two days before picking me up at the airport, Dad called to say that we would stay in a studio flat this time. I asked why, and he mumbled something about an argument with Simone. 'Why don't you just talk to her and say sorry?' I said (not knowing what had happened and assuming it was his fault). He said it was more complicated than that but didn't care to elaborate, reinforcing my assumption. Before I got on the plane, I tried to shake off the suspicion: *It's July. July means I'm going to see Dad, Simone and Rita again. It is going to be fun, as it always has been.*

When I landed in Natal, I still hoped she would be at arrivals, but she wasn't, and I felt a pang of something. Dad hugged me, took the handle of the heavy bag I'd brought, and started walking me to his old orange Beetle. He loved that car. I liked it, but to me, it was just a car. He named it Jerimum, which is the word for pumpkin in the north of Brazil. He had bought Jerimum two years earlier at a scrapyard and had spent the little spare money he had changing its parts. The latest upgrade had happened the year before when he installed a horn that sounded like an annoyed goat telling people to get out of the way – hearing it had always made me laugh, but not that day. I smiled instead when he pressed it for no reason other than to cheer me up. I didn't want him to think I wasn't happy to be with him after a year apart.

On the contrary, I was happy. I just didn't know what to do with the lack of Simone in that car. I didn't know how to act in the front passenger seat. She was always sitting there; I was always in the back with Beatriz. That's where I belonged. That's where I knew how to be. How to be me. How to be happy. Not just a bit, but very. Something felt irrevocably broken.

There were no goodbyes – he didn't think it was a good idea for me to visit or call Simone then, which was a big enough hint that their break-up wasn't friendly – and just like that, in what felt like a very sudden, sharp turn, life's paths disentangled, and I lost one of the most influential presences in my formative years, her extended family and Rita, all at once.

With a million unanswered questions in my head, I was left to mourn their absence the only way I knew: by bottling it all up.

With my second family out of the picture, I had to find ways to entertain myself all day, every day, for four weeks while Dad worked as a car salesman in the neighbouring area. The flat he had moved to was small, damp and mostly empty. And so I begged him not to leave me alone there. Instead, I turned fourteen, alone in a shopping centre, watching a movie I can't remember the name of or the plot, killing time by window shopping, and eating at McDonald's.

Later that day, I met Dad at his workplace. Upon picking me up at the reception, he gave me a big bear hug, asked about my day, and walked me to what he claimed to be the most expensive car model in the shop. We took our seats in the BMW: he was the driver, I was the passenger, we went nowhere. He explained each thing in the panel, showcased the embedded six-disc CD player, demonstrated the automatic gearbox, taught me how to change gears and talked about the engine. Something about horses. Hundreds of horses.

I tried to understand his words, but my mind wandered off: *Did he know what to do with me? The daughter he had seen only once a year for almost a decade. Did he wish he had a son? Did he wish he had no kids at all?*

I forced myself to listen – not to what he was saying, but to his voice. It felt good to have someone talking to me. Not around me or about me. *To* me. I missed Simone terribly and I wished my parents talked to me like she did.

2000

New Ground

In late October, I learned that I had passed the entrance exam to study advertising and the classes would start in February 2001. Mom and Tácio seemed pleased with the news and invited me for dinner, saying we should celebrate my university attendance. We had just arrived at their favourite steakhouse in Brasília when a couple approached our table – a congressman I recognised from one of the dinners hosted at our house and a woman at least twenty years his junior whom I had never seen before. I looked confused as they took their seats. I thought this was going to be a family dinner, but no – no such thing.

The topics of conversation were the same as always: the current state of the government, the next elections and party alliances, upcoming bills the Parliament and Senate were voting on, how hard it was to find qualified people to work as press secretaries, why the sirloin cap was overcooked, when the chicken heart was coming, what our plans for the holidays were, what the children were up to these days. The 'children' – that must be me.

'Well, Nicole just got accepted at the University of Brasília,' said Mom, sitting on my right.

'So exciting! Tell me, what are you going to study?' the woman inquired with a tone that made me feel like a toddler.

'Advertising,' I said.

'Advertising. That's handy. You can help your *father* with his campaigns,' said the congressman across the table, eating the olives from his dry Martini.

Feeling like I had been put on the spot, as political marketing wasn't what I intended to do, I tried to sound casual: 'I want to be a copywriter and write ads, slogans and scripts.' Tácio nodded from the head of the table as he forked a piece of grilled sausage. I nodded back.

'We see these ads but don't realise how much work goes into them. I always think about that when I go to New York and see all those billboards,' said the woman, sipping her margarita.

'True. It's everywhere. Billboards, in print, online, on the radio ... ' I said.

'Capitalism, young one. Capitalism,' said the congressman. The woman rolled her eyes.

'And then what? Move to the US? I'd think they have the best advertising agencies, no? What I wouldn't give to live there. We have been there a few times, haven't we, Carlos?'

'Yes,' said Carlos, the congressman, gesturing to the waiter that he wanted another round. The woman he never bothered to introduce was annoying, but she was listening, so I continued.

'No, not the US. My best friend also got in. She'll study psychology, and we're considering doing a student exchange in London for a semester or a year. We'll see.'

'Uh oh. It's looking like you are going to lose your little girl, Mom and Dad,' poked Carlos.

Tácio's uninterrupted chewing indicated he was unbothered by my plans, but Mom's face had mutated from a proud smile to a sinister grin. Grabbing her caipirinha, she said: 'No. We won't lose our little girl, Carlos. Before Nicole decides what she will do with her life, she has to be able to pay for her expenses. Things like housing, utility bills, food and toilet paper. As long as she is in my house, and I'm the one paying the bills she will stay in her country and help her *father*. She will archive his speeches, photograph him at events and help create the website for his next campaign. It will be good not to have to pay someone to do these things anymore.'

I was astounded. I looked at Tácio, hoping he'd say something. But his eyes went back and forth between his plate and the window on the far side of the restaurant. The congressman looked triumphant, and his nameless companion looked embarrassed. Placing the caipirinha back on the table, Mom looked me directly in the eyes as if saying *Do you understand?* I did. I had to get out of her house. There was just no future for me there. I mean, there was: the future she had designed for me – which I'd make sure would never come to pass.

By the end of that year, what used to be overwhelming gratitude towards my mother morphed into a complex set of negative emotions that felt increasingly alarming. It had become so hard not to resent her for the undivided attention she expected me to keep giving to her husband and her son that I split all my time between Gabriela's house and being locked in my room, carefully listening to the surrounding sounds and using the service door to go in and out without being seen.

Sometimes, she would come to my room to say that the maid had made one of my favourite dishes or to offer to drop me at school as if she'd forgotten what she'd said in the restaurant and how humiliating that whole speech of hers had been. Upon hearing my 'I'll eat it later' or 'No, thanks', she would look hurt, as if not understanding why I was being indifferent when she was being so nice. Then she would walk away, saying, 'You, my daughter, are weird. I worry about you and your heavy heart.'

In those moments, I hated her. I hated her as much as I had loved her all those years – seventeen years of sharing the space, the food, the toilet paper and the things that lacked or existed in excess in the houses where we had lived. In those moments, I cried in bed or in the shower, feeling that all-consuming hate erase all of my good memories with her. Then, I'd ignore her even more, ashamed for having hated her. Even if only for a millisecond.

My mood started fluctuating so violently between needing isolation from her and feeling guilty for having stopped trying to make our relationship work that I wondered if I had bipolar disorder. Concerned that my repressed feelings would manifest in explosive ways, I packed for my next visit to Dad, knowing that I wouldn't use the return ticket.

Leaving my mother's house was harrowing but the right thing to do. I held on to the hope that the distance would stop our bond from eroding. I also held on to the prospect of getting to know the paternal side of my family better. Unimaginable then was a life without Gabriela. My first real friend. My bunk-bed buddy. My English skills mentor. My hair stylist. The person who had heard more words from my mouth than all my relatives combined. The only one who had read the journals hidden under my mattress. Not knowing what else to do, I wrote a long letter telling her that I loved her beyond Brasília's coral skies and promised to always write to her, no matter where I ended up or who I met next. Then I cycled to her house as fast as my asthma would allow me to say goodbye.

2001

Little Chimp

It took me two weeks from the day Dad picked me up at the airport to gather the courage to ask if I could move in with him. In his mid-forties and twice divorced, he had returned to São Paulo to be closer to his parents, who offered him his old room.

He wasn't pleased to be living there. He wasn't pleased that I wanted to live there – even if both arrangements were temporary. But he didn't say no. He only asked, 'But why now?'

'Because the best advertising universities and agencies are here,' I said, trying to make the story I had spun about my reasons for moving stick.

'I hear you, but there's barely any space here. Also, your grandfather is very old-school.'

'I don't mind any of that, Dad. I'll keep to myself. And I can find a job to help with expenses.'

'No. You focus on your studies. I'll talk to him, but I can't promise anything.'

We both heaved a sigh of relief when my grandparents later accepted me as the fourth occupant of their modest residence and welcomed me to stay until I graduated.

Grandma Beth tasked me with cleaning my newly assigned bedroom and my father's bedroom every week, and I took the chance to go through his things. The wardrobe, the drawers, the boxes . . . I knew I shouldn't, but I couldn't think of a better way to learn about him. It didn't take me long to discover that he loved Sade Adu, wished to learn French, knew how to draw maps, bought far too many bottles of eye drops, carried nail clippers in the front pocket of his trousers and collected magazines about cars, travelling and naked women. When alone, I'd lie in his bed to read the 'Hottest destinations of the summer' and compare my skinny body to the body of the 'VIP girl of the month'. When together, we'd reminisce about our time in Natal and bond over watching Formula One.

In one of the first telephone calls with my mother after moving out of her house, she mentioned she was considering sending Davi to live with me. She reasoned that he listened to me and that it would be good for us to reunite. By us, she meant Davi and me.

After the initial shock, I managed to say: 'I don't think so, Mom.'

'Why not?'

'There is no space here.'

'I can send money and help your dad move out of there.'

'I don't know if he wants to move out of here.'

'Of course he does. Why wouldn't he?'

'Maybe he does, but not this way.'

'Don't be ridiculous.'

'Mom, this doesn't feel right.'

'He is your brother!'

'Yes. But he's not his son!'

It was true. My half-brother was not my father's son, and I didn't think it made sense for my father to become responsible for his ex-wife's child with another man. But what I wanted to say was, 'Yes. But he's not *my* son.' Still, I never did. I had caused her enough pain by leaving.

While saying no to her meant standing my ground, it also meant leaving my brother behind. To this day, I don't know how he felt. Did he realise at once or over time that I had left? Did he feel abandoned or think it was normal that I went to live with my father? I didn't dare ask, but I soon noticed that he suffered more fractures and became more unruly. I'd blame myself for almost everything bad that happened to him from that day onwards.

No later than midday, Grandpa would join us at the kitchen table for lunch, finish eating without saying a word, and walk towards his dark brown leather reclining chair in the living room. From there, he'd shout, 'Woman, coffee!' and Grandma would go, 'Yeah, yeah, Mauro. It's coming.'

This scene repeated daily like a long-running play, with only me as an audience. Occasionally, I'd get on stage to say my short line, 'It's okay, Grandma. I'll do it. You finish your food.' Seeing first hand what she had to put up with from her husband stirred many negative feelings in me. My first instinct was to spare her. The second was to defy him. So whenever I brought him coffee, I acted as if it was the last thing I wanted to be doing.

'It needs more sugar.'

'Go get it. You have legs.'

'Woman, sugar!' he'd shout in her direction through the wall.

'In a minute!' she'd shout back.

'I'll take care of it, Grandma,' I'd say, walking back to the kitchen. But I'd drag my heels.

More often than not, Grandma would let us spar, intervening only when she felt our exchanges were getting out of hand. 'He has a pacemaker. He's fragile,' she would say, even though he was the one shouting at us for no reason.

She was right to be concerned, as things often escalated. During a heated argument that started when I told him to stop whistling to call Grandma as she was not his pet, he raised his right arm well above his head and lowered it full force in my direction, only to lose his balance and fall over a twisted leg. Expecting me to help, he looked up at me from the floor, but all I could see was his arm, ready to strike me a second before. I turned my back and left the room. In my father's man cave, I cried. A cocktail of anger and fear mixed with regret as I heard him call Grandma, who rushed from the laundry area to check what he needed this time.

Standing on the other side of the closed door, next to their bedroom, I heard him shuffle his feet and grunt slightly as they talked:

'What happened?'

'I lost my balance and fell.'

'Just like that? Are you getting old, Mauro? Why didn't you call Nicole to help you up?'

'I didn't want to bother her.'

'You silly man. You fell. She's right there. Or is it that you wanted *me* to pick you up, *huh*?' she continued in a high pitch, trying to cheer him up while checking whether his leg was badly hurt.

I wasn't sure if he didn't tell her what happened because he worried she would know he tried to hit me or because he didn't want to get me into trouble. Despite his seemingly impenetrable ways, he could sense that the one I was terrified of upsetting was Grandma, not him. Because I respected her. I knew I had pushed all his buttons that day, and I wish I hadn't done that. I also wished he hadn't done what he did. But there was no turning back. Projection on my part or not, I could swear I had heard regret in his voice.

The next day, as soon as he woke up, I asked, 'Can I get you something to eat?'

'No.'

'How about some coffee?'

'No need. I'll get up soon.'

I didn't move. After a while, he reached for my hand and squeezed it. Two words escaped his mouth, 'Macaca Chita' – the nickname he gave me when I was little, and my parents lived next door. The legend goes that because I was his first granddaughter, Grandpa was incredibly affectionate and named me his little chimp after watching me crawl up to his lap. Having accepted my new name, I used to shout, 'Macaaaco Chiiito!' at the wall that separated our houses until someone took me to him. That scene too would repeat daily until just before I turned five years old and my parents divorced.

I don't recall any of that, but Grandma had shown me some pictures that proved it to be true. And I felt in my heart that it was. I loved him. I just couldn't remember why.

2002

Silent Pact

He was a glassmaker; she was a seamstress. When they got married, he forbade her to work but continued working himself even after cutting parts of his fingers off making windows. Money was always short, so three children in, she expressed concerns that a fourth one would be the end of them, to which he replied, 'We will have as many children as God wants us to.' The next time he tried to find his way into her body, she had stuffed it with pieces of fabric to stop his semen from reaching her womb. Grandma would tell me this and other such stories while we bonded over rolling her husband and son's socks into perfect balls. Things weren't that different from my previous house, after all.

'Did you dream of becoming a mother?' I asked as I followed her to the 'messy room' at the back of the house, filled with fabric rolls, sewing machines and colourful threads.

'Dream? I don't think I dreamed of becoming a mother. But that's what women did back then. We were trained to get married and to run a house. The men paid for it. The babies came in the package; that was it,' she said, pulling a pin from a square piece of cotton and placing it in the pincushion.

'But did you want to get married?'

'I wanted to make clothes. I was very good at it.'

'How did you learn to make them?' I asked, opening the ironing board.

'We were very poor, so I only studied until the fifth grade. After that, I had to help my parents make money. Your great-grandma taught me to sew when I was thirteen, and I started hemming trousers and fixing broken zips for some change. At sixteen, I made all my clothes and my parents and siblings' clothes too. Then I got a job in a boutique making clothes for rich people. The owner took a liking to me. She'd bring me fancy magazines and I'd copy the designs. She told me I had the gift of making dresses come true, wedding dresses especially. I loved making them! Many important women got married in dresses I made.'

'Really? How many did you make?' I said, reaching for another shirt in the ironing pile.

'Dozens. The last one was my own.' She stopped pressing the foot pedal for a second, raised the needle on the Overlock, and took a deep breath. Then she rubbed her green eyes behind her old glasses, looked at me and said, 'I have a picture of it. Do you want to see it?'

'Yes!'

She told me to get the '1950s' album from her wardrobe. There were more on the top shelf. All labelled by decade. I brought it to her. She flipped through a few pages and said, 'There it is.' My mouth hung open at the sight of her. At twenty-one, she was a double for Ingrid Bergman. Her hair had been grey and fixed up with bobby pins for as long as I could remember. I had no idea she used to be blonde. And those waves! I had always wondered where my wavy hair came from. And the dress: the endless amount of ivory tulle on the skirt, the lace sleeves bejewelled with pearl beads, the matching tiara and the elbow-length veil.

'My goodness, you look like a princess! You made all of that?'

'My boss gave me the materials as a wedding gift, but I made every inch of that dress. Now I'm here making napkins and bedsheets,' she said, her voice trailing off.

I put my arms around her. 'That is a perfect wedding dress, and so are your napkins and bedsheets, Beth Louie. You should be proud of yourself.' She kissed my cheek.

On Easter Day, while making fish pie, I asked what it was like to have children. She told me that with my dad, she felt she was being cleaved in half. The midwife wanted to use forceps, but she refused, and Dad eventually came out intact. She was mad at her mother for not telling her the first thing about giving birth and made her promise she would move in for the last month of her next pregnancy. With her second baby, a girl, she constantly felt like she had to poop. Her labour was mainly in the bathroom, with her mother kneeling next to her. Her third child, another girl, was born as she made the dough for a carrot cake. She barely felt a thing and only had time to squat and catch the baby between her legs.

'It's different every time and for everyone,' she said with her head inside the fridge.

'Do you know how it was for my mother?'

'Yes. Much worse. But we don't need to talk about that.'

'Why not?' I raised my eyes from the half-opened tuna can.

'Because you are not pregnant.' She cracked two eggs into the blender.

'Why do I have to be already pregnant to know more about giving birth? What if I don't want to go through it?'

'Nobody wants to go through it. Still, we do. Children are the glue of a marriage.'

'What if I also don't want to get married?'

'Then you don't need to know more about giving birth, do you?' She turned the blender on.

'Jesus Christ, Grandma!' I roared, 'Your mother told you nothing, my mother told me nothing, you don't want to tell me more; what's with the silent pact?'

'It's not my story to tell.' She put the pie in the oven.

'I get that. But it's also my story; I was born that day, wasn't I?'

'Let's sit down,' she said, taking her apron off and walking to a chair. 'Are you sure you want to hear this?' I nodded. Then she started speaking with a heaviness that wasn't usually there. 'Your mother's pregnancy was high-risk. Doctors didn't explain things to women then. They'd talk to your dad alone and say she had to rest. When she went into labour, it lasted for over a day. We took her to hospital twice, and twice they sent us back, saying she hadn't dilated enough. The hospital was full. No space to wait there. The third time we went over, there was little time left to get you out, so . . . ' she paused. 'They cut her. A big cut from where you poop to where you pee. No anaesthetics.' I covered my mouth with my hand. 'It was so deep that you were born with a cut on your hand.' I looked at the scar on my thumb.

She continued for a while: my mother developed sepsis and had to stay in hospital. When they visited her, they found her on a makeshift bed in the corridor, wearing only a hospital gown and shivering. They noticed bruises on her legs and tried to file a formal complaint against the hospital, only to be told that it was a hospital, not a hotel. One of the nurses told them she was horrified by how women were being treated there and that she wanted to help. They forced the hospital to discharge Mom. Grandma cared for her at home, and the nurse visited daily until she recovered.

My face had turned fiery red. My eyes were puffy. Grandma reached for my hand, caressed it, and continued, 'Your mother was nineteen, Nicole. That's you in three months. She fought for her life for weeks, and you had to learn very early on to survive without your mother as she could not nurse you. You were so small, almost premature. Your dad had to work during the day, so you stayed with us. I'd look after your mom, and Grandpa would look after you.'

A whistle came from the living room, followed by, 'Beth, you are going to scare the girl.'

I called my mother that night just to hear her voice.

2003–2005

The Female Eunuch

If Grandma saw me reading a magazine, I'd soon hear, 'As you're not busy, you can help me water the plants or sweep the floor.' I was busy; I was reading. But for her, the only thing worth reading was the Bible. If Dad or Grandad graced us in the kitchen with their presence, Grandma's requests would double: 'Go get your dad a glass of water', 'A piece of chocolate cake', 'One of those cookies I made'.

Before taking two buses to arrive on time for my afternoon class, I'd make the beds, fold the laundry, help her cook lunch and take the trash out. Sometimes, I'd also clean the two toilets and the garage, but by 10.30 a.m., I'd be free, so I'd do my assignments and try to read for a couple of hours. Meanwhile, she would clean the cupboards and the wardrobes, wash the pavement in front of the house, clean the fridge and the stove, or dust the furniture as if her life depended on it. Perhaps the lack of work outside the home made her feel that the work she did inside was what made her valuable.

I tried to understand her life, her routine. Until one day she found me reading *The Obscene Madame D* by Hilda Hilst.

'Better than reading porn stories would be to help me organise your dad's clothes.'

'It's not porn, it's erotica, and what do you think your son's magazines are?'

'Boys will be boys.'

'And girls will be slaves, it seems. I already folded his laundry and put them in the drawers.'

'You could organise his shirts ... '

'They are all clean, ironed and hanging in the wardrobe.'

'They are a mess. Long sleeves together with short sleeves, colours all mixed.'

I stopped complying when she asked that I colour-code my father's clothes. I continued to help out of respect for her while I lived under her roof, but the path was clear: I had to get my degree, get a job and steer clear of men who expected me to roll their socks and turn their wardrobe into a Benetton showroom. I also had to avoid women who expected me to do that for their sons.

Over the next three years, I found different ways to keep myself out of my grandparents' house: a part-time internship as a proofreader, advanced English classes twice a week, and reading at the university's library. Those moments of learning and voluntary isolation elsewhere were the much-needed breathing room from everyday domesticity and helped me make the best of each space I had access to then.

As a result, Beth and I grew closer. She taught me to cook, bake, sew and run a house on a tight budget. I showed her how to use the CD player, fix the TV antenna, send texts and top up her mobile phone. I also started watching the morning news with Grandpa and bringing his coffee with the right amount of sugar when he agreed to ask for it without shouting or whistling.

Weekends were for rest, barbecues with friends, and off-road competitions with Dad. We were now at ease with one another and had become confidants. I would watch him drive muddy Jeeps and flirt with his new girlfriend, and he would ask me if I was dating anyone. Some of my dates would last for a night, others would go on for weeks, maybe months, but none seemed important enough to be called a relationship.

In December 2005, at age twenty-two, I got my bachelor's degree in advertising. In the five years living with my dad and grandparents, I had managed to save some money, and it would have been enough to start a life on my own in a small town in São Paulo state or to live on the outskirts of São Paulo city. Instead, I convinced myself that it would be a good idea to spend time with Yara, Davi and Tácio in Brasília again before I took off to god knows where, which I knew I would one day soon. So I returned to the place I still called – but that had never felt like – home.

2006–2008

Déjà Vu

The dynamic Mom and I had developed in the years I lived away from her but visited twice a year had worked well for us. There was enough distance to stop us from being annoyed at the smallest things, but we remained curious about each other. And so, with enough new stories to keep one another amused, we had a grace period of about six months until I made the mistake of accepting Mom's generous offer to pay me to help with 'some things around the house'. 'I need someone organised, responsible and trustworthy. I can't find anyone who will last, and it's exhausting having to start over. Why don't we try?' I was aware of some of the pitfalls, but the desire to please her and the 'easy money' made me go through with it. Bad, bad, Nic.

Only too late did I discover the help she expected included but wasn't limited to ad-hoc and planned grocery shopping; dog walking three times a day; typing legal documents; booking beauty appointments; cancelling and rescheduling trips to Fortaleza several times a week; paying utility bills, car insurance and Davi's school fees; firing the driver; telling the maid she had to wear a uniform; preparing a weekly menu for the cook; making sure Tácio's shirt matched his tie ... I was now the governess and her personal assistant.

The more time I spent in Brasília, the harder it was to ignore the feeling I was going back in time. Skidding through a life that was not mine. Somebody's house, husband and son needing care. All the time. Davi's condition had improved, but the medical check-ups and the extracurricular activities were still frequent. Tácio remained the quiet authority whose face was often behind the computer as I brought him appetisers and newspapers, and picked up the discarded pages from the floor and abandoned cups from his desk. He never whistled or shouted and was rarely in a bad mood. But in that house and the house I had lived in for the past five years, the expectation was for the women to place the men at the centre of their lives. My grandma, my mother and I were but satellites.

I wondered if there was more to women's lives than that. Then, I began to seek more out of life. I told Mom I'd help her find and train a new assistant. I started offering formatting services to students writing their monographs and taking on freelance work as a copywriter so I could make money some other way. I enrolled on a postgraduate course in translation and another on teaching English as a second language. On weekends, I embarked on adventures with Gabi. My plan still was to leave my mother's house a second time and move in with Gabi in a future that seemed more and more compelling.

*

The last straw was when, after leaving the house at 9 p.m. for a night out with friends, I turned my phone off for a few hours only to find nine unanswered calls when I turned it back on at 2 a.m. Worried sick, I raced back as fast as I could. Everybody was sleeping, so I woke Davi to ask what happened. He told me Mom was looking for a document but couldn't find it.

The next day, I woke up to her barging into my bedroom long before my alarm went off.

'Where were you last night?' Her voice was harsh.

'I was out with Gabriela. I told you so before I left.'

'Do you think you are so important that you have to turn your phone off to avoid being bothered by anyone?' She closed the door and walked away before I could answer.

That was it. The switch. Another one, like in Grandma's house. A crushing certainty that I belonged elsewhere. I called Gabriela.

'Seven a.m.?! Did you fall from your bed?'

I couldn't speak.

'Hello? Nic?'

'Yeah, I'm here.'

'What happened?'

'I need to get out of here, Gabi.'

'Of where? Where are you?'

'At home. Her house. I need to get out. Please, can I stay there with you for a few days?'

'I have to check with my mom, but we'll figure it out. When do you want to come?'

'I don't know. I need to pack. But today. One p.m.?'

'That works. I can go there during my lunch break.'

'Okay. Let's do that, then.'

'Wait, are you sure about this?' she asked.

'Yes.'

'Sure, sure, sure?'

'Yes.'

'All right. See you then. I'll text you when I arrive and will be in the parking lot.'

'Thank you, Gabi. So, so much.'

I filled two big bags with clothes and hid them in the wardrobe. Then I cleaned what would no longer be my bedroom. Even in my state of extreme agitation, I didn't want to leave a mess behind or make my departure look insulting. Although it probably would anyway.

When I finished, I walked into the room next door and asked Davi if he wanted to have lunch. It was only 11 a.m., far too early for lunch, but maybe he sensed something in me. During our meal at a restaurant down the block, I didn't tell him what I was going to do. I asked him questions instead. How were things in seventh grade? Was he in pain when he played football? Was he sure football classes were a good idea when he had titanium pins in his limbs? Did he know what he wished to study after school? Did he know I loved him?

Once back home, I typed a long letter to Mom. I printed it, folded it in half and placed it on her bed. When the clock struck one o'clock in the afternoon, I asked Matias, the driver, to help me carry my things downstairs and put them into Gabriela's blue Chevy Celta. I thanked him and left without saying goodbye to anyone. Again. I didn't have it in me then. The strength. It took me hours to stop crying. And years to make peace with it.

It was in that last period at my mother's house that I met

Erik online. Very quickly we entered a secret space where everything seemed to be on pause. A pause that made me forget that I was not where I wanted to be. So I kept reaching for it, and so did he. In the spring of 2008, after he visited me in Brazil three times in less than a year, I boarded the plane to Sweden.

2010

Alexandria

Looking back on my early life helped me understand that not becoming a mother had presented itself as the magic shield that would protect me from the bad experiences my mother and grandmother had gone through. So I held tight to it.

Up to that point, not having a child had made me feel like I had complete control of my adult life. And that was important to me, even if it wasn't true. Continuing to have Erik by my side was also important to me. But my love for him needn't be my only compass in life. I could shift my focus to the present and think about motherhood pragmatically, without inherited trauma and associations with domesticity and entrapment. After all, I was an educated woman in my late twenties, married to someone I loved, trusted and respected, and who reciprocated my feelings. I wasn't earning much, but I was working in an area that I had studied, which gave me a lot of satisfaction. I lived in a cosy flat in a modern, secular country that supported new families in many ways. My husband, who did his fair share of house chores and cooked better than I did, wished to become a father and had pledged to be a hands-on dad in all aspects of parenthood. He had even mentioned he'd be up for being a full-time stay-at-home dad if I wished to prioritise my career and didn't mind becoming the primary provider for our household. These were not circumstances in which my mother or grandmother ever found themselves.

Unlike them, better even, because of them – and the amalgamation of sacrifices they had made to raise me as they did – I had been given opportunities that allowed me to choose my path, which included options they never had. I could decide if, when, how and with whom I'd have one or more children. First with their help and then as a product of my efforts, I had become my own person, and was building my own life. I could let go of the shield for good now and move into my future without carrying a weight that was not mine.

With that in mind, many times that year, I pondered motherhood from a different angle by seriously considering the possibility that it could be a positive experience for Erik and me, both as a couple and individually. I tried to imagine someone who would be 'the product' of our love, 'the glue' that would keep us together and 'the legacy' we'd leave behind. I thought about how watching someone grow so closely could be a journey filled with endless tasks but also with immeasurable moments charged with bliss. I thought about the daughter of a friend of ours who had come to our house, and when I offered her the ice cream and cookies I had bought for her, thinking that's what a three-year-old would want to eat, she asked me for cucumber and plucked leaves from my basil plant. Would we have one of those cute cucumber kids too, if we were to have one at all?

I had really given it thought, but still, whenever I tried to envision what it would be like to bring another human being into this world and become half of the duo meant to raise, protect and love it unconditionally until death did us part, I felt no inkling of interest or excitement to move in that direction. Not once.

How was that possible? Motherhood as the epicentre of women's lives was all I'd ever witnessed, so how was it that the centre was not there when it came to my own life?

Was I hollow, or was my centre elsewhere?

The peaceful days we spent attending to our art forms and each other were everything to me. And I was happy with things exactly as they were. But Erik was older. Twelve years older. So my twenty-eight was his forty, and his clock was the one ticking, while I just wanted to make time stop.

Are there others like me?
Where are they?
I had to find them.

I had searched for books about women without children at my local library for months. There were a few, and as happy as I was to get my hands on them, they ended up being like fireworks that brightened my dark sky only for a moment – dense with traumatic miscarriages, stillbirths and abortions written in torturous technical terms, filled with numbers but no insights about what it was like to have no children by choice or circumstance; melodramatic testimonies that made motherhood sound like the only thing worth living for; and anti-natalist books on the verge of referring to children like the plague. They were too academic, too dogmatic or too radical. I had no use for any of them.

Frequently, this quest felt like work, taxing my time and energy reserves. I spent nights reading those books, checking their bibliographies and looking for clues, only to find nothing that spoke to my curiosity about living without children. Deep down, I knew that the fact that I couldn't find anything helpful in those books meant something. Maybe I was looking for a book about a *feeling*. Maybe the question was not what childlessness was but who had no children and how they felt.

I googled 'famous childless women'. The results seemed endless: Dolly Parton, Oprah Winfrey, Stevie Nicks, Billie Holiday, Maria Callas, Helen Mirren, Katharine Hepburn, Billie Jean King, Eva Perón, Carmen Miranda, Yayoi Kusama, Coco Chanel and even *Mother* Teresa!

Running a new search to narrow the results down to female authors, my mouth hung open as I read the names on my laptop's screen: the Brontë sisters, Emily Dickinson, Jane Austen, Louisa May Alcott, George Eliot, Christina Rossetti, Virginia Woolf, Katherine Mansfield, Zora Neale Hurston, Edith Wharton, Octavia E. Butler, Elizabeth Bishop, Gabriela Mistral, Hilary Mantel, Bernardine Evaristo, Arundhati Roy and many more.

All this time, they had been there, lined up on bookshelves like an army of goddesses and I had not noticed them. Suddenly, I could see them watching me from above and saying incredulously: 'We were wondering how much longer till you stopped looking at your belly button, Nicole.'

A bit harsh, I know, but I don't blame them. I had been walking around thinking I was following a secret path unknown to all humans before me. When, in reality, some of my favourite authors had been there and done that many decades, even centuries, ago. The only way to redemption was to read their books back-to-back. I started with the ones I already had. One by one, I reread them, this time with new eyes. I felt less lonely when immersed in their words and decoding their lives. And, for a while, that was all I wanted.

2011–2012

Palm Reading

My mother and I never spoke about my departures. At our own pace, years later, we'd find a way back to each other's hearts. Although I suspect we had always been there, only silently.

If, as a kid, my mission in life was to be invisible and never show her when I was struggling with anything, this changed pretty soon after I got married. I don't know how the change came about, but one day we started talking on the phone, not as mother and daughter, but just as two women who happened to be alive at the same time. And it seemed not only possible but necessary to share our experiences with each other.

It had been almost three years since I moved abroad. I had sent emails with photos, but we had not seen each other once. Then, one day in early January 2011, she decided to come to Sweden with little notice. Tácio came along too. It was the harshest winter in a century in Europe, and we enjoyed each other's company by being out most of the day playing in the snow, visiting museums and trying cuisines that weren't as popular in Brazil – seafood pad Thai, chicken tikka masala and beef pho made it onto our list of favourite dishes.

While it was wonderful to have the two of them visiting, I didn't get to spend time alone with my mother because she couldn't fathom telling her husband she'd be going for a walk with me. That was hard for me to understand. But her symbiotic relationship with Tácio didn't seem to have space for any ... space. So when she left, we both pretended that her visit had been more conciliatory than it was.

This visit happened right after things started to derail in my marriage. In the twelve months since that first night spent awake by the window, I had told Erik that I didn't want a baby, and Erik had repeatedly said that he wanted me more than a baby. At first, all seemed well enough, but I gradually started to sense a deep sadness in him. The sadness extended into withdrawal, and I didn't know how to bring him back.

Longing for a resolution and assuming the reason for our marital discontent was the limbo state of not knowing if I'd change my mind in the future about having a child, I started considering permanent contraception options. One made available about that time was Essure, a non-incisional birth control system that used small devices to block the fallopian tubes. Considering my near phobia of doctors and hospitals (developed after having taken Davi to a gazillion medical appointments), that minor procedure seemed like a good compromise compared to major surgeries, such as tubal ligation or hysterectomy.

To my surprise, Yara returned for her second visit later that year. I don't know why she came back so soon. Maybe she noticed something was off between Erik and me. All I know is that she came by herself this time. During her week-long stay, we finally got to be together. We exchanged tales about her life before and after my birth and my life before and after I left her house as we strolled through the botanic gardens and picnicked at the Sofiero Palace. On her last day in the country, we took a train to Karen Blixen's house in Denmark. Blixen is the author of the memoir that inspired one of my mother's favourite movies, *Out of Africa*. Diagnosed as having syphilis soon after her wedding, Karen never had children. We took pictures of each other under Karen's apple trees, and Mom wrote her a note and pinned it to a message board as we left the property.

At some point, sitting on a bench next to the cathedral and sharing a ham and egg salad sandwich, I mentioned that I was considering going through a procedure that would permanently implant a birth-control device in my body, but that I wanted to do some more research after reading about a campaign by women who reported side effects the implant was having on their health, sex lives and ability to work.

'What kind of side effects?' she asked.

'Skin rashes, joint pain, fatigue, hair loss and, in some cases, perforation of the uterus.'[10]

'Oof ... It sounds dangerous. Why would you risk any of it?'

'Because I'm tired of trying to convince myself I want to have a child.'

'What's the latest from Erik on this?'

'He said he no longer wants a child.'

'Doesn't that alleviate the pressure?'

'I don't believe him.'

'Why not? Why would he lie?'

'He's not lying. He's sacrificing his wish to have a child to be with me.

The sacrifice. There it was again. I had developed an irreversible resistance to sacrifices after growing up hearing my mother list all the ways in which she sacrificed herself for me: to feed me, to shelter me, to send me to the best schools, to university, and to allow me all the privileges she never had. I could acknowledge them and be grateful for them. I knew they had been made out of love. But I also knew where that road led: to resentment on both sides. And I was terrified that one day Erik and I would have a conversation ending with him saying he had given up on fatherhood for me because he loved me. And that he now regretted that decision. But I wasn't ready to share this with my mother yet.

After a long silence, she asked for my left hand. I laid it over hers. She flipped it and started running her fingers across my palm. It took me a second to understand what she was doing.

'This is the life line. Yours is long, see? It curves around the ball of the thumb and ends at the base of the palm. Very thick at the start, then smoother, almost transparent in the middle, it means a stable phase, and then it gets thick again, but fragmented: full of choices. Too many even, which could be confusing. This is the heart line: yours splits in two. See the split here? Up to here, it could be Erik. After that, who knows? Your head line is long and curved. You're creative, a dreamer, someone who adapts easily to situations, a sponge that picks up and retains emotions from those around you. You must learn to shut your body to other people's energy.'

'I want to shut my body to sperm,' I said.

We both laughed. This pushed her out of the trance state. She stared blankly into the mosaic windows of the cathedral; her voice changed into a softer tone I had never heard before: 'Look, fifi, you may feel that having a procedure that would stop you from having a child is a good idea, and maybe it is. Not having a child doesn't make you less of a woman, and had I had the chance, maybe I'd have chosen the same. I understand that not having to think about this anymore can seem like a relief. I'm just not sure that will be the case. You are only twenty-eight, and a lot can happen that could change how you feel. You could both be happy without a child; you could break up; you could meet somebody else. If you are certain that you don't want a baby now, use contraception, but give yourself time to let life happen to you. If you still feel this way five, ten years from now, try something permanent, but why shut a door you are not using?'

My mother's visit gave me a lot to think about: not only my dilemma but also her feelings regarding motherhood. She had confessed her ambivalence. Could it be that what I perceived as her being half-hearted towards me was her feeling overwhelmed and lost? It didn't surprise me that she may have chosen a childfree life had she been given time to think about it or the conditions to follow through with it. But hearing that made me feel better, not worse. Instead of taking it personally, as if it were an attack on my existence, I saw it as a confession not by some holy mother but by a woman who grappled with some of the same questions I had been grappling with. That made me feel closer to her.

*

After she left, Erik and I agreed that the way forward was for me to believe him when he said that I was the family he wanted and that if I didn't want to become a mother, a life without a child was right for us. There was no need to undergo risky procedures or to drive myself mad. We would be fine. We would go back to finding purpose in our vows, verses and notes. We would go back to each other. Wishful thinking wouldn't be enough to glue us back together, though. We needed a fresh start. The novelty of the winters in Sweden had faded away, and I had become a snail, inching myself through the snow on the roads, my limbs turning blue, my lips cracking, my layers of clothes never enough, my hat always missing. I was miserable. Doing laps around the frozen lake near our home, the wish to live in a new country became a recurring topic until Sweden became a roundabout with three exits: Portugal, Scotland and Ireland.

We spent most of 2012 trotting between them. After confirming we were ready to leave Sweden, we started applying for jobs in those countries. He practised for auditions with orchestras, and I sought copywriting and translation roles. There was no job too hard or land too far away. His cello was an extension of his arm. The pen was an extension of mine. And, after four years of marriage, we had become an extension of each other.

PART II

Looking at Others

2013

Bookbinder

After hearing about a site called Meetup, where people from all over the world organised events in person based on common interests, I invited translators in the south of Sweden to share industry knowledge and have cake together. Once I received confirmation that six people planned to attend, I called a cafe in town and booked a table. I had no idea who would show up or how the conversations would go, but the possibility of making new friends motivated me to show up and talk to strangers for an afternoon.

The first person to arrive was Lucy. The first thing you notice about Lucy is her golden dreadlocks, which cascade down her back like the ponytail of a majestic horse. Lucy is witty, sarcastic and a bit cranky. She speaks in spurts in a distinctive British accent. She gets easily annoyed, and she will tell you all about it, whatever it is, whether you want to hear it or not. And I did want to hear all about her. Other nice people came along too, but no one with whom I'd click so fast or laugh so hard. And no one else who did not have children. We exchanged phone numbers and texted each other soon after. We were going to be friends.

Another day, another library. This time, I had taken an early train to a neighbouring town to get some work done in one of the places I had come to cherish the most in Sweden: the Malmö City Library. Walking from the central station took me about fifteen minutes before I'd reach the palace gardens and a cluster of three buildings would come into view. From left to right, I'd first set eyes on 'The Castle', a ludic space inspired by Renaissance castles. Then I'd gain access to the information desk and the cafe by entering 'The Cylinder', and by turning to the right, I'd reach 'The Calendar of Light', an immense hall filled with windows so large that all I wanted was to spend my days there all year round, watching the seasons change.

The biography section was my treasure trove, so I sat at a table next to a double-faced bookshelf where I had found a book about Selma Lagerlöf (a Swedish author who became the first woman to win the Nobel Prize in Literature) and the third volume of Anaïs Nin's uncensored diaries (a French author who wrote explicitly about sex from a female point of view). Both never had children. Both fascinating. And I craved more books about them and other women like them.

There was an hour left until I'd meet Lucy for coffee, so I had time, which I spent tracing the spines of the books aligned with the edge of the shelves and whispering each title with a female author's name as if summoning the subsequent discovery. Surname by surname, it took me a while to go over the alphabet, but when I reached P, there it was. A thick book with a black and white photo on the cover of a wooden chair, a painting and an open door, adorned by a burnt-orange strip of wallpaper with a pattern of leaves, flowers and berries. The book was *Paradise, Piece by Piece.*

I opened it gently and read from the quotes on the cover flap: 'The life of a poet that is a life for all women: an extraordinarily honest, moving, and lyrical exploration of what it means for a woman to come into her own.' 'Out of a consciously chosen childless relationship sensitively explored emerges a new emancipated vision of marriage.' That was it. I was hooked. I sat down and started reading. Several pages in, I glanced at my watch and saw it was ten minutes to the time I had agreed to meet Lucy in a car park twenty minutes away by foot.

Thankfully, Lucy didn't seem too bothered by my being late. We strolled through Triangeln mall, stopped by a cafe and continued to Pildammsparken, one of the many city parks, carrying an extra hot cup of coffee and two cardamom buns. Then, at Lucy's request, we tried to stop our teeth from chattering by sitting on a bench on the sunniest side of the canal and away from the playground. I reached for the bag of buns as Lucy reached for the book.

'*Molly Peacock.* I like her name. "The president emerita of the Poetry Society of America,"' Lucy read with a pompous voice. I handed her a bun and started eating mine.

'Thanks,' she said. 'What's the book about?'

'A poet who chose not to have kids.' Crumbs fell out of my mouth.

'Did she feel she had to choose between being a poet and a mum?'

'Don't know. I found it today. I've been looking for books about women who don't have kids.'

'Why?'

'Because I want to know how they live.'

'Why don't you find out for yourself?'

'How am I supposed to know what to do if all I see is moms and the odd cat lady in movies?'

'I have cats. I don't need to know what else there is.' She sipped her coffee.

'Well, I do. I want to write a book about it. For now, I'm sharing what I'm finding in a blog.'

'Why don't you ask me how I live?'

'Can I?'

'Of course, Nic. Don't be daft!'

'Daft indeed. I need time to come up with a questionnaire, though.'

'How long do you need?'

'Not sure. I've been quite busy preparing for job interviews.'

'How many do you have?'

'Five,' I said, scrubbing sprinkles of pearl sugar off my hands.

'*Five?* For the same job?

'Yep.'

'Did you apply to work for NASA or something?'

'Sort of.'

'Are you going to space?'

'No. But maybe to Dublin.'

'Dublin?! Nooo!'

A few weeks later, Lucy sat on my red sofa for two and half hours and answered all sixty-five questions of the earliest version of what would become 'the official questionnaire'. The whole thing felt like another of our long conversations, except that I was recording it this time, and we were sharing a bottle of terrible red wine.

Lucy, 45, British, translator

I'm from the Isle of Man, a small rocky island in the Irish Sea. I lived there until I went to a university in Wales when I was eighteen. I did a degree in archaeology, then a master's degree in archaeological heritage management. It sounds impressive, but it's no use for getting a job. It essentially means looking after archaeological sites, monuments and museums. Helping to protect, interpret and present. Generally, in the UK, you work for local public authorities. I started the degree and everything was fine. By the end of it, we were in a major recession, and they were shutting museums down at the rate of three a week. And that was it. By the time the recession was over, I'd got a job in IT, and I never got to work in archaeology. I moved to France, where I became an estate agent, selling property to English people.

Now I live in Sweden and work as a French to English and Swedish to English translator with my husband, David, and a cat. We've been together for twenty-five years. Neither of us is into the idea of marriage, but in 2010 we decided that we needed to put our affairs in order in case one of us died.

When I'm not working, I spend my time renovating houses and taking pictures. I'm also into geocaching: people hide little things out in the woods, and you take your GPS phone or machine, and it tells you the coordinates, and you go and find these things. There's a site where you can find other people who play it, and they're everywhere! So I keep busy and love life.

Having children was never a desire for me, and I'm certain about not wanting them now. I met somebody who didn't want them either, which is really lucky. I didn't want to have children for years because I believed my parents were crap parents. From an early age, I got this impression that if that's what you're going to be like with your children, then just don't have them. My parents weren't suited to being together at all. They were twenty-one and twenty-two when I was born, and they just didn't get on. She was far too intelligent to be married to him, and he was far too much of an egotistical sod to be married to her. And she doesn't know how to handle him. It's possible they never expected me to have children. My family is incredibly uncommunicative, so if it's not food, we don't talk about it. They've never put pressure on any of their children to do anything. They've been happy with whatever we've done, but other people don't feel the same.

There was this time when David and I were going to buy a house in France. We'd made an offer; the owners accepted it. We asked them to fill in the paperwork and the day that the notary sent us the document for us to fill in our piece of it, they showed the house to somebody else. To somebody who had a kid. And they decided to sell it to them instead, even though we'd agreed and we were going ahead with it. They actually said that. They said: 'You're a long way away, and we don't know you. And they've got a child.' And I felt that If I'd been somebody who had been trying to have a child my entire life – which I could have been, and they wouldn't have known, they didn't ask – I would be really upset about the whole thing.

The people who feel that having children is everything don't treat me the same as I treat them. This type of behaviour never happened to my husband. He came from inner-city Birmingham. You didn't ask personal questions because you'd have got your face punched in. It was easier in the UK to be childless. I was mixing with people who didn't have kids or didn't care much. In Sweden, kids are the centre of the universe. In the cities, you can go out and do things socially if you don't have children, but there's nothing to do outdoors in the countryside, where I live. You meet people when you go to the playgroup and the school and stuff like that. You relate to people because you've got kids in the same class. So we don't know many people here, even though we've been living here, on and off, for years.

Still, I'm beginning to think I've led a charmed life as nobody's asked me much about why I don't have children, I haven't had any pressure to have children, and I don't regret not having them. I must have just breezed through a load of unpleasant situations. There is only one moment when I regret not having children: when I go to a funfair and I see the rides for kids that you can only go on when you've got children, and that is the truth. Right there and then I'd quite like to have a kid to go on the ride with, but that's what, five minutes a year? So, no. I'll go on without them.

There are lots of people who have children and who I like and am friends with, but it depends on how they raise them.

If they're the sort of person who is subservient to the children, then I have nothing in common with them. Whereas I respect people like my sister, who has got three children and made sure they've got boundaries. She's tried to keep it subtle but, if you've not got kids, you can be somewhere in her house without being inflicted with sticky fingers and daft anecdotes.

The fact is that I've chosen not to have children because I'm perfectly happy being me. I'm being selfish in that I want to treat myself and not have to think about anybody else. If you have children, then you owe it to the children to treat them the best you possibly can because you chose to have them.

I'm not bothered by the lack of maternal instinct in me. I think it's not that 99 per cent of women have got it but that 99 per cent of women have been brought up to believe that they should have it. It would be important to me, if I'd had children, to not treat my children like they were an inconvenience, which is what my mother did to us. It's going back to this selfish business again. You know, we've got a cat. And the good thing about a cat is, if he pesters you too much, you can stick him in the bathroom and say, 'Shut up!' and just leave him there. But you can't do that with a child. (Well, I mean, people do it with children, but they shouldn't!)

The social aspect of not meeting like-minded people is a problem. And maybe because of that, there was a brief moment, a couple of years ago, when my husband thought it was a good idea to adopt. He said, 'Well, you know, if you need to have a child to meet people, and we're not going to have one ourselves, let's adopt and give that child a chance!' Which is not the reason you're supposed to want to adopt, but I think it was probably one of these things where you explore something for a bit. So I checked on the internet and looked at the rules, and it turned out that I was too old to adopt. I told him, and he didn't seem to be that bothered. I mean, he doesn't even clean up after the cat when it's been sick. But I don't know what would have happened if the rules had said we could.

We went from never wanting children to looking into adopting. It was a big leap. But in the end what remained was a sense of 'we didn't want to do that anyway'. I think that, at the time, we were trying to work out how we could make Sweden feel more like home, and we've since come up with the solution of just not spending all the time that we've got here. Now we spend half the time in France and the other half here.

Because deep down I didn't want to adopt, I didn't feel sad about the age limit in relation to me, but I felt sad for the people who actually wanted to have a child. It's a stupid age limit. There are a lot of children who need looking after, and the fact that some potential parents above a certain age are not given a chance when there's a shortage of people adopting is very short-sighted. Adoption is an even more profound path to parenthood, in my opinion, because you've chosen to do it. You haven't just got knocked up by somebody. Everybody has sex, but you don't have to get pregnant. Whereas the things you have to do to adopt . . . That's for people who are certain it's what they want.

If we were spending some of the resources that we've got as a race of humans on trying to make the world better instead of just having more children, then I think we could actually get somewhere. As it is, we're drowning in our population,

and we're never going to get anywhere until we stop repro-
ducing all the time because it's just what animals do. We
should be better than that. We shouldn't just be born, get to
adulthood and then have kids incessantly. Why not look at
the world around us and think, *What can we do as a group to
make things better?* We can feed everybody if we try. We're
not trying. Why are we all driving around in cars with fumes
coming out of them? Why are we polluting the sea at the rate
that we are? Why aren't we spending more of our brain power
on doing useful things? Because we're stuck in the same old
grind of having to have housing, an income and kids. We're
at such a low, basic level.

Much more thought should be given to educating people
that you don't just have to go and have kids. Society as a
whole needs to take responsibility for looking at things that
are viewed as being normal, and parenthood is the one that
nobody questions.

It was only in my forties that I started to look at myself and
think that I've done some really interesting things in my life:
I've lived in lots of different places. I've had lots of different
jobs. I've created a successful business. Now, I would like
to do more things that I enjoy and less of things that I don't
enjoy. So I'd like to go out and walk around in the countryside
more. I'd like to do things like go on meetups and meet new
people, and have tea and cake with them. I just want to make
the most of what's here now instead of always having to long
for something else I don't already have.

Twenty years from now I'd like to be back on the Isle
of Man. I feel that as I get older, I'm going to want to be
somewhere where I don't have to think about which language

I'm speaking. If you get dementia and you're in a country where you don't speak the language as your native language, I think you're going to feel even more alienated than you are to start with. And I think that by then, the energy to cope with being in a foreign country all the time is going to wear off. But I don't really think much about that time in the future. I've given up planning for things. I'd still like to be translating if I can or finally get around to writing. Writing would be perfect.

2014

Emerald Isle

I got the job. And once I signed the offer to be an in-house translator for the biggest tech company in the world, Erik and I could finally see our fresh start.

We arrived in Ireland in late March when the cherry blossoms were nearly in full bloom. At the end of our first week in a family-owned guesthouse, we found a 'bright two-bedroom flat' in a charming building next to a train station and rushed to express our interest in renting it. Despite only being offered a ten-minute viewing slot, we finished going through the documentation required by the estate agent right before a couple with a bouncy toddler knocked on the door. Lucy's story about losing a house to a couple with children came to mind, and I couldn't help but wonder what the outcome would be this time. The estate agent informed us that a decision would be made by the end of the day and showed us out.

We both jumped from the bed when my phone rang a few hours later. I put the call on speaker mode, and the voice on the other end announced the good news: 'The property owner would love to have you as tenants. You can sign the lease and collect the keys tomorrow.' We hugged and did a little dance in celebration. The rest of April was free of work commitments before I'd start going to the office and Erik would go back to auditioning, so we made the most of it by walking on the seaside and along the Liffey. We spent days exploring new parts of this old city we were happy to be living in.

For the first time in years, I could talk to strangers: bus drivers, people in the supermarket, at the pharmacy and in clothes shops; I could read all my correspondence, including utility bills, medical tests and the pizza delivery leaflets. I could understand the announcements in train stations or hear what preachers shouted on Henry Street. It felt good to discern and be part of the world outside my head again. What didn't feel good was to move away from Lucy, but this didn't stop us from growing closer. Quite the contrary. We kept in touch by exchanging postcards and emails, and I knew I had won the friendship lottery when I received a basket of lilies from her on my first day at work.

I was nervous. There was an onboarding event I had to attend. Three full days of immersion with the other 'newbies' landing on the same strange spaceship. In an auditorium with more than a hundred seats, there were people from all over the world in roles very different from mine, and we each had to stand up, introduce ourselves, and participate in group activities that lasted an hour each. We got temporary badges, T-shirts, hats and a bag of branded goodies. We heard recordings of vice presidents talking about the company's mission and senior employees giving an overview of their departments and how they fit in the well-oiled machine that creates software and hardware for billions of 'users' all over the globe. And how we were part of it now. And how happy they were that we were there. Or so they said.

Everything looked elaborate, synchronised and calculated. Every slide in each presentation, every free item in that goody bag, every slot into which those days had been sliced, including the main meals on rooftops and coffee breaks in the five different buildings that conjoined the company's European headquarters, with its mini-golf course and terrace with swings and high-back beanbag chairs in the colour of the company's logo. I was dizzy in the middle of it all and often felt like I wanted to find a secret passage to get myself out of there unnoticed.

On the third and last day of the boot camp, they had kept the agenda light so we could tour the south of Dublin. Andrés sat next to me on the bus that took us to the neighbourhood where both Bono and Enya lived, which also had a city park with stunning views of the Emerald Isle. On the way there, our conversation ranged from the differences between being a large accounts sales manager for the Spanish market and a localisation specialist for the Brazilian market, the shared appreciation for our national cuisines, and the delusional hope that we'd able to keep our creative projects going on top of our new tech jobs. Then we got off the bus and walked up Killiney Hill side by side.

'You said you're also a musician. Which instrument do you play?' I asked Andrés.

'The keyboard, but the hobby I was referring to is not

something I do with an instrument. I walk around the city, recording street sounds. Then, I go home and combine them into different tracks using effects and transitions. One album for each city.'

'So that makes you what? A street DJ?'

'I might put that on my business card.'

'Wow. I never knew this was a thing.'

'It is. How about you? What's your secret project?'

'I'm collecting stories about women who don't have children.'

'Really? My wife and I are *childfree*. Her name is Elena.'

'Fabulous! Can I meet her?'

'I'll put you two in touch. What's your number?'

A couple of weeks later, I got a message from Elena.

Elena and I met for the first time at a Spanish cafe in Dublin's Creative Quarter. We shook hands, smiled at each other, and sat down to have lunch. It wasn't long before we realised neither of us drank coffee and we both avoided sugar. We settled on a big pot of jasmine tea and a few tapas to share. Then we started doing yoga on Tuesdays and taking salsa lessons on Thursdays. Andrés, Elena, Erik, and I hung out a few times, but mostly Elena and I met on our own. She was the first friend I made in Ireland, and I'm fortunate to still count her as a friend.

Elena, 38, Venezuelan, graphic designer and wellness coach

I'm from Venezuela, my father is from Costa Rica and my mother is from Spain. I wanted to embrace all the possibilities in life, so I made a point of arranging to have all three passports. Still, I don't particularly feel that I belong or represent one nationality more than the other: I'm a good blend.

Just like with my roots, my career is also a mix. I have a bachelor's degree in art history but got quite bored while studying it – it was basically reading and writing non-stop – and I felt the urge to do something else with my brain. So I took a graphic design course and got a job as a graphic designer.

I lived in Venezuela until I was twenty-eight, then I married and moved abroad. First to Spain, then to Ireland. For the past six months, I haven't worked by choice. I was diagnosed with multiple sclerosis (MS) when I was sixteen, so now I'm using my time doing yoga, reiki healing sessions, cooking, discovering new places and focusing on maintaining a blog where I write about my experience of living with this illness for more than half of my life.

Studying health and nutrition in Madrid, I realised I needed to change my daily pace to improve my quality of life. Then I studied professional coaching to combine both areas and offer my services to people who suffer from MS.

Throughout the years, I became very active in researching ways to cope and live well despite this condition. It often meant being open to experimenting with things that are not within the realm of conventional medicine. I spent a lot of time and energy reading, which led me to learn what's good, what's bad, what's hard but worth it, what might be good for others but doesn't work for me and vice-versa. At some point, I felt I had enough information that could be useful to someone else, as I would have loved to have had something like this when I was diagnosed but simply couldn't find it. That's when the idea of creating a blog came along.

Unfortunately, when I got diagnosed in the late '90s, the internet was still very new. There was no easy access to it in South America and certainly not as much information readily available as there is today, so I was stuck with what my doctor told me back then.

MS is a neurological disease for which there's currently no cure. In simple terms, it's the equivalent of your immune system being constantly attacked and affecting the cable connecting two neurons. At some point, the information that should go from A to B doesn't get there correctly, so your body stops working as it should, which can affect different things, such as mobility, sensations, vision, speech … And it's exactly this aspect of the disease, the range of symptoms being so broad, that makes both the diagnosis and the treatment so complicated.

Also, doctors don't know what causes it, so there are many theories, and it can be hard to know what to believe. Diet can help. Exercise can help. Certain weather conditions can also help. But is this related to my body specifically or the illness in general? I don't know. I know that certain weather conditions benefit or compromise my health, and the changes are quite obvious, as I haven't had an episode in two years where I live now but had several the year before when living elsewhere.

The episodes vary a lot. Once, I suddenly stopped feeling any sensation on one side of my body. Half of my face, one arm, hand and leg were completely numb, so I lost balance and strength. Another time, I started seeing double. I was still working as a graphic designer at the time, so you can imagine how hard it was for me to get anything done.

I don't have any children and don't know if I can have them. What I do know is that, while I don't wish to have them now, I did want to before. I started wanting them when I got married in 2009. I thought that sometime soon in the future would be a good time for my husband and me to start a family of our own, but we didn't make it a priority because we wanted to enjoy our married life with just the two of us for a while.

Then, about six years later, I had a massive emotional crisis. Out of the blue, I quit my job, moved to a different country, and felt that something big was missing in my life. At first, I thought it was my body asking me to have a kid right away, so I spoke to Andrés about it, and, after a very difficult conversation, it became clear that he didn't want to become a father. Knowing that shook me quite a lot, as it had the potential to break my marriage and change what I had expected my life to be by then.

After thinking long and hard, I decided not to ask myself *how much* I wanted to have a baby but if I wanted one. And I concluded that I didn't. The preconception that I'd want a baby was a product of being a woman and observing the lives of others around me without ever stopping to think or question any of it. You grow up, find someone, marry that person and then ... babies. I was following a path.

When I felt my life was empty, I jumped to the conclusion that a child would fill that gap. But the emptiness came from being in Ireland, away from my family and friends, spending my days mostly alone at home, and having a hard time finding a job in an English-speaking country while Andrés was out working all week. I was feeling the lack of something that would keep me busy, not the conscious desire to become a mother.

In many ways, I'm happy that Andrés told me how he truly felt because I was then able to stop and consider how I too felt about parenthood, and by doing that I was able to stop us from having a baby to fill a void that was caused by something else. And, without having a child to distract me, I chose to keep looking inside myself to understand the source of my unhappiness and how I could change things for the better in a way that was true to me and my nature.

Another thing that contributed to my decision not to have a child was its physical aspect. The first doctor who treated my MS gave me a supplement and warned me to be extra careful because it would make me very fertile. I did not think about getting pregnant until after my thirties, but when I did, I also remembered him explaining to me that during pregnancy, the disease stops manifesting itself, only for it to come back stronger afterwards and cause your body to crash. I thought a lot about that and realised I didn't want to take that risk. Who would take care of the newborn while I recovered? It could take weeks or months. Also, why put my life at risk? If it was something that I wanted, sure. But that was not how I felt.

Living with MS already presents so many challenges that I didn't want to risk losing the limited control I had over my health, independence and freedom. So this was part of what led to my childless life.

For a long time, my parents would ask me when I would have kids. Not if, when. My father, in particular, often brought up the topic until I had had enough and managed to have a serious conversation with him. Finally, I said that I wanted him to stop asking me this because I had already told him several times that I was not going to have kids, and the fact that he kept telling me I'd change my mind in the future meant he was not listening to me. And the fact that he wanted grandkids (his other argument) was not my problem. I told him he already had two grandsons and that if he wanted a third one, he could adopt a baby and take care of it. He got very frustrated, but it was the only way to make him understand. He stopped asking after that.

This is the right decision for me, my current reality and the life I want to live, and it works for me now. If something makes me change my mind later in life, I'll consider adopting a child. I make sure to keep an open mind to change because I think it's important not to live a rigid life, but I know the chances of this change happening are minimal because I didn't decide to remain childless lightly.

As much as I don't appreciate my family pressuring me about having kids, I can understand it up to a point. The same is not true when it comes to strangers, though. I did a job interview once, and they asked if I had children. I said no. They asked me why. I said I didn't want to. They asked how that could be. It was endless questioning into something that should have nothing to do with my ability to work. I was shocked to realise that our notions of privacy can be so different.

Another notion that puzzles me is having children to add meaning to a marriage or life. There are many other ways of finding purpose or fulfilment. If you are not able to take care of yourself, if you are not capable of improving yourself, there's no meaning in having kids just for the sake of it. I think that before having a child you should feel satisfied and be in a good place so you can welcome that new presence into your life.

People worry about dying alone and ask me if I don't feel the same. I do think about it, but I don't want to think about it too much. And I certainly don't want to make decisions based on that fear. Because the truth is, no matter how much we think about it, it won't change the fact that we still won't know when or how we will die. Let alone if someone will be there for us. Having kids is not the purpose of human lives. It's an option. A possibility. Just as devoting your life to yourself or to something or someone else who is not related to you. Every day we have the chance to learn new things, go to new places, and help people around us. There's a lot that we can do to improve life in general. We just have to keep our eyes open to how we can contribute. In my case, my dream is to open a wellness centre to provide emotional support to people who suffer from MS.

2015

Hypothermia

The Irish winter was shorter, the people were friendly and the certainty of a monthly salary was a balm. Some old problems were gone. Then came new ones.

While being a freelance translator in Sweden was by no means easy, I didn't have to attend meetings every day, report on metrics every week or present the impact of my work to my team every quarter. What I was experiencing in the new job was a very different type of stress. One I didn't know how to handle. In multinationals like this one, people are hired in levels. Mine was 3, which made me feel like one of those wooden spoons found on pub tables with numbers. As a 3, I was under a strict schedule of hitting targets in different areas while being reminded that my 'performance' would be evaluated twice a year. The environment felt competitive and oppressive. The office was designed to keep the employees there for hours on end, embellished with far more than anyone would ever need to get any job done. Organic ingredients freshly picked for meals, the gym and a massage parlour were all free! Well, there was a price, but the bill would come later.

I'd leave home before 8 a.m. and return by 8 p.m. if I had managed to catch the train. But I'd often feel so tired that I'd get confused about which train to get or read the platform number wrong. Then I'd have to wait another half an hour to be on my way home. I'd open the door with enough vitriol stuck in my throat to ruin any possibility of having a pleasant dinner with Erik, and I'd fall asleep ten minutes into watching a movie together.

My way of coping with the pressure of keeping our new life going was to learn as much as possible as fast as possible. I'd work on weekends and sign up for in-house courses to learn how to 'communicate efficiently', 'design beautiful graphs' and 'give and receive feedback'. It took me less than a year to succumb to the gamification system designed to make me believe I was never doing enough. My manager's favourite mantra, 'If you achieved 100 per cent of your goal, you didn't aim high enough,' was the poison that clogged my thoughts to the point where 2014 became the first year I did not write a single line not related to visa, work or household administration. I felt dead inside and hated most of my days. Especially Tuesdays.

On Tuesday mornings, I'd spend the journey to work thinking about excuses that would prevent me from attending the meeting with my manager. One day, I imagined missing a step and twisting my ankle, and that's when it became clear that things were out of control. My mind going there, even for a moment, scared me. It's nearly impossible to explain how working at the corporate version of Disneyland for adults with a compensation package three times higher than I was making before could have damaged me, but it did. And the reason it did is that I had never wanted to be there. I was simply trying to fix things in my marriage and thought that less snow and more money could save some of it. But the dread continued and extended to meeting my director, who would conclude her newsletters with 'fun facts' and photos of her toddler. In our fourth one-on-one inside a straight-out-of-a-Kubrick-movie red meeting pod made of acoustic foam, she asked, 'How is everything going?' I told her I was thinking about quitting. After follow-up questions, which I answered with calculated brevity, she diagnosed me with burnout, reminded me of how lucky I was to be working in a company that receives a million resumes a year, and informed me about the 'emotional support' offered in-house.

Alone in a white room with two chairs and a coffee table, I filled in the form.

'Dr Una will be with you in a minute, Nicole,' said the receptionist as she placed a glass of water on the coffee table before closing the door. A short woman with vibrant auburn hair cut in layers to her shoulders entered the room smiling and extending her hand. No older than fifty, she wore a blue viscose midi dress that matched the eyes in her oval-shaped face.

'Thank you for filling in the form, Nicole. Let me have a look. Right, all good. Do you want to tell me more about what brings you here?' she asked tenderly.

'Many things . . . ' I replied, almost stuttering, and I never stutter.

'What's been on your mind lately?'

'It depends on the day . . . Sorry, I haven't done this before. I don't know what to say.'

'Don't worry about not having done this before. There are no wrong answers. You mention whatever brought you here, and I'll do my best to help you deal with it. Is that okay?'

'Yes.'

'What is the main challenge at the moment?' she asked.

'I'm worried I will divorce my husband.' The words had rocketed out of my mouth.

'I see. How long have you been married?'

'It will be seven years in July.'

'Why are you thinking about divorcing your husband?'

'I don't know where to start. How long do we have?'

'Fifty minutes. I'll let you know when we are close to the end. So tell me, why are you thinking about divorcing your husband?'

'Because . . .' I stopped and took a deep breath.

'Take your time.'

'Because he wants to have a child, or wanted to, and I don't want to, nor do I believe that he doesn't want to anymore. Also, because we can't find a place that is good for both of us: I'm from Brazil, and he's from Sweden, where I moved to be with him, but I couldn't find a job there, so I worked from home as a translator and earned just enough to get by. After a few years, Sweden didn't feel right. I found this job, and we moved here thinking things would get better, and they have, financially, for me. But he is a cellist, and there are few orchestras here, so he had to start going back to Sweden for work, and now we spend weeks apart. I thought we could make it work until he spoke about quitting because he didn't want to be away from me. Now I feel responsible for him giving up his career and for the life he'll not have if he stays with me.' At this point, my rambling speech came to a sudden halt.

'It's okay. Do you want to stop?'

'No,' I moved my eyes from the floor to the wall. 'It's just that I've never said these words out loud before. Maybe a version of them when talking to the women in my book, but not the whole thing.'

'Your book. You're writing a book? What about?'

'About not wanting to have children,' I said, looking at her for the first time in minutes.

'I see. And when you say "with the women in my book", what do you mean?'

'I interview them to understand how they feel and what their lives are like.'

'How long have you been working on this?'

'Since 2013. I've interviewed two women so far. I want to get to twenty.'

'And have you been doing this while working full-time?'

'Yes.'

'Do you like your job?'

'I like being a translator, but I don't like doing it where I've been doing it for the past year.'

'Is going back to Sweden an option?'

'No. The winters, the language – I tried learning, but I think deep down I knew I wouldn't settle there. No family, few friends. We tried other places for shorter periods but couldn't find work.'

'Right. Sounds like a lot, Nicole.'

I reached for the glass of water and drank it all. 'It's fine. I applied for a family reunion visa to get me out of the work permit here.'

'No, I mean everything that has happened in the past few years. It would be a lot for anyone. It's natural to feel overwhelmed.' I stared at the bottom of the empty glass.

'Have you been thinking about divorce for a while, or is it something new?'

I looked at the cherry blossoms outside. Flashbacks to our first week in Dublin a year before flooded my mind. The walk in our new neighbourhood, the pictures I took of the blush petals above Erik's head, the sunlight on his face. There was hope on that walk. We both felt it.

'I was focused on fixing it all. But I've been thinking about it lately.'

'Why do you think that is?'

'Well ... this new job and all the pressure that came with it didn't really help.'

'What's your husband's name?'

'Erik.'

'Apart from the external factors you mentioned, are you in a loving relationship with your husband?'

'Oh yeah. We wouldn't have done all of this if we didn't. He is a wonderful man and husband. It's just that ...' Unzipping my backpack, I grabbed my woollen scarf and wrapped it around my neck. 'The time I've spent away from him has given me some perspective. Although my days here are a repeat of working, eating, going home and falling asleep, I get so caught up in this routine that I forget everything else. But then I feel guilty that I'm relieved when I'm alone and try to carve energy out of thin air to spend quality time with him like we used to. But being together brings everything back. All the things for which I see no solution. So it's easier when I'm alone, but also hard to imagine a life without him.'

'How do you feel when you think about divorcing him?'

'Lost. It's unbearable. It makes me want to quit and go away, but I don't know where to go.'

'Look, you're not quitting your job. Not today. You'll be all right. We'll talk through everything. What else do you feel when Erik is here with you?'

'Not too long ago, he mentioned how it felt like we were flatmates, and I agreed. Even though we are comfortable with each other and love each other, there's an emotional gap between us.'

'I'm afraid this is us for today. But there's a lot to unpack, Nicole. And we will if you want to.'

'If you think it can help, I want to because I don't know what else to do.'

'Yes, I think it can help. I'll book you for next week. How about that?'

'Okay, thanks,' I said, rubbing my hands together.

'Are you that cold?'

'I'm always cold.'

She got up, came closer, touched my hands and then my forehead. 'Nicole, I think you should go home. Tell your manager you are not feeling well and go home. Would you do that?'

'Yes.'

Once I got home, I went to bed and slept for fourteen hours straight.

*

In one of our monthly lunches, Ali – a Turkish engineer who spoke Portuguese and wished to practise it more often – asked if I wanted to interview a Turkish woman. I said yes with a spark in my eye that was impossible to miss. By the end of that day, I got an email introducing me to a friend in his hometown. Her name was Burcak.

So far, Burcak and I have only spoken on Skype, but I hope we will meet one day because I'd like to thank her in person for introducing me to the physicality of life, to the rewards of learning to control our own bodies and training them to do what we want. Our conversations made me understand that it's not the body that carries us around but we who tell the body when and where to go.

Burcak, 37, Turkish, academic

I'm very much an outdoors sportswoman. So I keep myself occupied with running and travelling around for climbing. It all started when I joined the mountaineering club at my university, attracted by the social aspect of it. My then-boyfriend, Serhan, who later became my husband, also joined that club and it became our way of life as a couple.

We've been married for eighteen years, and I consider our marriage a happy one because it's not traditional or conventional. The university where I work as an instructor has a campus in Cyprus and I was appointed there for a while. That meant that, for eight years, I lived in Cyprus while he lived in Turkey. It was not convenient to travel every week, but this arrangement was not a problem because we have a solid relationship.

While doing my PhD studies in employment relations and organisation studies, I lived in the UK for a year and a half, and I really enjoyed it. I can say that I was happier there because my country is very complex in terms of the political environment and social and political issues. Being away brought me relief. But, at the same time, I found it hard to be away and hear the news from abroad, knowing that my husband, parents and friends were all back in Turkey. That made me want to come back.

I like my job, but being out there in the open and up high in the mountains speaks much more to me. I'm proud of having climbed Mount Everest and Gasherbrum II, and my dream challenge is to climb the top fourteen tallest mountains in the world with my team. Two down, twelve to go – although I realise this is not very realistic, because climbing such high mountains takes a lot of time as they are all taller than 8,000 metres. Still, that's my heart's desire.

Doing things as a group is very important for us in the mountaineering club. The best part of climbing Everest was that we decided we would do a collective expedition with ten people from the beginning. Our golden rule was that we wouldn't reveal the names of those who had climbed to the summit until we returned to Turkey in order for it to be the success of the whole team and not of that one person. That moved us to work so hard that all ten of us reached the summit. Six men and four women, which is such a hard gender proportion to achieve. Not only that, but the four of us became the first women from Turkey to ever get to the peak. All ten people felt proud of being part of that team while on top of the world.

When I think about these two achievements, there are so many challenges. First, it's very expensive. You need lots of money. And it can take a long time to find a sponsor. Then, you never quite know how your body will react to the whole thing. I was unconscious once during the climb for about half an hour. I had some hyperventilation issues and it was very serious, but I'm well now thanks to the Sherpas who were with me. And finally, there's the time it takes to do the whole expedition.

Everybody talks about the summit, but everything before and after that summit moment amounts to something like sixty days, meaning that you cannot just care about that one bit. It's a journey. A journey filled with challenges. And these challenges are a big part of my life, and they are like my children. The children I chose to have.

As far as I know, I could get pregnant, but I never have, and I don't recall ever desiring to go through this experience. I also didn't want to get married when I was young, but that changed. Serhan and I were classmates in secondary school, then we moved to different cities until we met again when we went to the same university. After nearly nine years together, we decided to get married because in Turkey it's not very easy to live as a couple if you are not married, and it's also more advantageous to be legal partners for things related to employment and travel permits. Another thing that influenced our decision was the feeling we had that our families would be happier if we got married.

While getting married was a choice influenced by external aspects, not having kids was natural. This way, I felt I could be my own person, instead of being an emotional sponsor of someone else in life. Not being a parent means you don't have dependents, but also that you have to build a strong self as you won't be able to count on your kids when you're old. And I'm fine with that because there is just no place for that someone in my life. For someone to occupy that much space. I didn't decide not to have kids per se. I don't remember ever asking myself the question and telling myself I would not do it. I simply found out I would not have kids by having to answer to my parents and my in-laws asking us when we'd have children. That's when we said, 'Look, we love kids, but we don't have time, so we don't plan to have them.' And I think they got used to it. To our reality.

Other people, on the other hand, didn't seem to really grasp it. One example would be a previous mentor of mine, a professor, who would openly express his discontent about me not having kids and would lecture me during our academic discussion sessions about how I should have them and why, according to him. I found the whole thing so weird, and it really annoyed me being questioned and told what to do like that. It was a time in my life when I could still get pregnant – maybe he felt the need to push me in that direction. Still, it doesn't make it right.

Recently my husband and I asked each other: 'Did you ever think about having kids?' We both said no, which was great to hear; I just don't know how we got there. The lack of this discussion within our relationship is very contrasting to how many times we have to deal with it externally. But it makes sense when I think about how Turkish culture is so communal and how people pay attention to and talk about other people's lives.

Yet, I want to be known as an individual based on my lifestyle, political identity and cultural identity. Someone autonomous and capable of making my own decisions. And I believe the same should be the case for parents. They could work more on their own sense of identity and on being part of society without feeling that their lives have to revolve solely around their kids.

My mother showed me that this is possible. Being one of five children in a working-class family in a small town, she lost her mother very young and was the only daughter to continue education after high school. She was a great mother, but she made sure to be a part of the household, not just someone who lives for her family. She cooked us meals and took care of things, but she was also a university instructor with her own routine and interests. I appreciated that while growing up and do even more so now that I understand how that has shaped me as a person. I believe that we can choose the weights that we carry in life. Life as a parent or as a childless person doesn't have to be hard, as a rule. It doesn't have to be always challenging. Being alive and a woman in Turkey right now is already a challenge and not something I can change, so I try to stick to the things that I feel will make my life easier and more pleasant to be lived, and I wish others would do the same.

Rage Against the Dying of the Light

I had been climbing a mountain too, but a different one. Looking back, it's easy to see how therapy helped stretch our marriage further, but 2015 was destined to be the last leg of our journey together. In many ways, it had been a long time coming.

After eight years together, we reached the peak, saw the abyss, and came crashing down. The difference between our falls was that mine had started six years before, when I watched the light dimming from the window of our flat in Lund, and that was something I could never unsee, not with the interviews or going to Ireland. I had been living with the realisation that we'd have to go our separate ways sooner or later and bruising myself in silence on the way down while he was still at the top, alone, hoping we'd be rescued.

A rainy night in Dublin in the last days of autumn meant a walk with my hands under my armpits and my head tucked under the hoodie. On the way home from work, my red coat seemed to want to turn into a cape. When I got to our door, I hesitated to open it for a while, and when I finally did, I could feel a lump forming in my throat. He heard the door opening and came to the hallway.

'Welcome home, *amor.*'

'Thank you,' I said, removing my wet coat and ankle boots.

'You poor thing, you're freezing. Come here. I was about to heat the soup.'

'Quick hot shower, and I'll be right back.'

'Okey-dokey.'

I hugged him tightly.

After drying my hair, I went to the living room in flannel pyjamas and sat silently on the old love seat, watching him place cutlery on the kitchen counter. He was wearing an old Yoda T-shirt I had given him on our third anniversary, washed-out blue jeans and colourful socks. I kept scanning his face, his body and his movements.

'Can I get you anything to drink? A cup of tea to warm you up?'

'No, thanks.'

'*Amor*, are you all right?'

Holding my chin and covering my mouth with my left hand, I stared at him.

'Hey, are you okay?'

'No,' I said at last, but very low as if wanting to swallow it back.

He put the spoon down and walked towards the love seat. 'Did something happen?'

'Yes,' I said decidedly without looking at him.

He sat down cautiously next to me and put his hand over mine. 'What is it, Nic?'

'I can't do this anymore,' I said. I had said it some years ago and again a few months before, but my tone had a different ring this time. It sounded dry and resolute.

He went silent. I waited for a minute. 'I'm sorry. I'm really, really sorry.'

'You almost begged me not to come back from Sweden. I found it strange. But, still, I came. You don't want me here anymore, is that it?'

'It's not it. It's not about here or there. It's about not knowing how to do this anymore.'

'This? Do you mean us? Is this about the baby? I already told you I don't want a baby. I want you more than anything. How many times do you want me to say it?'

'It's not just the baby thing, Erik.'

'What is it then? Tell me, and we will find a way. Is it the job? I know it's been tough on you. You don't have to do it. We can go back to Sweden.'

'I don't care about this job. I can quit. But I don't want to go back to Sweden.'

'Then we stay. We can rent the flat there, and I can come back here full-time.'

'No, you can't.'

'Why not? What's going on?'

'You can't just quit your career, come here, and expect us to be okay. How is this meant to work if we keep leaving everything behind to be together?'

'It will work because we love each other. I'd do anything for us; you know that.'

'You've been trying for over a year. I don't want you to give up on more things.'

'I don't understand it. I don't understand any of it. Don't you love me anymore?'

'Yes, I do.'

'So what is it then? How can this be? Have you met someone? Something is not right.'

'Erik, it's not one thing. It's not the baby, my job, your job, someone else, or something else or somewhere else. It's everything. All of these things haven't been right for a long time.'

'But why would you give up on us like that?'

'Like *that*? Do you want me to list *all* the things I've done for us to get this far?'

'I know it's a lot, but these things can be solved. Why would you stop trying?'

'Because trying is all I've been doing! Trying to adapt to Sweden, trying to get visas, trying to adapt to this new job, trying to believe you don't want a baby anymore. I don't want to think about any of these things. I tried everything. You tried everything.'

'That's not true. I can still try. You can't decide for me.'

'No, but I can decide for myself and I'm done. This is it. I have nothing else in me. I'm sorry.'

He let go of my hand and looked outside through the balcony's glass door for a while. I heard a dog barking in the garage, the next-door neighbour's TV, the clicking from the heater on the wall behind me, my heavy breathing . . . I heard everything but another word from him. He got up and left the living room, closing the door behind him. The next day, he flew back to Sweden, taking most of his things. Several days passed without us making any contact. Upon checking his Instagram account, I saw his latest post: a picture he took of a stormy sky in Brasília. The city where we spent our first month together. The place where, with petals and candles, he designed a question mark on the floor big enough to fit him on his knees and asked me to marry him. The place where I said yes to a lifetime together. In the photo's caption, he wrote: 'Rage against the dying of the light.'

By the time the twinkle lights were on in all flats but mine, the flood of tears I cried seemed to have crawled up the walls and claimed the ceiling – now covered in mould – and the last thing I wanted was to spend Christmas in a damp Dublin flat watching *Home Alone*. When my phone beeped and Lucy invited me to spend the last week of December with her, I only needed a second to think. 'On my way!'

Together we went for walks around her village in the rural south of Sweden; we cooked batches of salmon with creamy dill sauce and aubergine lasagne; we watched old black and white movies curled on the sofa; we took turns untangling her cat's fur and making fresh cups of herbal tea; we spent hours assembling the pieces of a jigsaw puzzle until we could finally see Mona Lisa's half smile as we ate chunks of cucumber, apples and walnuts from a ceramic bowl; we snort-laughed and choked on white wine while filling in 'Fuck this shit' in rainbow shades on the swear words colouring book I had brought as a gift.

For five days straight, we enjoyed each other's company. Sometimes in chatterbox mode. Other times in silence. There was no emptiness there, in our nest. No loneliness. No lack of a family in the traditional sense of the word. We were a family. For five days straight, I almost forgot I'd have to go back to my empty flat.

On the last day of 2015, Lucy drove me to my old flat in Lund. She parked in front of the kindergarten across from what used to be my living room, and I sat on her passenger seat, looking around. Having lived there for almost six years, I knew where everything was, every building, every tree, every parking space, but now I was visiting a movie set – nothing seemed real. Nothing felt the same. After trying three times, it was clear I had forgotten the code to the main gate of my own flat. Luckily, I had it camouflaged as a contact on my phone. Carrying one big piece of rolling luggage each, we climbed the stairs. One bag was full of clothes Erik had left in Dublin; the other was empty and meant to carry my things. Flat 48. The one we bought a year after getting married. The one with the chunky metal door that made me feel safe. The one with the vintage green wallpaper we weren't sure we liked at first.

Going inside without looking up or around seemed the right thing to do. I followed my feet to the living room. The red sofa was still there. Right next to it was the Ikea book-case. A glance at our photos on the wall caught me off guard. I felt my whole body shake. Lucy kept her distance as I paid my respects to the symbols of my defunct life. I didn't want to make her wait and I didn't want to risk being there when Erik got back from work, so I started piling books, clothes and shoes I didn't remember I had into the bag, and old family pictures and outdated immigration documents into a plastic folder. She followed my lead.

Then came the hardest part. I marched slowly to the

bedroom, dragging the other bag behind me, sat on the dark wooden floor and started unpacking his clothes while buttoning the shirts and folding the trousers just as Grandma had taught me. I placed them carefully in the drawer under our bed. Now *his* bed. I needed fresh air. We carried the bags downstairs. I heard the chunky door shut for the last time and watched the key slide through the grey letterbox – the one with both our names still on it. Back in Lucy's car, I was numb. I asked her if she could drop me at the station so that I could take a train to Stockholm. She asked me if I was sure I should be doing an interview instead of going back to her place. I told her I would make the four-hour journey to meet Candice, a friend of a friend who wanted to tell me her story.

Later that day, I was welcomed into a spacious flat in Solna and set up camp in the pillow corner on the floor. It had been a while since my last interview. I was tense and distracted. Having forgotten to charge my computer, I asked where I could plug it in. Candice pointed to a wall next to me. I got on my knees to reach the electric socket, and by the time the questionnaire loaded on the screen, I couldn't see a thing. I couldn't find a tissue. I didn't know I'd need one. She kneeled next to me and hugged me. She hugged me for a long time without saying a word. There was nothing to say but the actual thing, so I hiccupped that I had separated from my husband. She comforted me until I felt more like myself again.

My sense of time about that day is a bit fuzzy, so I don't know how long it was before I felt ready to listen to her story, but I'm so glad I did because it taught me a great deal about empathy and sisterhood. A stranger opened her house and sat with me while I stained her pillows with my pain, and that's hard to find. Someone who will do just that: sit with you while you ache. Not talking, not advising, not trying to fix you or fix what has broken you to pieces. I knew how hard that was because I had realised in therapy how much of a chronic fixer I was and how I wish I could have seen earlier that I had failed, time and time again, to do that in my relationship with Erik. To sit with him and listen to him instead of always looking for a solution for his wishes, for the lack of my wishes, for the incompatibility of our future selves. But that time had passed, and the lights were out. Still, if I wished to be better or do better, there was an opportunity right before me. 'Sit with Candice,' I said to myself. 'Listen to what she has to say.'

Candice, 49, Rhodesian,[11] Swedish, psychosynthesis therapist

The world I was born into was that of the Rhodesian Bush War when Rhodesia, now called Zimbabwe, fought to claim independence from Great Britain, yet maintain the minority rule of Caucasians. Growing up in a war seemed normal to me, which also meant living in constant fear of losing my beloved father, who was recruited to the war, as all young able men were. There was also fear of an attack and our home being invaded.

War and fears aside, I've incredibly beautiful memories of a place that seemed to be a paradise to me. The people were unusually united, regardless of skin colour. I remember honest, decent, hard-working people trying their best to survive something we did not want. We were subjects of the tragic result of politics.

My mother was young and smart, yet insecure and scared, just twenty years old with strong codependent and egocentric tendencies. I was told she experienced terrible labour. It was she who told me I was the ugliest baby she had ever clapped eyes on when I came out. I imagine there was no proper connection between us during my first breaths, nor later, since she suffered from postpartum depression. Although she loves me and is physically warm, I've never really *felt* her love.

My father welcomed me, his firstborn, with an open heart. I quickly became the apple of his eye. According to my aunt, my mother never expressed the joy of having a child before or after her pregnancy. Perhaps she felt trapped within the expectations of society. It could not have been easy to try to raise a family when she herself was in constant fear of what was happening around her, not knowing if her husband and the breadwinner of the family would return from the war.

We lived on the outskirts of Bulawayo and were urged to be vigilant for the unexpected. My one-year-younger brother and I were brought up in a strict Victorian manner. He and I cycled three kilometres to school daily, unsupervised, from the ages of five to twelve, whatever the weather conditions. We were taught to have good morals, that children were to be seen and not heard and that we were born to take care of our parents when they grew old.

The stories that returned with my father painted a harrowing tale. He told me of witnessing friends being killed and finding people in small tribal villages who had been barbarically butchered by terrorists. Soldiers had to go undiscovered, be forever on the run, taking catnaps when they could, leaving no trace of scent in the wind. They experienced extreme heat and floods; they walked for days with wet blistered feet; no fires nor flashlights were allowed. It was a vile war in a naturally beautiful country that had no importance in the world.

My father imprinted in us that we needed to be

independent, to be tough and not show weakness. Should he die and leave us, we were expected to be able to cope. I'm grateful for his warmth, his titanium psyche, his attitude towards survival and his jovial nature. He did his best to be a provider and create security for his family, despite his harsh upbringing and being in the war.

Ironically, it was not my father who left us, but my mother. My parents separated when I was seven. My mother moved to the United States to be with an ex-boyfriend. She had sold most of our things to buy her ticket to leave. It was a tumultuous time. It was very unusual for divorces to occur at all back then, let alone for a mother to leave her children. We never knew when we would see her again.

Growing up, contact with my mother was sparse. No telephone calls and half a shoebox of letters testify to that. We met for a week almost every two years when she came over with her new man, a Swede she'd met in Chicago. After visiting and spending a week with my brother and me, they would leave us to spend seven to ten days on their own. At times it felt as though my brother and I were orphans in some sense.

I was invited to visit my mother in Sweden for six weeks after I graduated from high school. It was a wonderful experience. I had dreamed for so long about discovering new parts of the world, a hunger for new experiences, new cultures. The people I had met there were so well-educated and well-travelled, I was entranced. Returning home to Africa after that vacation made me yearn for a new start in life where the culture was less patriarchal. The silent rebel in me wanted a place where I could grow beyond the confines of what is expected of women in the shadows of their husbands. I also hoped that somehow my mother and I could bond and mend the mistakes of the past.

After that visit to my mother and her new husband, I decided I would like to live abroad. I completed my training as a radiographer in South Africa and applied for a permit to work in Sweden, which was approved. Then I worked with adult education in the MedTech industry, mainly in radiology and neuroscience. As an idealist, my aspiration is to improve patients' quality of life. After having spent so many years learning about the brain and its functioning, I felt an urge to learn more about the mind. I left the corporate world in 2016 to become a qualified psychotherapist in autumn 2019.

There was no single defining factor as to why I decided not to have children. As a child, I instinctively felt that I would not have a child. Although I like children, I never felt a yearning to have them. Somehow, I subconsciously willed my body to be under par when it came to the procreation process. I started menstruating at the age of ten. It was not an easy start. I bled copious amounts of blood and clots every month. It was quite common that I would bleed through onto my school uniform and clothes.

When I was fifteen, we were shown a film on childbirth in class: a horrifying and gory video with plenty of screaming. It scared me away from ever wanting to have a natural childbirth. I remember thinking, why would I want to put myself through that pain and possible injury? How is it possible for a baby to come out of a little opening in the cervix and through the vagina?

Later, I found out I had numerous fibro-myomas on and in my uterus and fibro-adenomas in my breasts. I had a hysterectomy in 2018 and the gynaecologist confirmed that my chances of having a child would have been slim. I also learned while studying to be a radiographer that my pelvic measurements and pelvic floor are quite narrow, which would also have been a hindrance to natural childbirth.

I questioned why I would want to bring children into a grossly overpopulated world full of egos, mind games, violence and chaos, where natural resources are constantly being depleted by the human race. I failed to provide myself with a good enough reason to defy my decision. It seems I have the ability to love very deeply. I may appear to put up a hard exterior to protect the loving, vulnerable, sensitive part of me. I imagined I would overcompensate any children I had with so much love that I would be an emotional walkover, easy to manipulate. It would mean I would risk losing my own self.

I also felt the age-old fear many have of becoming our parents. I think my mother and I have a yearning to be free spirits. I cringe at the idea of having somebody being dependent on me. Would I turn into my mother if I had children? Oh, the strategies we form to survive, hide and cover up past hurts. I found myself choosing to be in longish relationships with three men over time, whom I did not wish to have children with, who were either chronically ill, had children of their own, or were workaholics. Each relationship was meaningful in its own way at the time.

My last love, Ulf, who had been healthy all his life, suddenly got acute myeloid leukaemia. We spoke of growing old together, but never about raising a family. We were both focused on our careers and doing our best to live healthy lives, which unfortunately were far from balanced. The ultimate test of my earlier decision not to have children came the day he got his diagnosis. We were told that if we wanted to save any of his sperm, we needed to do so immediately, since the chemotherapy would diminish his chances of having healthy sperm.

I was forty-two years old then and loved him deeply. We were both very scared and sad at the time. It was a very tough decision during an incredibly absurd time. I could not bring myself to even think of him going off to jerk off into a jar when he had just received such devastating news.

Simultaneously, so many questions and fears arose within me. Would I give Ulf's wonderful parents a much-longed for grandchild to continue their line? If he was to die, would I want to bring up a child alone? Would I slowly die from the pain of seeing a child who would remind me of him daily? We jointly decided against that opportunity. The ticking clock was never louder. I gave up thinking of 'my or our children' when, tragically, Ulf died just four weeks after the diagnosis.

A few years ago, my father did a genealogy tree of everyone in my family who has had children. My name was not there. I found that hurtful and offensive. If a person has no children, does that mean they do not exist? Is having offspring the only true contribution to mankind? We spoke about it. I cannot remember if he did include me or not in the end, but I was upset by the thought of my life not having meaning in his eyes.

I have younger nieces and nephews as well as friends with children. I rather enjoy being able to pamper, feed and laugh with them for a little while and then give them back. They bring out a very playful and fun aspect of my personality which I enjoy connecting with.

Admittedly, procreating may be the meaning of life, a chance that humanity will continue to evolve. It provides an instinctive driving force to get out of bed every morning, to feel as though there is a purpose. A child's unconditional love and *joie de vivre* is a truly magnificent thing. There is an unspoken promise of a strong bond, of being taken care of, of creating mini-mes or better versions of ourselves, and the hope of not dying alone in the winter of life. There is much allure in this.

There is of course more freedom without children, but being single takes a lot of time in other ways. Everything is done by one person, there is no sharing of responsibilities. For couples, children are usually a natural glue in a relationship.

I sometimes wonder if those who are parents truly are selfless. I have experienced countless occasions where parents have assumed that childless people are natural back-ups: at work, in families and among friends. It is as if an unwritten code exists in society. Mentioning the word 'kid' allows for any number of perks, and singles or couples without children are expected to plan around this.

The relationship with yourself is the most important one in this life. The plasticity of the brain is absolutely wonderful. Once we start to understand we are in fact not a product of the viewpoint of others, we can begin the work of becoming who we were intended to become, but got lost on the way. It takes a lot of courage to grow old. It's vital to live with determination and a sense of belonging with others. I'd like to continue to spend my time indulging myself in meaningful encounters and relationships with those who I feel a strong connection with and vice versa, to build up and maintain my tribe. Nature is my haven. I now have a budding interest in macro photography. I look forward to capturing details in shadow and light unseen by the masses and sharing this.

As I age, I see myself constantly evolving by concentrating on being healthy and embracing my senses. There are pros and cons to everything. We are the result of how we have chosen to act on our choices. We are our thoughts and these are what we project on the world.

I long for a society that has a broader perspective on life, that views varying outcomes by 'standing in another's shoes'. I am committed to utilising the power within love, healing, play, joy, presence, creating, empathy, acceptance and forgiveness, which we all possess. Developing these qualities is a lifelong journey and a purpose in itself, with or without children.

2016

My Body, My House

Once back in Dublin, illness struck like never before. I'd wake up being sick and go to bed with a raging fever. Bedridden, I'd read all the letters Erik had written, flick through our photo albums to the point of awakening my arm tendonitis, and binge our wedding video as if I was about to lose my sight.

That went on for days. The forceful removal of weight too heavy to carry from my back. The violent extraction of a gravid mass of conflicting emotions that had solidified on my spine and twisted it so badly I couldn't stand erect.

At some point in the first months after the break-up, I counted how many houses I had lived in. Fifteen. No wonder I felt so disoriented. On my way to the supermarket, I'd take the wrong turn and end up in a part of the city I had not seen before. On business trips, I'd pass the airport's security point only to realise I had left my luggage at the restaurant. I'd lose my reading glasses, groceries and house keys. I was barely there. As a matter of fact, I don't think I knew where 'there' was, so I left traces everywhere. My place in the world had not just been houses but also people. My mother, Simone, Rita, my grandmother and Erik. Now, all gone. My existence resembled an explosion of breadcrumbs that led nowhere.

Therapy once a week helped me understand that I had to start building a shelter from which I could never be displaced again. I had to allow myself to live the life I wanted even if I saw most people walking the other way. Even if it meant losing everything. But going against the current for so long had sucked the life out of me. I felt drained, and the battle then was to learn how to turn a carcass into a vessel.

The first sign that I wasn't quite there yet was my metabolism. It slowed down to the point where every meal prompted me to bloat. One day, on the train to work, someone thought I was pregnant and stood up so I could sit. I indulged in the scenario for a bit: the baby's foot above my belly button, the elbow poking my ribs ... But the illusion wouldn't last. I wouldn't let it. Doctors, family and friends started nagging me lovingly: 'Eat more veggies, drink more water, exercise regularly and take some time off.' I nodded as I knew I needed it all. I also needed a shelter, however small, without memories. So I broke my rental contract and moved to one of the two bedrooms in a flat a couple of streets away from the office. I'd be there in five minutes. No more taking the wrong train.

My flatmate was a German geek with a gentle soul who loved to play video games through the night. We mostly kept to ourselves but ordered pizza and watched cat videos on Sundays. It was my first time living with someone who was not a relative or a partner, and my way to avoid codependency.

I also hoped to save for a deposit to buy my own place, making this new living arrangement convenient all around.

In a new tiny bedroom with a view of a canal populated by seagulls, I worked, read and planned more interviews. That was all I did. The interviews were the only antidote to my hunger for purpose.

That February afternoon could not have looked any greyer when my phone rang. I moved the laptop further down on the kitchen table and rested my forehead on the glass in desperate need of cleaning.

'Hello.'

'Thank God, Nic. I was starting to worry!' Gabi said.

'Sorry,' I said with a gulp.

'Why weren't you picking up? How was your time with your mom?'

'She didn't come.'

'What? But . . . Last time we spoke, you said she was arriving the week after.'

'That was the plan. I took time off, my flatmate flew to Germany to give us privacy, I had the fridge filled with food, I had booked a couple of local tours, but she was a no show.'

'What happened?'

'She sent me a message two hours before her flight was supposed to land saying she couldn't make it. I had already spent the night awake, uncertain if she had gotten on the flight.'

'Did she say why?'

'First, she said her legs were swollen. Then she said Tácio was giving her a hard time. Who knows? I don't. I'm not even angry. I'm just hurt. This was the only time in my life that I

called her and told her I needed her. I actually said the words:
"I can't do this alone, Mom, please come." She said she would,
so we talked about dates, and I booked the flights.'

'For Christ's sake. I'm so sorry, honey. I really am.'

'Thanks. It will pass. I used the time to rest, and it did me
good. How are you?'

'Me? Well. Yeah . . . I have some news, but I don't know if
this is a good time.'

'Oh, please! Go on.'

'OK. Well, I'm getting married!' she shouted.

'Woah!!!'

'I was dying to tell you, but I didn't want to talk about me
getting married when you are—'

'Getting a divorce. Of course, I understand. But Gabiii, I'm
so happy for you! When?'

'17 May 2017. And I had to tell you soon because I need
my bridesmaid here!'

'Your bridesmaid . . . I'm your bridesmaid?!!!'

'Of course you are, dummy!'

I cried happy tears as I asked her to tell me all about the
proposal. And she did. Fernando, her close friend for many
years and boyfriend of over a year, had asked her to marry him
by surprising her with her grandmother's engagement ring.
As Gabi's grandmother was German, Fernando proposed in
Gramado, a mountain town in Brazil's southernmost state,
built by nineteenth-century German settlers, with Alpine
chalets, chocolatiers and artisan shops. Gabi is addicted to
chocolate, so the ring was inside a chocolate egg. He'd thought
of every detail, and they indulged in what she called the hap-
piest weekend of her life.

More sniffles and giggles followed as she shared what she had in mind for the hen party, the ceremony, the reception and the honeymoon. Life was suddenly a list of special dates duly added to my calendar, and I was going to help plan and attend all of them!

That same week, I got a notification about the first comment left on my blog: 'I found this blog last night, and I'm so relieved. I thought I was losing my mind because I didn't want children. So I'm not the only one? I bought one of your recommended books and I'll come back once I finish it. Thank you for creating this space! Anonymous.'

Being found by someone who felt the same felt like nothing else. There was so much comfort in knowing others were out there that I had no option but to keep looking for them. So I started sharing links to my blog posts on Twitter and tweeted a call-out for women without children who wished to tell me their stories.

*

The first person to send me a direct message on Twitter was Andrea. Her bio said, 'Anthropologist, feminist, bi, atheist and autistic.' There, I found a link to one of her latest studies about the role 'whiteness' takes on in Mexico, where colonial, religious and social heritages elevate it as an aesthetic ideal, simultaneously denying its underlying racism. I knew that to be the case in Brazil too, and I remember thinking: how I wish Mexico were closer. I considered visiting her, but it wasn't possible. Still, I wanted to hear her story, so we booked a video call. I was in my flat in Dublin and she was in a crowded cafe in Mexico City. The background noise was intense, but as soon as the face behind those big black glasses started talking, she had my full attention.

Andrea is straightforward and assertive in the way she communicates. Listening to her speak made me feel braver, and her story taught me to accept my thoughts and desires, however misunderstood they might sound or seem to others.

Andrea, 34, Peruvian, anthropologist

I was twenty-six years old when I was diagnosed with autism spectrum disorder, but, at the time, I didn't feel that I fully fitted into the category of that syndrome. I simply had some characteristics associated with it. And that meant that, when I was a child, I couldn't speak well or easily talk to other people. I got too easily overwhelmed by noises to enjoy playing with other kids, and I was way too rational to relate to them, or even less make friends with them. There were times I didn't feel like a child.

Becoming an anthropologist was my way of trying to understand the many things about the world and what people choose to do that didn't make sense to me. One of them was choosing to have children. Through studying this area, I discovered that not all choices are completely logical or evident. Some are subconscious or symbolic, and they vary in different cultures, ethnicities and genders. This realisation fascinated me so much that I pursued a PhD in anthropology in Mexico. As it can be hard for me to understand very abstract concepts, I chose to focus on themes that I could touch, hear and feel, such as body issues and material culture.

I was born in 1985, at a time when there was massive conflict – the biggest in the twentieth century – in Peru. A civil war between the military and two terrorist groups led to violence everywhere and, because I was living in such a poor neighbourhood in Lima, it was even closer to me. Worse than that, it was inside my house.

Many of the neighbours' girls my age were kidnapped and raped, and some would never be seen again. This made me grow up feeling like I had to protect myself at all costs, and part of that was to make sure I didn't get pregnant, which may have had some influence on my decision not to have kids. But I think that the focus on protecting myself was mostly unconscious until I was in my mid-twenties. It was only after my mid-twenties that I caught myself thinking about the practical aspects of having and raising a child and how I did not think it would suit me.

During my second year at university, my classmates and I had to do research outside of Lima. We went to Ayacucho, in the heart of the Andes, to spend time in a very remote community, in a rural area. I remember being asked every day by the locals why I didn't have children. All of us women visitors would be asked that, and because I was the oldest one in the group, I was asked about it even more. It was inconceivable for them that an adult woman would not be a mother.

Once we were back in Lima, the whole group started talking about it. It steered a collective sense of reflection about the future and motherhood. Through the discussion, I thought about how children made me feel nervous, and how I felt I would not be able to take care of them properly simply because I didn't feel I would understand them. At some point, I heard myself saying: 'I just don't want them in my life.' Somebody asked: 'Never?' And again, I heard my voice say: 'Never.' And that was it. It made sense to me, and I have carried this feeling with me ever since.

Before I met my husband, I never had a boyfriend. I couldn't connect or put myself in the place of others. As a kid, I could only think about myself and my needs. And while, to some extent, I was worried about my mom, my brother or my sister, I could never understand what they needed or try to feel like them. I didn't have a framework to do that. So I learned it very slowly over time and by living in society. Then I learned some more at university, by studying anthropology, psychology and sociology, and connecting the dots that showed me that there was a way. It's depressing, but everything can be reduced to laws and methods. And it was a method that I learned. Before that, I didn't have a good relationship with my family and I didn't have any friends because they couldn't trust me. And the reason they couldn't trust me was that I couldn't be empathetic towards them. That empathy was something I simply wasn't born with.

Then, in 2009, I met Gonzalo and I remember talking to him and being very aware that it felt different. I could see myself in him. And I could tell that he could see himself in me, not the autism spectrum disorder, it was a rapport that I had never had with anyone before. It was strange, but it felt good.

Things got serious; I told him I didn't want to have children and that this wasn't going to change. At that point in his life, he hadn't seriously considered parenthood so my feelings about it were not an issue and we moved on. A couple of years later I brought the subject up again by saying I wasn't going to marry him if he was thinking about having children in the future. He then told me he didn't really want to become a father and that his confusion was more about the fact that he had grown up thinking that this is what you do as a man. So he had to work that out in his own mind first, but once he could finally see a future without children, we got married.

In 2015, I chose to have my tubes tied. This type of surgery was not allowed to be performed in my country until 1995, because of the Catholic Church's heavy influence on government issues.

Alberto Fujimori was the president, leading an anti-democratic government at the time. He wanted to stay in power for ever so he started taking measures that would keep people quiet and gain allies, such as international organisations that took the opportunity to pursue their own agendas. One of the measures was that voluntary vasectomy or hysterectomy needed to be approved by a doctor. And one of the reasons it was difficult for me to have the surgery, even though there was a law allowing it, was because between the years 1995 and 2000 in Peru, Fujimori put in place extreme measures for rural women to be sterilised without their consent. And that's something that has also happened in other underdeveloped countries in South East Asia and in Africa.

The United Nations Fund for Population Activities suggested to local governments that they should reduce the number of children that were born from each woman and a quota system was implemented. So, each hospital, especially in rural areas, had to sterilise a certain number of women. And the number of sterilised women in Peru got to over 285,000.

In numerous cases, the women didn't know they had been sterilised. They just knew they had gone through some surgery. The whole thing happened so fast and was done in conditions that were so unsafe, many women died from infections or had other organs compromised. The practice was denounced in the late '90s, but involuntary sterilisations continued.

After Fujimori's presidency, more documents from those hospitals were recovered and Peru was investigated for its mass sterilisation programme. A group of the women affected started demanding answers and justice from the state, but, to this day, not much has happened.

At first, when I requested to go through the procedure, there was a lengthy protocol that doctors had to follow in light of the recently forced sterilisation of so many women, which meant that it was hard for the next generation of Peruvian women to have their tubes tied. For two years I tried to find someone who had gone through this surgery to give me more information about the procedure itself and the paperwork that needed to be done, but I just couldn't find anyone. The only explanation I'd get from doctors was that this procedure was usually done after a C-section and that it would be hard for me to get it done without having had children.

Finally, I had to go to the head of gynaecology of the public maternity centre in Lima and ask him for advice, as I knew that women were legally allowed to request that their tubes be tied. The doctor was very surprised by my request – in many countries, doctors are seen as this authority who has power over your body, so I don't think he was used to women expressing their opinion and requesting procedures that would allow them to control their biological future – but he listened and helped me.

It took three and a half months to get the paperwork ready and, because I went to the public maternity centre, the costs were minimal. The procedure was quick, it lasted only forty minutes, and there were no complications.

I remember Gonzalo's reaction. At first, when I mentioned the surgery, I'm not sure he fully understood what it meant. He knew the procedure was surgical and that the risks to my life were small. But one of the things I had to go through was a psychological evaluation to certify that I was sane. Then the psychologist asked to speak to the person that I consider to be my closest relative or friend. That was Gonzalo, so he too had to go and talk to him.

On the day of the surgery, he came to the hospital with me and while he waited for me, he could see and hear women giving birth. He later told me how shocking it was to realise that I was the only patient there who did not have kids and who was going the other way in life. And the truth is, I felt that too. So much so that I heard a medical assistant to the main surgeon say, 'Oh, I'm so happy to be here to see this, because we see many births every day, but not this type of surgery, so we want to see it, so we can learn how to do it.'

That didn't surprise me, as I knew only one other woman who'd had her tubes tied, my former boss, soon after her C-section. I had friends who were interested and who asked me how I had done it, but I don't think they went ahead themselves. They were afraid. Not of the surgery, but of the system. Of having to explain themselves and their reasons to so many people. Of having to repeat that nobody was pressuring them. Of confirming that they were fully aware of what was going to happen to their bodies after the surgery and to their lives in general. All the forms they had to fill in ... The whole process was designed to make you give up on taking control of your reproductive rights.

I didn't feel emotional then, but it hit me a couple of days later. I felt angry that everyone could be so amazed by a woman who was choosing what to do with her body. I could see the surprise in the eyes of the women who were in the observation room with me. I could hear it in the tone of their voices and in how it changed when they spoke to me. Then I got angrier that I had certain advantages that other women might not have and that would enable them to follow the same path as me, if they wish to, such as education. The simple knowledge I had acquired that tying my tubes was possible and that it was an option available in my country allowed me to pursue it. I knew I had rights. I could also speak Spanish fluently. Many women in Peru don't. Their mother tongue is Aymara, Quechua, Asháninka, or any of the other forty-three languages that are spoken in my country, but if you go to the doctor, he is going to speak to you in Spanish. So many women end up not going to the doctor because they don't understand what is being said to them and they are badly treated.

Another aspect that contributes to the low number of requests for this procedure is the personal support system that is needed for you to go through it: I was told by the doctors that my organs would rearrange inside me in the following days after my discharge and that this type of surgery would demand complete rest. So during the first four days, I was stuck in bed, and, while that was not at all pleasant, I had a husband who took care of me. Who went out to buy food, cooked for me and fed me, gave me my medication, bathed me, helped me change clothes, took me to the bathroom several times a day. Not many women have that. And without that, you just can't handle the postoperative phase.

After the surgery, Gonzalo changed. He became more sensitive. It's as though he too went through a transformative process, and I think it went beyond understanding that the procedure was irreversible. It was also about realising what I had to go through, what women have to go through and how difficult it can be. He had to sit and listen to a doctor saying 'We are going to cut here and there, then we are going to open this part and remove that . . . ' It's all very graphic and it's the body of his wife they are talking about. And he understood we had to go through all of that to be sure that we would live a life without children if he did not want to go through a vasectomy. He became more informed, more open and more understanding about women's issues.

In South America, generally speaking, there's this assumption that if you are a woman and you don't have a child, it's probably because you couldn't have one. For example, in the neighbourhood I come from, many women couldn't get pregnant because they were malnourished. So people assume that something like that must have happened to me.

Long before I could rationalise most things or understood what a body is, I already felt a distance from it. So when I got

older and learned what a female body is and what the reproductive system is, I already knew that my body is a body that
could not have kids, but not in a biological way. I knew I was
fertile, it was just not the way I saw my own body.

After going through the surgery, I was finally able to see my
body the way I had always felt it. Certain things only become
real to me once I can see and touch them. So now I touch my
scar and I know it's real.

Contraception in general is a big issue in Peru. In theory,
you can get it for free. But in reality, you go to hospital or
someplace that the health department has authorised to
dispense free medication, and you get there and they don't
have it, or they want to sell it to you. But because not a lot of
attention is paid to health in general, sexual and reproductive health fall low in the list of priorities when it comes to
investment.

To make things worse, most contraceptives are sold at a
very high price in Peru, a country where not everyone has
enough money even to eat. So it's difficult and there are just
too many barriers that prevent women from controlling their
own bodies.

I look forward to talking to younger women about my
experience. There are many in my class and I've noticed that
when I tell them about my choice and how it happened, I
give them something I didn't have before: a true possibility
and lots of information. I'm open about it and happy to share,
so they call me, they write to me and we talk it all through.

As I don't have contact with my relatives and I won't have
children, sometimes I do wonder how this is going to affect
me in the future, but there's not much I can do about it. I

try to save money. I know that if I finish my PhD and start working I can save some more. For better or for worse, we live in a capitalist society, so a part of me thinks, *Well, if I have money, I'll probably be all right.*

Children of No One

Unlike Andrea, I had no scar to touch, so it was hard to know when I'd fully heal, but I knew things were getting better when I stopped getting lost on my walks.

I'd enter the glass building where I worked with a badge hanging around my neck. The security team guarding reception would glance at the worst picture ever taken of me and compare it with my real-life, ever-sleepy facial features. A green light and a beep would indicate I was allowed access to the seven commercial floors and the rooftop with the canteen. Most days I'd head to the canteen, and 'A latte, please' would be the first words to come out of my mouth.

My newly acquired addiction to coffee was slow burning and mostly due to post-break-up aftershocks mixed with early-morning video conferences with colleagues in Asia. Back then, the only way to drag myself out of bed and sound like a fully functioning human being by 8 a.m. was to drink coffee, even though I didn't like the taste and I knew I'd develop a migraine soon after. It didn't take me long to get used to the long hours of temple pounding and eye stabbing; what took me a while to recognise was the soothing effect of new chat notifications on my corporate computer screen. But not any notifications.

Notifications from Ben – a tall, blond, athletic drummer in his late twenties whose unassuming smile lit up any room.

Ben and I worked for the same company. We had worked on some projects together in the past and had always been friendly, but the smiles we'd direct at each other on our way to meeting rooms evolved into direct messages, and soon every click on our chat window felt like unwrapping a gift. Lunch once a month turned into once a week, until one day, a concert turned into a date, and we started going for long strolls on Sandymount beach on Sunday mornings.

We only talked or saw each other a few times a week, and only made plans a couple of weeks ahead. I had time, space and energy for other things. So did he. We liked it this way, so we kept going. On the last day of our first weekend spent together in the countryside, I gave him a handwritten note:

I'm learning to dissolve myself in time without ceasing to exist. Like yesterday, when your head was resting on my lap, my fingers were buried in your wheat-coloured hair, and I watched the giant shade of a tree spin from the corner of my eye. I didn't make that up. It was all there: first waiting for us, then savoured by us, mostly in silence, like a sanctuary of all things magnificent.

He smiled as broadly as the Wicklow Mountains, then kissed my hands. That day, whatever was left of the fog in my life was finally gone.

Weeks later, I placed my cup of coffee on a table in the back-yard of a cafe in Greystones:

'The barista made you a heart?' Ben asked.

'He did.'

'Bastard. Why didn't he make you a panda or something?'

'I think pandas are hard to make.'

'I'd make you a panda.'

'You don't even drink coffee.'

'Yes, still I'd make you a panda.'

'Oh, how very cheesy!'

'Of course I'm cheesy. I'm Dutch!'

Surrendering to the comfort of those egg-shaped suspended chairs, we stretched our legs out as if teasing the sun to come and tan our vitamin D-deficient bodies. I felt calm and happy. And not knowing what to do with any of it, I repeated Dr Una's words in my head: *It's okay to let things happen to you. Things you may not have planned or don't fully understand yet.* For about an hour, that's all I did. I savoured every second spent at that table with a view of the ocean, inhaling the salty breeze while Ben people-watched over an overpriced glass of orange juice. My senses were unclogged and I started writing again. I took a pen out of my bag and wrote some words on a napkin.

'Is that another romantic note?' Ben asked.

'No, sorry. A question for my questionnaire.' He went quiet for a bit before asking, 'Are you completely sure you don't want to have kids?'

'Probably not. I don't think I'd obsess about women without children for so long if I was.'

'What if you change your mind?'

'Then I'll see what my options are.'

'Like what? Adoption?'

'That too, if I'm still eligible. What about you? Do you want kids?' I asked.

'I don't know. I've never given it serious thought.'

'Never?'

'No.'

We both went silent and tried to fill in the awkwardness of having started a conversation that felt too early to be had. I doodled on the napkin; he looked for sunscreen in a tote bag and applied it to his fair skin.

Noah

That same week, I dreamed of a baby with blue eyes. His name was Noah. His golden locks and tiny hands caressed my face. His sense of humour, like his dad's, brushed away my sadness. Noah was a projection in my subconscious of that first baby talk with Ben. And I knew it because, before Noah, there were others. Baby talks and babies that visited me in my sleep.

Peter and Paul

When Mom was pregnant with Davi I noticed her near obsession with twins. After he was born, I had a phase where I used to say, 'When I grow up, I'll have twins, and I'll call them Peter and Paul.' Did I think I wanted twins because I knew she wanted them? Was that one of my early attempts to give her what she wished for and make her happy?

Sofi

Erik and I both dreamed about a girl called Sofi. Even when we both knew I didn't want to have a baby. Why then? Why did we allow ourselves to dream about her? It wasn't much. It wasn't often. But it did happen. And it added to the confusion in my head. Maybe in his head too.

There were other dreams with babies, but I didn't get to hear their names.

In another one-on-one with my director, she expressed her satisfaction about me not having quit the year before and recommended a two-day course on leadership for women. *Nothing to lose*, I thought. And signed up.

The first half hour of the course was reserved for introductions. The instructor asked us to say our names, our current roles, what we expected to get out of the course, and mention something that meant a lot to us. It could be a person, a moment, a trip, a hobby, anything. Twenty other participants and I formed a circle and started introducing ourselves. Most of them mentioned their husbands or children. I mentioned the book I was writing as the most important thing in my life at the time. A young woman with short brown hair and almond eyes asked about the book. I told her and the women in the circle I was writing about the lives of women without children. When her time came, she mentioned she was building a mathematical model that reflected her understanding of how the economy works. I memorised her name: Janka.

At lunchtime, Janka approached me and asked if she could join me. Janka and I had several lunches and dinners together after that. I felt motivated by her passion for her career and inspired by her idealism. When she said she wanted to make the world a better place, she really meant it, and she made time for it. She had concrete plans and ongoing projects. I had never met anyone like her before.

Janka, 31, Hungarian, software engineer

I was born in Transylvania, and the good thing about that is that nobody knows much about the place. Transylvania was part of the Hungarian kingdom and is now part of Romania. Most of my family lives in present-day Romania, but my whole family is Hungarian. I have a Hungarian passport, and that was the language I spoke as a kid, so even though I was born a Romanian citizen, I feel very much Hungarian.

My parents were the first in my family who decided to pursue higher education and move to a city. My grandparents and all their ancestors lived as farmers in remote villages. Very little education, very little high culture; they were mostly working the fields, and their thoughts revolved around very basic things like: How do I get food? How do I make children? How do I keep a roof over my head? That was about it.

My father is an engineer. He used to design electrical engines in a factory. Around the time I was fourteen, the factory closed down and he lost his job. He couldn't find engineering jobs after that, so he works at a gas station now. My mother studied textile engineering and the factory she worked for also closed down, so she mostly worked in administrative jobs. They did try to break free from the traditional way of living, but by staying in a small place where all the factories closed down, they got stuck and couldn't go further than that in life.

There's no question that my inclination towards maths came from them, especially from my mother. She was always at the top of her class. So I ended up with two master's degrees: one in computer science and one in mathematics. And I'm a software engineer.

I started taking computer science lessons in 1998, but we didn't have a computer at home. Nobody around me had access to the internet then, so we just wrote programs. At that time, I had the idea of becoming an architect, but then two things happened: first, I met a really nice female computer science teacher and decided I wanted to be like her. And then I got interested in a guy who was a programmer and thought to myself: maybe we can talk about computer stuff. He knew so much about computers and it motivated me to learn more so that I could impress him. They were my two role models for this profession, and the guy became my husband.

When we met, Tamás was married but in the process of getting a divorce. I had nothing to do with it. I knew the woman better than the man in that marriage, and I saw their marriage break down right in front of my eyes. I remember not understanding why she was leaving him as I saw him as a really valuable person. So, in a way, I felt free to let my feelings for him grow over time and within a year of their divorce being finalised we fell in love. I was still in high school back then.

We've been together ever since, and we've been through so many things and changed so much. In my case, I guess I mostly grew up. It's crazy to think that I've spent more years of my life with him than without him.

When we first started dating, my mother didn't like him because he was too old for me and she hoped that both my aspiration to be a programmer and the relationship were just temporary. It turned out that neither was. Once my family realised that what we had was serious, they accepted him as part of the family.

I have no reason to believe I could not get pregnant but I never have. I take contraceptive pills. I never wished I'd have children strongly enough. When I was young, I thought I would eventually have them, but the older I grow, the more I find that I'm so interested in intellectual things and in how they fulfil me that I could channel all my energy into that direction and be happy without becoming a mother.

Having an older husband contributed to the decision not to have children, as this is a special situation. He could make children at his age, no problem. But a child would require extra attention from parents who are in very different life stages. It would also feel awkward to have such a big age gap between a father and a child. He is forty-seven, so if he were to father a child now, when that child graduates from university, my husband would be around seventy years old. So I took this into consideration, but I don't think it was the main reason for the decision. I think it's mostly related to my personality. And when I fell in love with this man, I was already well aware of the big age difference. And I felt, already back then, that I had to choose what my future life would look like, and I chose to be with him. So, in a way, I feel like I chose it a long time ago.

Another thing that puts me at ease is that he already has two children from his previous marriage, so he feels like he's done his duty in that area, and I didn't have to feel like he was missing out on it because of me. But he made it clear that he was open to having kids with me if I wanted to.

There was a window that for years I felt would close, but it didn't. In the end, I was the one self-imposing deadlines and part of that was that I felt that if I were to become a mother, I'd want to have more than one child. And they would be planned. I am a rational person, and I always have a plan for everything. So with motherhood, things would be no different.

Growing up, nobody had only one child, and if someone did, it was an exception. In the last century, people tended to have more children. It's quite a new thing for people to only have one or two. One of my grandfathers had twelve siblings.

Tamás didn't want to push me in any direction. We discussed it at the beginning of this decision process and at the end, but most of the time I was going through it alone. The most important things in my mind were: what happens when I'm old? And why do we make children for society? What a selfish thing it is to make children only for them to take care of you when you are old. If this is the main reason you want to have children, don't have them. I can take care of myself by working and saving money, by taking care of my health so that I can at least try to grow old in good health, I don't need children as a safety net. And, the second thing is that people make children because they think you have to keep

humanity alive. And to that, I thought, I want to contribute
to society, but I don't feel that having children has to be
my contribution. Maybe I can give something else which is
equally valuable.

For example, because I worked in the financial industry, I
have this ambition to understand the world economy better,
which led me to build a mathematical model that reflects
my understanding of how the economy works. So every now
and then, I refine that model, gather data and write little
programs. My intention is to publish it, and if it proves to
be a valid and useful thing to others, then great. My main
influence was the financial crisis of 2008, when I lost a lot
of my savings. Many people lost so much in the crisis; some
even lost their lives.

I know I can change my mind about motherhood, but I also
know that only a very drastic change in my life would make
me start thinking about the topic again. For now, a decision
has been made and I'm pleased with it.

Because I was brought up in a traditional environment, I
still remember being quite young and noticing a woman who
lived nearby and the fact that she had no children. I asked my
mother why she didn't have kids. And I didn't get a direct
answer, but I had the feeling that my mother felt sorry for
the woman, and I don't think she was the only one. There's a
sense of societal pity towards childless women.

I'm not sure to what extent I was projecting those collective feelings, but I remember noticing that she had a job and
her own flat. To me, as a kid, it was sad to think of someone
living alone in her flat, but now, as an adult, I think: she had
a job and her own place to live. She was independent. I don't

feel sorry for her. I was just seeing her through somebody else's lenses.

Somewhere along the way, I realised that even though society has expectations laid out for me as a woman, I don't have to follow them. I don't have to get married or marry someone people expect me to, I don't have to have children or pursue a profession that is deemed 'feminine'. I can be the only or one of the few female software engineers in the office. I can be the childless woman in the village. It's okay to be different. It's not a bad thing. And it can drive a change of perspective in society.

A few years ago, when I was younger and a lot more insecure, whenever I met with distant relatives, they'd ask me when the stork was coming, and I'd say 'maybe later' just to avoid the conversation. But I don't do that anymore because I'm no longer afraid that the conversation will hurt me. I find the same resolve about this that I found with other things in my life.

In the software engineering industry, there are few women. Not only that, there are very, very few women who have kids. People who choose this direction are more likely to go against society in other ways, too, not just in their career, because that's what it takes. It takes so much energy to go against the current. In order to keep going, you have to keep reminding yourself that your condition as a human being, regardless of your gender, comes first. And you have to ask yourself: are you happy? Do you feel free? Are you doing what you want to be doing with your life? *Your* life. Those are the questions that have guided me here. To where I am, who I am and how I spend my time and my energy.

My first ever work experience was in the Netherlands,

and I was there for less than half a year when one of my colleagues – they were all men – announced he and his wife were expecting a baby. Once the baby was born, he took two weeks off, which was a surprise to me: *Wow, fathers take two weeks off for a kid here?* To my bigger surprise, he came back from his paternal leave and said: 'From now on, I'm going to work four days a week because I want to spend a day every week with my kid.' That was something I never imagined possible! I had never seen or heard anything like that. It was a complete culture shock to me.

Another example of culture shock was realising that harassment towards women on the streets is less accepted here. Whereas in Eastern Europe, it's so embedded in society to catcall a woman or call her a bitch if she doesn't respond to a stranger's advances that people seem much less aware that this is a bad thing. They will ask: Why would this be a bad thing? What's the problem with 'complimenting' a woman in the streets?

I have this strong core intent to be useful to society. To channel as much energy into it as I would put into raising two children, and I'm most interested in lowering economic inequality between people because there are very, very poor people and very rich people. There is also inequality in salaries between men and women. I'll keep developing my economic model, but I also volunteered to translate a programming book and a website into Hungarian. Both projects aim to help women learn programming.

As I grow older, I'm more conscious about what makes me feel happy. And it's not as simple as having or not having children. It's so much more. You will always miss out on something. You can't experience everything available to you in life. So you make choices, and you decide which paths to take and which ones to leave behind without trying. And that's okay. What's important is to move forward with intent.

Head Space

Ben wasn't a fan of big changes. The last one had happened four years before when he moved from the Netherlands to Ireland for the job he was about to lose. That Monday morning, his manager dropped the redundancy news and told his team they had ninety days to find new jobs.

It took Ben three weeks to get to the last step of the recruiting process for a role that was perfect for his multimedia background. The final call with the recruiter had just ended.

'So ... Did you get it?' I asked.

'Yes. They just sent me the offer,' he said, smiling but without showing excitement.

'I'm so proud of you. Well done!'

'Thank you,' he said, looking at me as if trying to read me. I smiled for a second. Then my eyes welled up and I looked away, embarrassed.

'I know. It's okay. It's okay,' he said, wrapping his arms around me.

The news was bittersweet because the job, while indeed perfect for him and still in the same company, was not in Ireland but in the UK.

*

Having read novels and journals by pioneering travellers who had no children, such as Sanmao (Chinese), Isabella Bird (English), Freya Stark (English-Italian) and Robyn Davidson (Australian), I made a point of booking solo trips after my divorce. My trips were nowhere near as long, challenging or groundbreaking as theirs, nor was I as fearless and resourceful as they were. However, arriving and exploring a new country alone reminded me that I could do many things on my terms and at my own pace. When the news broke that Ben would lose this job, I had a short trip booked to Iceland. When he got the job in the UK, it felt even more important to take some time to think through my next steps.

On a purple plane with big white letters that read WOW, the flight attendant announced that we were about to land in Reykjavík. I closed my bag of jelly beans and stowed it in my backpack, which held a portable camera, a BIC four-colour pen, and a spiral notebook. One hour later, I dropped my bag at the guesthouse and walked to the city centre.

It was September, but it was cold. I wore a beige turtleneck sweater under a black corduroy jacket, black trousers, combat boots, and a massive scarf that would make Lenny Kravitz proud. Still, I was cold. And hungry. From restaurant to restaurant, my eyes would jump out of my head when I read the menu prices hanging outside. The graffiti was equally eye-catching:

To be normal is to have the same disease as your neighbour.

Shortly after sunrise the next day, I headed to the southern coast for some of the country's best sights. The roads were in perfect condition and virtually empty, so the view was always clear. Every time the tour bus turned a corner, there was a new stunning vista. Staring ahead did me good and gave me a lot of head space.

For the rest of the weekend, I hopped on and off the bus shared with families and couples. An older man from Catalonia and I were the only two people travelling alone. The razor-sharp wind numbed my face as I walked on black sand beaches and photographed basalt columns. Sat by the window on the ride back to the city, I watched giants surrounding me, surpassing me, as I waved them goodbye.

Being in that part of the world made me wonder what it was like to be born and grow up there. What kind of social expectations and norms did Icelandic women experience? Did they have many children? Were they pressured into having them? I tweeted about it. And retweets led me to Jóna.

The tall woman I met in an artisan bakery wore a grey coat that reached her ankles. The lapels were turned up, covering her long neck. Her hair was short at the back and more voluminous on the front, where lustrous curls adorned her delicate features. Her eyes were a swimming pool, and her voice was as velvety as her coat. I could listen to her speak all day long.

Jóna, 31, Icelandic, actor, musician and composer

I was born in Húsavík, which is just one bay over from Akureyri, a big city in the north, but still far away from Reykjavík, the capital of Iceland. The place is quite small, and more of a village, with a population of only 2,500.

In my first three years of life, my family and I lived half an hour outside of this village, in the middle of nowhere, like proper hunter people. Then, between my fourth and my twentieth birthday, I lived in the village which, despite its size, offers everything one might need: a hospital, a primary school, and even a secondary school, which is why I stayed there for that long. But I wanted to go to university, and I knew I wanted to go away from Iceland one day, so I started by going to Reykjavík, to study music.

I've always been a geek. I liked anime and video games, and at some point, I realised how much I also liked languages. And then there was the fact that I didn't know what to do with my life after a music degree and that I was already learning Japanese in my spare time, so I thought why not just do it full time? I did a three-year degree in Japanese, which included spending a year living in Japan to experience it and to become fluent.

It was amazing. Especially because I could communicate and, every time you learn a new language to the point you can understand it, it just gives you a different way of thinking as the language reflects what's behind a culture, how ideas are formed and the native speaker's sense of themselves and others. A lot of people were surprised that a foreigner could speak Japanese. But I get it: I'm tall. I'm white. I've got big blue eyes. People looked at me and wondered, *What's happening?* I've also got tattoos and they are still quite taboo there, which didn't help with first impressions. People would often revert to English even if they could barely speak it. Then I'd say, 'I'm talking to you in Japanese, can we just do that? Because that's a lot handier.'

Luckily, I had won a grant to finance my studying, which enabled me to travel a lot and to truly experience the country. I miss it. I miss the smell of it. The air, the plants and flowers that grow there, the cooking . . . You can get the food sometimes, in other countries, but you can't replicate that smell.

The Global Gender Gap Report 2011 came out when I was in Japan and that year Iceland was number 1, the UK was number 16 and Japan was number 98. So Japan has a long way to go when it comes to women's equality and representation and there's also almost no access to childcare. That means that many women are choosing to not have partners, just to keep working, because they don't want to give up that autonomy. There you're still expected to become this second person to your husband, someone who has babies and stays home. And I just can't get my head around it.

After Japan, I did a master's in popular music performance in the UK. It was my way to change things up. My parents were in music school, and my dad was a pianist, piano tuner and a conductor. He taught me to play the piano. My mom taught me the recorder. So music was always in the house.

I live in London, and I realised recently that I'm the only one in my extended family that doesn't live in the capital of Iceland. And the good thing is that nobody makes me feel bad about it. My mom visits once a year and I go home a lot, so all is good. Depending on what or with whom I'm working, I'll tour in Iceland, the UK or Scandinavia. It's a continuous up and down and everybody is used to it by now. But I think it's surprising for everyone that I'm the only one abroad and living this life because I was very quiet and reserved as a kid. I was scared of new things. I had two older brothers who were very loud and took up a lot of space, so I kept to myself. And then, all of a sudden, that kind of flipped. I'm also the only one with tattoos in the extended family, the only one with a foreign boyfriend, and the only one that's travelled further than Scandinavia. It's strange how that's happened.

Still, I feel very Icelandic because we're very harsh, very direct people. We don't have a word for please. We say thank you, but we don't say please. So I had to practise saying please a lot so people didn't think I was rude. And I know that sometimes people are startled when I say something that an English person wouldn't say, but I don't want to give that up.

In Iceland you have to pay for higher education and for your healthcare. So our country isn't this free, equal utopia that a lot of people think it is either. With that said, I'm proud of what Iceland has achieved so far. We had the first democratically elected female president in the world: Vigdís Finnbogadóttir. She was in power from 1980 to 1996 and we loved her. She has no children, so, back then, people would ask, 'Why don't you have children?' and say, 'You're not motherly.' And she would say. 'That's irrelevant, next question.' And I remember thinking: *You go!*

Then, years later, we had the first female prime minister, who was openly lesbian and this aspect of her life was not part of the conversation. We were happy to have her running the country. Can you imagine a lesbian or a gay man leading the UK? Would people be okay with that? I doubt it.

However, and unfortunately, I think we may have stagnated a little in recent years. Iceland is so small that changes can happen fast. If an idea is formed in a little pocket, it spreads very quickly, because there aren't that many people to get to. So while things can move forward quickly, they can also go backwards.

You can never quite realise how different the world is out there until you go elsewhere. The fact that I was twenty-six when I got my first catcall, and I didn't believe it, says it all. I came to the UK for an audition to go into the interview for my university, and I walked past this group of builders. It was just like it happens in the cartoons: 'Oi, darlin'!' Then I thought, *Did that happen? No, that didn't happen. Forget about it* ... But then I had to walk past the same group on the way back, and it happened again, and I thought, *That did happen! How has this happened?* Because it doesn't happen in Iceland, and, if it does, it's at 5 or 6 a.m. when the drunkest guy from the dodgiest bar is outdoors and says something silly to you and you think, *Oh, well, that's just sad.* But it's not widespread. Not there. And not in Japan. So they have that in common.

I like to read. I'm into humanities and feminism, and I do a lot of research on that. I would like to be more involved than I am in activism, but I try at least to be a voice. Just having conversations with people. I try not to shy away from it, so that we can stop this idea that all feminists are the same person, and they all have the same opinions and they all agree on everything. Whereas no group of people is like that. Imagine that you're a bassist. You don't agree with every bassist in the world. You don't all have the same opinions. You can't just say that everybody's like this and they all think that, and this one rotten apple ruins the whole bunch. That's not how it works. So these conversations are important.

Another important topic is female sexuality or sexuality in general. Why is it taboo? Why are there things that we don't know about our bodies? In Iceland, when we were thirteen or fourteen, we were taught about sexuality and sex and how it works. It was controversial at the time and critics said it was too early, but, no, it was too late! Because I know there were girls in my class who weren't virgins anymore and who didn't get the information they needed before they were active.

Also, why do we accept pain in sex? Why is it so common and why don't we talk about it? Why are we led to believe that we shouldn't need lubrication outside of our own body when there's at least a week and a half of the cycle where we don't make as much lubrication? So why would we not then buy lubrication if it exists and makes things easier and nicer? Because people associate it with anal sex? So what if that's what's happening? Why is that a problem for others? Again, taboos. And once you realise that often women around you are going through the same thing as you, but we suffer in silence, I can't help but feel the need to learn and talk to each other.

Then there's also the importance of expanding these conversations to men who have sex with women about how our menstrual cycle works, and how it affects sex, and different positions, and the cervix and loads of things that contribute to sex being pleasant or not, so all of us can benefit from that knowledge.

The morning-after pill is readily available in Iceland. You don't have to do anything. You just go in and say I need the morning-after pill, and there you have it. But when I needed it in the UK, I had to have a chat with the pharmacist and I couldn't understand what was happening. Why are you asking me these questions about my sex life? On which day and at what time I had sex? With whom? I'm an adult. I need this, and I should be able to have it without feeling embarrassed about it.

I've never got pregnant. There's nothing indicating I can't, but I've never tested it. When I was younger, I presumed I would because that's the thing to do at some point. I like kids, and I'm good with them, which reinforced the presumption. As I got a bit older, established a life that I liked, and got to think about what life I wanted to provide to somebody and what I would have to do to do that, I started to get iffy about it.

This change happened between twenty-five and thirty, and I met my current partner, John, when I was twenty-six. Back then, he said, 'I want kids. And if you don't want them, that's not a good thing to do, for us to get together.' And I'd always assumed that I'd have kids, so I wasn't going to make this the cause of separation. But over time we have both gone from yes to I don't know, and we're currently undecided about whether we want kids. We're in a place in our lives where we don't know if or where they would fit in.

As artists, we both work evenings, we tour and we live a life that's financially up and down, never quite knowing what our income is going to be. Still, we have no deadline to decide since new research shows that women can have children up to the age of forty and often beyond.

Part of my ambivalence is to do with too many people being in this world already. There's not necessarily a need to create your own. Even if you want a kid. The other part of me is apprehensive about the changes a pregnancy makes to your body. I've got chronic pain, so I wonder how my body would handle it. It's not just giving birth, it's all the changes and procedures you have to go through for months.

I learned a great deal from my friends who had babies. They told me how much it hurts to dilate and to have their dilatation checked, and, again, why did nobody tell them this would happen the way it does? Why are we taught logarithms at school, but not how our bodies function? You go into something that big so unprepared because we treat it as natural when natural doesn't necessarily mean you should do it, or that you should do it without thinking or being informed about what it's going to be like.

I went to the Festival of Choice in 2017,[12] and there was a talk about obstetric violence and procedures that are unnecessary during pregnancy, or that are still largely unknown by women but that are common practice. Such as episiotomy and the fact that in some countries it's used in 100 per cent of childbirths. How is that possible?

When it comes to motherhood, there's a lot to consider, so I am taking it day by day. Life is not so much what I plan, but what is happening to me now, and looking back at how careful I have been about not getting pregnant so far, it's quite obvious I don't want it yet. Still, I'm quite open to it and I think it's fairly possible that, in the future, I will choose to adopt, foster, or invite somebody into my life, in whatever way it's possible then. And if for some reason it doesn't work out for me, it doesn't have to devastate me, because I'll know that up to that point I will have been living the flow of my life. There's no right or wrong, there's just what feels right in the moment. And there's no one pressuring me, so I can take my time. If nature wakes me up one day with some sort of post-thirties feeling and says, *You're still fertile, let's do this!* then I'll deal with it.

I do look quite young, so maybe that's why I don't get asked if I have children a lot or why not. It's such an intrusive question, especially when you're just out and about and a random guy starts small-talking and asks you point-blank. What happens if you can't have them? Are you expected to open up? 'It's just because my stuff doesn't function. How about your stuff? Does it function? How is it doing?' Is that how that conversation is supposed to go? Weirdos. I don't understand why people think they're allowed to ask. And while it doesn't upset me to be asked because I can say I decided not to, unless I write a song with the lyric 'I don't have children', I would rather people ask me a different question.

I often ask myself if I want this experience as much as I want the experiences that I will have without the child. I know there is a life where I don't have children, and that will not affect where I travel, what I do, or what I can accomplish creatively. But will I be able to do all that is meaningful to me today and also have a child? I believe that many women are making the decision not to become mothers based on the fear that they just won't be able to.

Until this gets sorted in my head, I want to keep doing what I'm doing, and I want to go everywhere. It's just a matter of balancing it with being an artist. And I know for certain that my career is my passion. When I was a kid, and I thought about what I'd be when I grew up, it was always music, acting and being a farmer, because I love animals. So, first and second, done. Farmer? We'll see when that one comes in. It requires a lot of commitment. There's not a lot of touring that can happen when you've got cattle. You know, who's going to feed the sheep? Maybe someday down the line.

The Baby Matrix

Thursdays were Una's days.

In my first October session, I brought up the latest with Ben and how, initially, my instinct was to run away. I didn't want anything that would make me redirect my life or someone to have to do the same for me again. I told him I enjoyed our time together, but, above everything else, I wanted peace of mind. Although what I said was more along the lines of 'a fucking break'.

'And how did he take it?' she asked.

'He understood and said that the next phase didn't have to be demanding.'

'Exactly. Your life doesn't have to be about someone else, even if you love that person. Your life is about you. You get to decide how much weight you put into relationships.'

'That's it. We'll start with two monthly visits, taking turns travelling and paying for it. We'll talk about it again if it gets too much for either of us.'

'Sounds reasonable. So it might be worth giving it a try, after all?' Her smile was warm.

'I think so. But I'll pace myself. No living together or getting married, and still no babies.'

'Good woman. One step at a time. How about work? How does it feel now?'

'Same old.'

'Would you consider looking for a new job?' she asked, scribbling on her notepad.

'I haven't, with everything that was happening, but now that you mentioned it, I might.'

Once the lights in the office turned off automatically for lack of movement on my floor, I visited the internal jobs portal, typed 'writer', and scrolled through the results. Most were for UX writers and required the candidate to be in the United States. At the bottom of the page, I spotted the 'creative writer for a virtual assistant (Spanish)' role. A new team was looking for poets, comedians and fiction writers to craft the personalities of artificial intelligence tools.

When the divorce came through, I had no energy to think about another significant life change. But now, I could feel a reservoir of energy starting to bubble up. I wanted that job! I emailed the hiring manager asking if she already had a Portuguese writer. Earlier the next day, I got her reply. She would be expanding her team in the new year. 'If there's a Portuguese role, and I think there will be, I'll let you know immediately.' The thought of receiving another email from her soon filled me with hope.

On my first trip to London, after we decided to embark on a relationship across the Irish Sea, Ben picked me up at Gatwick Airport. On the train to King's Cross station, I placed the book I was currently reading on my lap and a blue leather notebook in Ben's hands.

'There. More romantic notes,' I said. His gaze moved between the verses and my face.

'You wrote these poems for me?'

'Yes.'

'I don't know what to say.'

'That's okay. You don't have to say anything.'

'I'm not good with words. I'm the guy who gave you a card with an ostrich shaking his ass.'

'Yes, and I love that about you. I love that you don't take everything as seriously as I do.'

'I take us seriously.'

'I know. Now shush and read a poem or two, why don't you?'

'On it, boss.'

I leaned against him and went back to reading *The Baby Matrix* by Laura Carroll.

'What's this one about?' he asked.

'It's in part about how humans unquestionably believe the desire to have children boils down to our biological wiring. Carroll argues it's much more than that.'

'Like what?'

'Pronatalism. She draws a parallel with the movie, *The Matrix*. The blue pill is continuing to live this way, with our society believing parenthood should be the central focus of every adult's life, even when this notion no longer serves us. And the red pill is shattering these beliefs, seeing through them and moving towards a post-pronatal society.'[13]

'Dang. I may read this one once you've finished. By the way,

I saved something for you.' He pulled out his phone. 'It's a thread that became viral this week from a Reddit community called Childfree. They have more than one and a half million members! Let me find it in my bookmarks.'

He found it and handed me his phone. I spent the rest of the train journey scanning through the top threads. In one about childfree women in Asia, I found Sherryn.

Sherryn, 30, Thai, gold jewellery shop owner

I live in a province on the east coast of Thailand. It's called Chonburi. I've been to Australia, Japan, Hong Kong and the United States, but mostly lived here. If there is another country that has good weather, no rain and is not too cold, I might want to move there one day. Why not?

In Thailand, when you want to go to university, you have to take an entrance exam. But because I was never really good at taking tests, my score was low, so I ended up choosing to study agriculture. Right after getting my bachelor's degree, I realised it wasn't for me. Then I gave up on it, forgot all about it, and ended up working for my family. We own a gold jewellery shop and I work there as a salesperson, which I enjoy because I don't like working under a boss.

My father was a jeweller too; he died when I was twelve. My mother used to sell all types of Thai food, but then, later on, she also became a jeweller. Of the five children they had, I am the youngest, and this is one of the reasons why I still live with my mom. Another is that it makes it easier for me to help her with the shop. It's common in Thailand, and other

Asian countries as well, to live with your parents when you are an adult.

Most Thai people are Buddhist. I'd say about 95 per cent of us. The other 5 per cent are Muslim and Christians. In the past, there was no conflict and we could live together. But now, in the south of Thailand, in three provinces at the border between Thailand and Malaysia, there's conflict between Buddhists and Muslims, and a lot of terrorism, which is very upsetting.

Buddhism suits me as it is not very restricting as a religion. There are only five rules for Buddhists: tell no lies, don't kill any animal or human being, don't steal, don't do any addictive drugs and don't cheat on your loved one.

As far as I know I can have children, I just don't want to. When I was little, I believed I would one day have two kids, but I was too young and I didn't know myself well enough. From ten or eleven onwards I already knew that I would not have children because I realised I don't like them. When I go to events or family gatherings with a lot of kids, I don't feel at ease. I think they are annoying with their screams and tantrums. When I have to stay home with my nephews, I put on my earphones and listen to some music because I just don't know how to interact with them.

There are a few restaurants in the Western world that do not allow children, but I've never heard of a restaurant like that here. I think that if we had a similar place here, local people would find it offensive. It simply wouldn't work.

Having children is a lot of responsibility, so that is a no for me. Nothing can guarantee that if you have kids they will be good people. It's hard these days when they have access to the internet from an early age and they are connected online to people who are not family. They get to see so much that as a parent you have no control over. And there are so many bad things that could happen to them. I don't want to take risks.

My parents seem to understand my decision, but in Thai culture in general, people push their children to have children. As soon as you get married, people will ask: *When will you have kids?* So for the longest time I worried about missing out on becoming a mother, but when I became aware of how many people regret having them, I realised I didn't want children anymore. Many people don't know what it's like to have a baby. They do it because everybody else is doing it, and some find out later that it's not for them, but it's too late. Women should be taught about motherhood at an early age at school because there are many teenage mothers around. Information could keep them from having an unwanted child.

One of my sisters is not married, but I don't know if she wants kids or not. I never asked. I also have some friends who say they don't want children and I have three aunts who don't have children. They are all in their sixties and still single. I'm not sure why, but I just don't speak to any of them about it. Maybe it's because they aren't childfree like I am. They are childless. There's a difference between people who couldn't have children but may still want to have them and the people who choose not to have children, and I'd like to connect with people who feel like I do.

There is one couple that comes to mind. A Thai TV actress, Piyathida Woramusik, and an actor, Napassakorn Midaim. They got married but they say they will never have children. When I found out, I thought, *I want to find a guy like him!*

I've never been in a serious relationship. I went to an all-girls school. Then, when I went to university, there were only eight boys in my classroom, and seven of them were gay. So I didn't meet many guys with whom I could go on dates. If I can find a good man, then I would like to marry, but if I cannot, then I would rather be single than marry someone who doesn't think like me. No kids!

Before I was twenty-nine, I used to be unhappy about not wanting to become a mother. Until then, I thought that even though I did not want a child, if I got married I'd probably have to have one anyway and that made me feel terrible. Back then I didn't even know that childfree people existed. I didn't know that there were so many people who don't want to have children in the world. Then I found a thread called 'Do you want to have kids or not?' in a Thai online forum, and many people replied that they didn't want to and that they called themselves childfree. I became familiar with the term and also experienced a sense of relief for knowing there were others like me.

Soon after this discovery, I made a commitment to myself. Becoming a mother did not define happiness, so I wouldn't be a mother and I should find a compatible partner who doesn't want children. Unfortunately, that's hard.

Dating apps are great, but only a few apps have a section where you can say if you want children or not, so they haven't really worked well for me so far. Even when I find childfree men, they are in another country. Also, I'm picky: I like handsome men. So even if they are childfree and live in my country, there are other things that don't match my preferences.

Being childfree is now part of my identity. I've made up my mind and I know I will never be a mother. I don't feel any pressure from friends or acquaintances to reconsider my decision, but, strangely enough, I feel pressure online. When the topic is being discussed in forums and I share the reason why I don't want kids, there are always some people who reply: *Who will take care of you when you are old?* They really try to make me change my mind, even though we don't know each other. Then I end up replying because I want them to let me be. People have to let you be what you want to be. When I'm asked why I don't want children, I tell them like it is. I never lie. I want them to understand my motivation.

Some people think that those who don't want children must come from an unhappy family, but that wasn't the case for me. I have a good relationship with my parents and siblings.

There are many people who don't like children, but have children anyway. They are not asked why they had them in the first place, but those who say they don't want to have children are asked all the time. I'm honest about not liking them and about not wanting them. It makes perfect sense to me. Not every woman has maternal instincts, because if that was the case there wouldn't be any news about mothers who hurt, abandon or kill their children.

When I feel the need for information about a life without kids, I go to online communities. I mostly just read what people say and don't participate as much as I once did. I no longer feel isolated, just curious.

Through my Twitter account, I looked for accounts of people who discuss not having kids and got more suggestions from the algorithm. As I could not find a childfree-focused account in Thai, I created one to connect with people in my own country who had made the decision to remain childless and who might want to talk about it.

Thailand is still conservative because we all think that you have to have children to take care of us when we are old. But what if they die first? The fear of not having a child to look after me in my late years on earth is gone; I just have to save money for my retirement. I'm not sure I'll be able to, but it is something I keep in mind. Thailand will become an elderly country in the near future, just like Japan. And I hope that there will be many places to take care of the elderly, so I could live in one of them.

Everybody deserves to live the life they desire. If you want a childfree life, I say, just go for it.

2017

Birdie, Birdie, Birdie

After celebrating Valentine's Day with Ben in Dublin, I felt ready to call my mother and tell her I was in love again. Despite some flings and a couple of short-term relationships, Erik was the only man I formally introduced to my family, and I didn't want to risk bringing someone new into their life if that person didn't have a fair chance to stay in it for quite some time. Ben did. And I wanted him to stay.

Her first reaction was to squeak on the phone, 'Tell me more!' I told her how we met, his name, age, nationality, and profession, and sent a picture. The usual checklist.

'He is gorgeous, fifi!' Then she went quiet.

'Mom?'

'Yeah?'

'What is it?'

'Does he treat you all right?'

'Oh, yes. He is marvellous. Don't you worry.'

'I do worry. Mothers always worry. And you won't

understand this until you have kids.' She stopped for a second, realising what she had just said, then tried again, 'I know you might not have kids, but this worry is hard to explain.'

'Mom, I don't have to have a child to understand that you worry about me.'

'Certain things are hard to describe, Nicole. No matter how old you are, I'll always be here thinking that you are alone on the other side of the world, and not a day goes by that I don't pray that nothing bad will happen to you. That no one will hurt you.'

'I understand. But if anything, I'm stronger now and more able to care for myself. And I'd love you to meet Ben. I'll be there for Gabriela's wedding in May, and he's coming with me.'

*

A brand-new Audible subscription led me to *The Story of My Life* by Helen Keller. After that, I listened to *The World I Live In*, in which she talks to Anne Sullivan and Polly Thompson about how she learned to inhabit the life of the mind and appreciate the world through the sense of touch.

Helen Keller was born in 1880 in the United States. When she was less than two years old, she contracted an illness that left her deaf and blind. It wasn't until she was seven that Anne Sullivan, a visually impaired teacher, entered her life and became her speech instructor and lifelong companion.

I searched for more information about both women and found a tribute post in Kay's blog. I contacted her, and we started exchanging voice notes on WhatsApp. She taught me how to lock the recorder on my phone so my finger wouldn't keep sliding and sending her empty or half-baked voice messages. And she added a ton of texture to my life.

I visited her in Canada and stayed at her house, where she showed me her Harry Potter books in Braille as we sat on her porch to hear the northern cardinal whistling a song that sounded like 'birdie, birdie, birdie'. Then she visited me in Ireland, where we walked along a long gravel path in the park near my flat and sat down on the grass and by the sea as she recorded the sound of the waves and the swimmers in Sandycove.

Kay describes herself as not having children by choice and circumstance, which made me understand that childlessness is nuanced and the places in which women will find themselves within its spectrum can overlap or change overtime.

Kay, 34, Canadian, writer

I could run and reach and run and never get to that distant line – so imaginary, begging to be defined. Risking fruitless pursuits, and still, I walk into a fathomless open sky, unsure of what might be out there, missing everything going by as I pass. And just how do I adequately describe this concept to him? I try to explain what the horizon is to my younger brother. He was blind from birth, but as a child I was low-vision and could still see a fair amount. I learned, early on, the line dividing the earth from the sky of Woodstock, near where I grew up.

When people hear the word Woodstock, they often think about Woodstock in the United States, where the music festival was. But I'm from Woodstock, a small town in Ontario, Canada.

As a kid, I loved drawing and painting so much that I aspired to be a visual artist. Then I lost the ability to see colours when, at twelve, I was diagnosed with kidney disease, and had to start doing dialysis which caused an unknown virus to attack my remaining sight. As I got older, I developed other medical conditions, so I was in hospital a lot. Over time, I started gravitating towards words, which led me to become a blogger and freelance writer with the help of the internet and assistive technologies like screen readers.

It took several years, throughout my teens and early twenties, for colours to completely fade from view. When I could no longer see them, I moved to soundscapes. Clunky tape recorders at first, and voice memos on my phone now. And this is how I remember things and how I got to know the sound of my own voice. I know many people don't like to hear themselves, but I became accustomed to it. It's just my voice so I like it. I have to. It's the key to finding my sense of self and the power that lies within me.

Another love is reading e-books with Braille technology, which has come a long way, or with my computer, as there is a voice that narrates the text to me. Audio storytelling is a very powerful thing and, as a blind person, it allows me to be on the same playing field with others because we are all just listening. This aspect of life in audio is so important to me that I now have a podcast with my younger brother. The podcast is called *Outlook* because it has to do with perspective, ours and others'. On Monday mornings we broadcast live for an hour from the radio station at a local university. The show's aim is to bring awareness to accessibility, advocacy and equality issues.

In addition to being a creative outlet, producing *Outlook* every week means I get to spend quality time with my brother regularly, as I go to London (Ontario), where he lives, and meet him at the recording studio. Then I return to my house in Woodstock, where I've lived alone, on and off, since I moved out of my parents' house in 2006. In this house, I've had two pets, a dog and a cat, and they gave me more reasons to get out of bed and helped structure my days, particularly when I was not in a relationship.

I've had three serious romantic relationships so far. The first one was with Ryan. He was my first long-term boyfriend and, at twenty-five, I was still learning what I wanted and needed from being with another person. He seemed like he wanted to get married and have children, but I ended it because I realised we were very different people and didn't share similar values and goals in life. I can't say how that might have turned out if I'd stuck around, but I had to make a decision, and at that time, that was the right one.

In the second relationship, when I was twenty-seven, Oliver had medical issues of his own, which at first seemed like a good thing as I figured he could understand some of my physical limitations. But he didn't think he wanted kids. Occasionally we would talk about it, and we'd say, 'Well, maybe we'll adopt, or maybe we'll find some other way.' In the end, that relationship too ended because of a lot of factors, but it was partly to do with the different ways with which we handled and communicated about our conditions.

Both Ryan and Oliver could see, but in my thirties, I met Ali at an advocacy event for blind people. He was living on an island on the east coast while I was all the way in Ontario. He was also losing his sight. We started a long-distance relationship, but dating someone who is losing his sight comes with its own struggles because an almost codependence can develop. Coming from Pakistan to study in Canada and having no family nearby meant we bonded very quickly. And so, one year in, when I decided to break up with him, not only did I feel that I had broken his heart, but also that I had taken away one of his lifelines. It was hard to watch him have to go through it practically alone, as he came from a society where disability was less understood and accepted.

Although I felt bad, deep down I knew I would need a solid partner if I were to ever have kids, but finding the right partner is just as tricky as finding the right time to consider all that it would take for me to become a mother. You know what they tell you: somewhere around forty, that's the line. That's when you won't be able to bear children anymore. But although this age limit is still a way off, I've long thought that it would be difficult for me to become pregnant because my periods have always been irregular.

Potential fertility issues aside, I know I'm not in some movie where the woman decides, 'the hell with it', and gets pregnant on her own rather than waiting for the right person to come along and do it together. It's me, and my life may never be suited for parenthood. I can't snap my fingers and make some dream of motherhood come true. Reality is more complicated. I must think of what's best for not just me, but for the child that's not even a child at this moment.

When I was about fourteen, I had a guide dog, Croche. Shortly after I got her, I thought I would be in high school, go to university, then out in the world with her by my side. But I started having chronic headaches and ended up in bed a lot for many days. And Croche was staying right there where I was. She was a brilliant and very well-trained dog, and I felt like her guiding skills were being wasted by the poor thing having to lay there beside me, guarding me.

That experience made me think that if I had kids they could also be missing out on a lot of activities with me – dance, sports and the after-school world – if I'm not feeling good, which is often. And that's the one thing that makes me feel better about not having children. My children would never have to go through what I go through. There is comfort in knowing that. Whether I use this as a reason to deal with my feelings about unrealised motherhood or not, now I can focus on myself and what I need and I don't have any little beings to worry about. It's what people often say: 'Oh, I can spoil my nieces and nephews and then send them home to their parents.' That's it. Now I have two nieces and two nephews and the children of my close friends, through which I get to experience being an aunt, which means that I get to help shape them, but I don't have to worry that I'm messing them up because I'm unwell and because I'm the one who is solely in charge of them.

At the same time, some days it can be painful to hear people around me talking so much about their children, as it's a constant reminder of what I don't have. Not having a child of my own means that's one less person in my life that I could probably count on. So, as the years go by, my parents get older, and my siblings get more and more involved with their own lives, my fear of ending up a burden on anybody grows.

The truth is that my life turned out differently from what I expected. Loneliness has reared its head, and so has the ache of missing the child I may never know. But I'm on the verge of accepting what will happen to me and preparing for a life without children, slowly, over time.

My family knows that I would like to become a mother, but they also know what I've been through, so they've never pushed me in any way. People will look at me and come up with any reason they want for why they think I'm not having children. I shouldn't have to say it, but blind women have children every day and are as successful at it as any sighted parent. There are as many stereotypes about childless women as there are about blind women. I'd like to break them, through my writing, my podcast and the way I go through life.

Childless is such a direct word. It's like blindness. I don't want to be thought of as just a blind woman. There are many parts to me and many things that make up who I am. Being childless is one of them, but that's not all of it.

If you live in a small town, as I do, it's hard to find perspective. You think there's nobody like you. So it's all about the horizon to me. As time goes on, I choose to focus more on what I can do, and on building a legacy through my skills and goals and hobbies. I also wish to expand my world to other possibilities still ahead.

Travel was always in my system, thanks to adventurous parents and grandparents who taught me to love and appreciate different people and places. They encouraged me to face my fear of the big, wide world when I travel. I have travelled to eastern Canada to see the world of *Anne of Green Gables*, to central Mexico to meet up with a writing group, and to Ireland where I experienced the Ring of Kerry. Looking ahead, I'd love to see Bjork's Iceland, and thought it was important to visit Anne Frank's house in the Netherlands and Flanders in Belgium – 'In Flanders Fields' by John McCrae is my favourite poem. Another place that I would especially want to visit is Louis Braille's village in Coupvray, France. Louis was the inventor of Braille, the code that enabled me to read and write independently.

Heading out for the horizon has become a way of life for me, just as the greyish water always did give way to the brightness of the sky. I can hardly describe something so visual, but it gives me hope, and I keep promising myself that I won't ever stop searching for my own definition of perspective.

London Bridge

If the days spent in London were eventful, the days spent in Dublin were quiet and restorative, and it was then that I got to focus on myself by having plenty of time to read and write. Those days had an almost tangible sense of progression about them. I felt revitalised and capable again.

Not everything was moving forward, though.

'Your days seem balanced. You sound and look good. Do you feel good? Una asked.

'I do.'

'So glad to hear. Now, I think it might be a good time for you to stop seeing me for a while.'

'What? No! Why?'

'Because we've been just chatting for the past couple of sessions, which I'm happy to do, but it could be a waste of time and money as you seem to have it all under control.'

'You're breaking up with me, aren't you, Una?'

'No, I'm not,' she said, giggling.

'It sure sounds like it.'

'No. What is happening is that you have the tools that you need, and you are doing well. It's time for you to go out there and enjoy it all. You can always come back if you hit a bumpy road.'

'I don't like this one bit,' I said, channelling my disappointed inner child.

'Come here,' she said, walking across the room and hugging me. 'It's like graduating. There's nothing left for me to help you with. You did all the work, and I'm so proud of you.'

There it was: another departure. Una and I would stop seeing each other, but that's because I was doing well. So it was good news and bad news bundled up together.

In our final session, which I insisted on booking, I gave her the most alien-looking thing I could find in the flower shop: a Persian shield. A flowering plant with dark green foliage and metallic-purple stripes that radiated zest for life and was reminiscent of the many dresses and scarves in shades of lavender, violet and fuchsia that I'd carried with the rest of my emotional baggage to her counselling room for almost two years. She loved it, or at least that's what she said. I loved her. And that's what I said the last time I saw her.

In early April, I got another email from the hiring manager, saying that the Portuguese role had just opened up. 'Here is the link. I hope you'll apply. By the way, the job is in London. Would you be willing to relocate?' A rush of adrenaline zipped through my body. I opened the link, attached my resume, and clicked *Apply*. Then came a writing test, a portfolio review and five interviews. By the end of the month, I got the job. Then it was time to talk with Ben about what my life in London would look like. He was in Dublin that Friday, so we discussed it over dinner.

'Now I'm thinking about the hassle. The waiting for the new work permit, giving notice in the flat here, finding a place there, packing, unpacking, registering with the immigration department, with the NHS, with the embassy.'

'You gotta enjoy this before your mind goes to these places,' he said.

'I am enjoying it.'

'Are you, though? This is huge. You got the job you wanted. You got it. This is great!'

'I suppose.'

'Would you move in with me?'

'No.'

'Jeez, that only took you a second.'

'Shit. Ben, look, I didn't mean it that way.'

'Yeah, you did.'

'No, not really. I'm sorry.'

'Yeah, okay.'

My heart sank. His gaze was down and his arms were crossed.

'Ben, please look at me.' He didn't for a while.

'Please?'

Then he did. Sort of.

'I'm touched by you asking me to move in with you, and I know I ruined this moment with my shotgun answer. I'm sorry. I am.'

'Look, Nic, I don't want you to hide your feelings. If you don't want to move in with me, it's fine. But it sounded like you'd already decided on that, and I didn't realise that was the case.'

'What I meant is that I don't want to do it now, but we could talk about it in the future.'

'So that I understand, what are you scared of?'

'Of things changing.'

'Like what?' he asked.

'Like us.'

'Why would it change?'

'Because we might feel that we need to do everything to-gether, and we'll start getting on each other's nerves.'

'No, we won't.'

'Yes, we will.'

'Not if we don't want to.'

'You don't know what it is like . . .'

'What? Living together? No, I don't. I never lived with a girlfriend before, but this is not my first relationship. And you and I? We never had a single fight, and we've been flying to another country to see each other for months. I don't see any red flags. Not a single one.'

'That's my point. It's been so good that I worry we'll mess this up if we change things.'

'I'm not worried. But if you are, it's not the time for this step. And that's fine. Take your time.'

While not ready to move in together, I was ready to meet his family, so we decided to spend the Easter holiday in the Netherlands. Two weeks later, I saw four hands waving at us at the arrivals area at Eindhoven Airport. Then there was a group hug. That was hard to describe. That family feeling. I was glad to be there and to finally meet his mother, father, sister and brother, to match names and faces in photos to real-life people, and to decipher which parts of Ben had come from which parent. We spent three days together playing board games, sightseeing and eating big chunks of Amsterdam Cheese and traditional Dutch pastries. I felt happy around them and so loved by them that I had to ask myself why had it taken me so long to go there.

*

By looking for blogs about intersectional feminism, I found 'Childfree African'. The top post was titled, 'Is being child-free only for white women?' The one before that: 'Being childfree is not an "interesting debate"'. I kept reading: 'My cousin said that it was an "interesting debate". This isn't interesting, nor is it a debate. I am an adult human being. I have the right to decide what happens to my body.'[14] I read the whole archive and was struck by the author's unyielding intent to share with the world what she thinks of it. The author's name was Doreen. And after exchanging some emails, I travelled to Geneva to meet her.

Doreen, 35, Ghanaian, international development professional

I was born in Accra, Ghana. When I was one, my mom and I moved to Japan to join my dad, where we lived for eleven years. Growing up in Tokyo was so much fun. It's an amazing, giant city with so much to do. The only complaint I have about my childhood there is that I was a Black girl in Japan in the 1980s and '90s and people were not so culturally sensitive about race back then.

After that, my mom, sister and I went to the United States. I started junior high in Tokyo and completed it in upstate New York, then I went on to complete an undergraduate degree in history in the US as well. While my travelling as a child had to do with my parents' decisions, as an adult, it had to do mostly with residency issues. At twenty-three, I was living in the States and my visa was running out. I started looking for a job anywhere. I found a job in Shanghai and moved there, staying for two years. It was a mixed experience. It was good and bad: it's a very racist society; they are not fans of Black people or really anyone with dark skin. There were times when I felt dehumanised. But, at the same time, it's a country with a rich culture and history, and with many interesting people. I met some cool Chinese people and some cool foreigners.

Several years later, I moved to the UK to do my master's degree. Just after I arrived, the government decided to get rid of a two-year residence permit that used to be granted to students so that they could stay in the country after graduating. I went there so confident I was going to find a job in London. I refused to go back to Ghana and moved to Senegal where I stayed with a friend for a while.

My master's was in peace studies, an interdisciplinary field where the main idea is that peace is more than just 'no war'. A peaceful society, in peace-studies theory, is one in which all people's human rights are respected. This means that, for example, any society in which there are people living in poverty is not a peaceful one; poverty is a type of violence. Throughout the course, we looked at how to build societies through policy and programmes, and at theory, literature and history concerning how to build societies that actually are peaceful beyond not having war or conflict.

In 2015, I moved to Geneva and took a job doing communications and research on human rights, gender and social protection. I've had jobs that weren't really what I wanted to do, such as English teacher, administrative assistant and business development manager, so it was fulfilling to finally be working in an area that I had always wanted to.

A few years ago, I came out as asexual. It took me a very long time to figure out that I was. Before that, I'd never even known that that was an option. While that was not at all clear to me, it was clear to other people: both an ex-boyfriend and a guy that I hooked up with asked me if I was asexual. Back then, I didn't let those thoughts go too deep in my head, but when I finally came out to a friend, she said, 'That doesn't surprise me.'

When I say that I came out, I don't mean that I told everyone around me about it; for the most part it's not really relevant to anyone. Some people do think it's weird that I'm no longer dating, but I stopped dating even before realising that I was asexual. That was a decision that I made because of some bad experiences with men. After a particularly awful one, I decided that I was not going to spend any more of my time doing that. It's different for everyone, but for me, being asexual and the bad experiences have fed into each other, and at this point I no longer know where one starts and the other ends.

I mostly learned about asexuality from online forums and groups. They helped me understand that sex and romance are separate things, which explains why when my ex-boyfriend asked me if I was asexual, my answer was 'Of course not!' When, in fact, what I was really saying was that I couldn't be asexual because I had romantic feelings for him, and romance and sex go together. At least, I had thought that to be the case.

Without knowing anything about the topic, or that other people felt the same, I resisted the idea of being asexual for quite a while. Especially because I'm an extremely romantic person, and I don't mean it in the commercial, capitalist sense that means heart-shaped chocolates and diamonds, but in the sense of developing feelings for men and how hard it is for me to get over them. It took me a long time to understand that I could have feelings for men without the sexual component being part of the equation. Upon realising that other people were romantic and asexual, I finally thought, *Yeah, that's it! That's me.* Now I keep in touch with other aces, as we call ourselves, on messaging apps, and we even meet in person.

In the mid-2000s, blogs stopped being online diaries of trivial daily activities and became places of discussion. I started reading about women who decided that monogamy wasn't for them so they decided to be in open relationships; 'women' who didn't actually identify as women at all, and the experiences of trans women, and most significantly on a personal level, women who didn't want to have children. That's when I realised that I actually had a choice in the matter. I was twenty-two when I decided not to have kids. It wasn't a hard decision for me because nothing about being a mother interests me. I don't want to have sex; I don't want to give birth; I don't want to be a mother. That was just one more decision that enabled me to be the person I want to be, and that gives me a sense of belonging.

After living in so many countries, it can be hard for me to feel like I belong anywhere. When I moved back to Ghana, I was twenty-five. Even though I thought 'this is my home country', there was only one moment when I really felt that, instead of forcing myself to think it. I went to a club, and I didn't stand out there like I did on the street. I was drinking, talking, dancing and actually *feeling* Ghanaian, even though legally and ethnically I've been Ghanaian all my life. The reason I didn't feel at home outside of the club was because I just 'look' different – my hairstyle, the way I dress, and even just the way I walk. My personal cultural traditions and values are also quite different from local ones.

In 'my' culture, it's almost expected that we all have to believe in the same things and behave the same way. This was very difficult for me because I grew up in Japan and the US and was not accustomed to how uncritically religious everyone was, even though I grew up religious myself! I didn't want to adjust, I didn't want misogyny to be 'normal' to me. But my extended family just couldn't wrap their heads around why I wouldn't want that. People aren't encouraged to engage in critical thought. Education is mostly rote memorisation, and everyone has scripted answers to anyone who questions things that they believe. I was never ready with a scripted response. I learned that there's no point in trying to change someone's mind if they've decided that this is the only way to live and you have to do it because you're African. Because then it's not logic, it's just dogma, and you can't really argue with dogma.

I used to think that my parents were very conservative until I went back to Ghana. I then realised that considering their upbringing and the first thirty-plus years of their lives, they are actually pretty liberal. They don't care about me not having kids and they spent money educating their female children when a lot of people wouldn't have. Nowadays, sure. Thirty years ago? Not many families would have prioritised educating their girls.

At a friend's birthday party in Ghana I was put on the spot regarding being childfree. There were Ghanaian, Nigerian, American and repatriated women like me, so it was quite culturally mixed. One friend, for some reason, announced to the table that 'Doreen doesn't want to have kids, because she doesn't want her body to change!' I swear to god, everyone at the table descended on me like vultures on a wildebeest carcass. Women from all different ethnicities and nationalities were arguing with me about why that was not my choice to make. One woman told me she'd just had a baby and her body bounced back. I thought ... *And?* That has nothing to do with me and the choices I'm making. I felt so disrespected.

My ex-boyfriend and I lived together for most of the year and a half that we were together. At first, he had said that he was fine with not having kids, then he changed his mind. Not only that, he also thought that *I* had changed my mind (even though I never said anything to indicate that I had), so we hit a wall. I started doubting myself. I was convinced that I needed to have children to be with him. Then, fortunately, he broke up with me. Looking back, it's clear to me that, had I had a child with him, our relationship would not have lasted long after I had given birth. I would have left him and the child. I do not want to be a mother. That's it.

One of my aunts in Ghana said that I should have been born a man, because I 'just make decisions'. Instead of being a compliment, that's such a bad mindset to have; it implies that women are not entitled to make decisions. But we are and we do. Not only do I make my own decisions, I also don't maintain relationships with people who are disrespectful of my choices. Being childfree is as much a part of my identity as being a woman, Black, asexual, feminist, vegan, a runner and a lapsed trombone player.

Switching to veganism a few years ago, I dedicated myself to learning more about the environmental aspect of eating animals and wearing leather and wool. It wasn't only the environmental aspects that convinced me. It was also the effects on other people, and how inhumane it is to the animals. I'm not even an animal lover – I don't have or wish to have any pets – but after learning more about the meat and clothing industries, I just felt that I could no longer support exploiting animals. Choosing what I eat and wear, and knowing where it comes from, and how it's made is part of that. Again, it comes down to education and choice. But it's also privilege.

It's important for me to keep learning and opening my mind so that I can continue to make sure that other people's opinions about me are not more important than my own. Childfree women are often labelled as bitter, undesirable for long-term relationships, being 'career women', and when as Black, African women, we choose not to have children, we are also accused of trying to act like 'white women', as if we have been whitewashed from living abroad. However, just because I think for myself, it doesn't mean I'm 'trying to be white'. If anything, it's insulting to all of us. It implies that because we're Black, we can't make individual decisions and have richness and variety in the way we live.

If I meet women who mention that they don't have children, I get curious, but I always try not to articulate it, because it could be something very traumatic for them. Maybe they couldn't have children, or maybe they had a child who died. You just never know, so unless the person wants to talk about it, I try not to go there. I don't want to make my interest in the topic more important than the feelings of the person with whom I'm having a conversation.

Writing about it helps. I started a blog called 'Childfree African' in 2015 because I couldn't find a blog about childfree African women. At first, it was a place for me to share my own experience, but then it evolved into a space for any woman who is African or of African descent to share their experiences about not having children. Interestingly, I got submissions by men too, which was great, because it gave me some insight into the fact that there are also African men who don't want children.

Reading other people's stories has been really important to me as it helped me feel less alone and to understand people's different circumstances and the emotions attached to them. If someone is childless and it's a choice that was made consciously or a choice that they're happy with, I think it's great. If it's due to infertility issues and they *would* like to have a child, I hope that they're able to get what they want, whether that's through adoption, in vitro fertilisation or hormonal therapy. But, ultimately, people with uteri have to be able to make choices about their own bodies and about what's good for them in general. And if they do choose to bring children into the world, I'd hope they make an effort to raise their kids in a good environment where they feel wanted.

Sometimes I fear not having a long-term social network when I'm old, but as someone who struggles with anxiety, the following lines by Ralph Waldo Emerson calm me down:

Finish each day and be done with it. You have done what you could. Some blunders and absurdities no doubt crept in; forget them as soon as you can. Tomorrow is a new day. You shall begin it serenely and with too high a spirit to be encumbered with your old nonsense.

Spellbinder

Twenty-four years had passed since I met Gabriela, and I kept my promise to stay in touch by writing, calling and visiting her. Our friendship made me believe it was possible to keep some things intact in my life even when the parameters and conditions of that life kept changing, sometimes by choice and sometimes by force.

In early May, I flew to Brazil for her wedding. Ben joined me two weeks later. On his first night in Brazil, he wouldn't say no to my mother, so he drank all the different flavours of caipirinhas she ordered: lime, strawberry, passionfruit and kiwi. For the rest of the month, I watched him playing dominoes with Tácio, watching wrestling competitions with Davi, driving up and down with Afonso, walking arm in arm with a frail eighty-two-year-old Beth, and doing his best to mirror every dance step Gabriela threw at him at her wedding reception.

During our goodbye dinner at Grandma's house, she looked at Ben, then at me and said out loud: 'Your children will be beautiful.' I felt a shiver down my spine. Something about how she said it made me feel like my destiny was set, and I had no control over it. I didn't want to talk about any of it.

So I pretended I hadn't heard it and got another serving of dessert. The next day, we flew back to Europe, headed to our flats, and took a break from each other. We loved each other, but we also loved being alone.

Candice came from Stockholm to visit me in Dublin in late June. This time she was the one needing a hug after going through a tough break-up. She longed for a change of air, and I invited her over for the weekend. We stayed at my place for the first night, then we rented a car and went on a road trip. Crossing the country from east to west, we bared our souls while trying to navigate love and the road supported by paper maps and a GPS device. We stuffed ourselves with shepherd's pie and lamb stew in little restaurants tucked in pretty villages with names that always seemed to start with 'K'. We stayed in a modest bed and breakfast atop the greenest hill, where everything was quiet except for the sheep.

There was a sense of freedom and traces of the sister bond we shared when we first met at her flat. We drove, hiked, ate, cried, laughed, slept and woke up together. Although she was in pain this time, she was kind enough to show interest in what was happening in my life.

'How is it going with Ben?'

'Are you sure you want to hear about a relationship still in the honeymoon phase?'

'Yes. I care about you, and, who knows, it might give me hope again.'

'All right. It's going very well. I feel so much passion for him and am so at peace by being with him that sometimes it's hard to believe it's all coming from the same place.'

'That sounds very good. And healthy.'

'It is. It's the healthiest thing I ever had, and it gives me so much joy that I find myself pressing the brake pedal most of the time, afraid that I'll lose control.'

'I can understand that after what you've been through. At the same time, make sure that your fear isn't the very thing that breaks you apart.'

Candice's words entranced me like a spell.

Later that day, after dinner, I called Ben and said I wanted to tell him my main reason for not wanting to move in with him. Something I hadn't known how to share before. He said he was listening. So I told him I feared he would want a child one day. I knew he was younger than me and that a lot could happen (I realised I was talking to him like my mother had spoken to me when she went to Sweden, and I didn't know how to feel about that), but that my way of protecting myself was wanting to keep my life independent from his.

'I get it. Look, I know how important this topic is to you, and I know about your previous relationship. I also see you reading books, watching movies, interviewing women without kids, and it's all there; it's hard to miss. And that made me ask myself about parenthood more than I ever would have at my age, which is good and what I wish most people did before they had kids. When I think about it, I feel no desire to have a child today or soon. And I wish I could tell you I won't change my mind. But I can't. That would not be right. I can tell you this is how I feel today and that if I felt differently, I would not be asking you to move in with me or be in this relationship with you. It takes two. And I'm all in. How you feel about that is for you to decide.'

The next day, the last day of the road trip with Candice, I found a picture of two rocks protruding from the deepest blue sea in a tourist shop in Donegal. And I thought about Ben. He came to Dublin the next weekend, and I asked if I could still move in with him. He said yes. Then I gave him the picture. On the back, I wrote, 'This is when and where two stones become a path.'

*

Before Candice said goodbye, she wrote an email address on paper and handed it to me. Next thing I knew, I was sending an email to Magdalena.

Magdalena's interview was a huge turning point for me. I was sitting across from a woman who would do anything to have a child, including risking her life. And I was doing everything I could to move away from the life she wanted. She was honest and told me she didn't understand me. That she couldn't possibly. She could understand my words but not my feelings. At times, our conversation was confronting and emotional. But our encounter was memorable because Magdalena is one of the kindest human beings I met on this journey and someone I admire deeply. We met again in Sweden and England over the next few years.

When I filed for divorce in 2016, I lost my family re-union visa and was told I had to leave Ireland and return once my new work permit was issued. That would take up to six weeks. I didn't know where to go then and contacted friends in various countries, trying to break the period down into smaller chunks so as not to bother anyone for too long. Magdalena spoke to a friend of hers, Ulrika, who was a single mother, and arranged for me to stay with her and her little boy, Pontus, for as long as I needed. Ulrika received me with an open heart. We cooked for each other and went for long walks in nature. Pontus and I played memory games and read comic books at bedtime.

At a time in my life when I'd felt the most lonely, the three of them made all the difference.

Magdalena, 44, Swedish, skincare therapist

It's not easy to be childless anywhere. And definitely not in Sweden, because the number of childless people here is much lower, so you feel like a minority, and being part of a small group of people means that it can be more difficult to meet others in the same situation. You feel isolated.

I live in Stockholm and I'm a skin therapist. I worked in this area for about eight years and always really enjoyed doing so, then a life crisis hit me and I started thinking that I wasn't a good therapist for my clients and that I should get a real Monday-to-Friday, nine-to-five job. So I went back to university and took a three-year course in human resources. The curriculum was huge and meant that I had to study everything from law to economics to psychology and sociology.

While I've never lived outside of Sweden, I love travelling and a very special place to me is Spain – the Camino de Santiago to be more precise. That's because when I was thirty-four, I met Johan, and he was the one. I had short-term relationships before him, but nothing like this. He is perfect for me and we've been married for seven years. On our first walk on the Camino, we decided to move in together. The year after, we returned and walked the second part of the path, another three hundred kilometres. In the last week of this journey, he proposed to me. He was just standing there in the rain going down on one knee, and I couldn't believe my eyes. After that, we came back home, started planning our wedding and I stopped taking the pill. We planned the wedding for nine months later so that we could have a baby right afterwards. And so we got married but nothing happened. We went on our honeymoon in Sicily and left the last part of the Camino for later.

Honeymoon over, no baby. Presumably I was fertile back then, but I couldn't get pregnant and, as far as doctors could tell, there wasn't anything wrong with us. It's easier if you can find a reason because you feel that you can then fix it, but we were never given one. In a way, I felt as if I wasn't infertile, so we kept trying. The IVF treatments began when I was thirty-seven, and it felt great to complete it, but after four rounds of IVFs and getting pregnant twice, I had early miscarriages both times. In Sweden, the government pays for IVF until you are forty years old. If you are older, you have to pay for it yourself. So I tried as many times as I could. Each time meant that I had to prepare my body for over a year with homeopathy, acupuncture, reflexology, diet, exercise, relaxing, meditation . . . and, after several rounds, unfortunately, I got breast cancer instead.

As soon as I was diagnosed, the treatments started. I was forty years old. First, came chemotherapy to make the tumour smaller, then surgery to remove the breast with the tumour. They removed everything, put in silicone, and reconstructed my breast using my own skin. After that, there was also radiotherapy. In the middle of it all, we started considering adoption. It was important that I felt healthy and like myself again, so we decided to go back to Camino. I believed it could heal us.

On the path you always follow the yellow arrows. You can find them on the walls of houses, on the streets, on trees, everywhere. They guide you so you never need a map to make it to the next milestone. But if you haven't seen an arrow for a while, you have to go back to where you last saw one. And it's the same thing in life. When everything is going in a positive direction, you are following the arrows. You are where you should be. On the other hand, if something happens and you are not satisfied with your life, maybe you should just move backwards, to where you last saw an arrow, and continue your journey from there.

The path pushed me forward. I wanted to recover quickly, so it felt good to be there and to be able to use my body again. I was very tired, so we had to take full days to stay in a hotel and rest until we could continue. Exercising was very healing for me. It was as if I was trying to run from something bad, so I started running longer distances. I'd get emotional from tiredness, and I'd fight with my body, my illness and my situation as a whole.

It took nine months to go through all the cancer treatments and another year to get myself back to physical health and feel that I had energy again. During this period, I wasn't in contact with fertility doctors. Since the tumour was hormonal, I knew I wouldn't be able to continue the IVF treatment as it could put me at risk of having cancer again. I'm cancer-free now, and I have been for the past three years. While the illness was hard, I don't regret the IVF rounds. It was something that I had to do. And even though I cannot continue trying to get pregnant, and, according to Swedish law, I'm too old to become a mother, the longing for a child still lives within me. My mother suggested surrogacy, but I've decided to stop there. I can't go any further than this. But she has a hard time understanding it. I know she means well, and so do other people. They want to fix you. They start listing all the things you could do to 'fix' the lack of a child in your life without knowing if you have anything left in you to give those options a try, or if you have tried them already.

If I say I can't have children, it's because I can't. I thought about every single possibility. What do they think? That I'd miss something? That they are so thorough with everything but that I could not think of that option myself?

When I was told that my last IVF treatment hadn't worked, I was already on the waiting list to adopt, as it can take years. We went to an agency and chose a country to be in the 'line' for. There are babies from all over the world and different rules depending on which country you are adopting from. You choose, and then you stand in line for that country and that country only. You can't stand in line for different countries at the same time as the process and the prices vary greatly.

Had we adopted it would have cost us a fortune, even though the government covers part of it. They check your financial situation before you start the process, and you can't be older than forty-two. When we started the process I was younger than forty-two, but health conditions were also taken into consideration, and, since I had had cancer recently, I wasn't allowed to continue the adoption process. That was hard. They told me we could wait a while to make sure that I was still in remission, but it was heartbreaking because another year would mean that I'd reach the age limit for adoption. I felt that this was it. This was the end. And when I finally turned forty-three, I thought maybe now I could start healing, because there's no other option.

The fact that I wanted to become a mother and couldn't caused me so much pain; I felt that I had to understand my grieving and I realised that I thought it would be a privilege to follow a child through their lives, watching them discover new things, develop and learn. I wanted to be there to support them throughout that.

I'd come home to my empty flat, and think, *Where are my children? Where are they hiding?* Something was missing. Something is still missing. I'm constantly reminded of what I don't have. It's a mixture of different emotions from day to day. Sometimes it's frustrating because I can't change it in any way. I feel helpless. But, even if I didn't choose it, I hope it will feel better one day and I try to make the absolute best of this life to compensate for the situation I'm in. It takes a long time and I'll probably have to put this philosophy into practice my whole life.

I wake up and ask myself, *What is important to you other than that? How can you make the best of your days?* When you have children you can barely think about yourself. But I can, so what do I want? Where do I want to live? Do I want to move closer to my sister's house? And what do I want to do then? Do I really want to start a bed and breakfast with my husband?

One thing that helped me through all of this was that I never felt any pressure from my husband. My health was always his primary concern. His mother died of breast cancer when he was twenty-nine and I remember thinking that going through this first with his mother and then with his wife is just not fair. Still, he was there for me all the time. He followed me to all my doctor's appointments and gave me everything I needed. Absolutely everything.

Having such a wonderful partner gave me strength and helped me focus on other things. Positive ones. I started wondering why living a life without children wasn't discussed broadly in Sweden. I wanted to fight for recognition and support other women who couldn't have children, so I started reading about this subject in my spare time. Then I started a blog. I expressed all the feelings I experienced as a childless woman. It was like starting to learn how to live again. I realised it was a sensitive subject for many. To increase the possibilities of communicating and connecting with others in the same situation, I created a closed group for childless women on Facebook. What I got from it was a great sense of relief and the possibility to freely discuss the situation with others. It was as if the love and energy I had kept for my unborn children were being used to understand and help start conversations about this topic.

I also took a course to become a supportive coach to help others and became an organiser of meetups for childless women in different places in Sweden. I travel to conferences about being childless and give talks. This topic is still not often spoken about in Scandinavia, so I started contacting people in Norway, Denmark and Finland in search of connections and aiming to help make sure we find ways to support each other and feel less alone.

After all of this, I can think about my childlessness without feeling too sad about it, and when I'm asked about my life, I tell it as it is. If people ask me about my weekend, I'll tell them I flew to London to attend a workshop for childless women and that I did that because I'm childless. Then they mention someone they know in the same situation, or they ask me for the link to my blog, and suddenly we are talking about something that needs to be talked about. I feel like I'm on a mission. It gives me purpose. It also diminishes the sense of shame that comes with not having a child, with not being in this normal situation with others when I wanted to be among them but couldn't.

The best way I can explain it is this: imagine you're sitting on a train, your carriage is full of people, and the train stops at every station. People get off with their baby prams. They walk away and fade into the distance while you watch them from the window as you keep waiting for your stop to come. But it never comes. Suddenly you realise that you are the only person still left on the train and that it has stopped and can't go any further. Not only that, you don't know how to get off either. You're all alone on this train, the doors won't open, and, even if they did open, you are not sure how to live among the people who have the baby prams.

That's how you feel every day when you want a child but don't have a child. And it becomes a huge elephant in the room: people don't talk to you about what it's like for you not to have a child. They either want to fix you or they want to talk about how *they* feel about it.

When you have cancer, you have access to support groups, to forums, you go to rehab with others in the same situation, you do group therapy to talk about what it's like to have cancer, but when you end up being childless, there's nothing like this available. With cancer there's also a chance that you will recover from it, move on and leave it all behind. But with childlessness, there's no recovery. It will be there your whole life and you have to learn to live with it.

Childless women are not invisible, incapable of love, caring or giving, and we shouldn't feel that we are. If we could count on the support of others to release all the energy that we put into our grief, then we could use that energy to help other people, with or without children, once the grieving process is finished. And that would make the world a better place.

Upstream

By the end of the summer, everything I owned – three boxes of clothes and shoes, five boxes of books and one big plastic container with miscellaneous papers and items – arrived at the flat that Ben and I started renting and sharing in Islington, a residential district in London, only twenty minutes away by foot from the office where we both worked. There was a view of a clock tower from the living room, a small green area with a running track, an Italian deli and a pharmacy, all within a few blocks of our building. The two-bedroom flat was plenty for us – we slept in one and the other was a shared home office. The furniture was basic, but everything worked. A couple of extra pillows and plants, and we were all set.

It felt good to have a life companion again. To sleep and wake up next to someone I love. To stand behind each other while brushing our teeth. To share the house chores. To have someone to talk to on the way to the supermarket. I enjoyed the added dimension of his presence in my life when doing most mundane things. We walked to work together most days. Sometimes we'd eat together, but more often than not, we didn't. We'd invite our colleagues for lunch or enjoy some alone time on one of the eleven floors of our office building.

After three years working in the tech world, I had learned not only to cope but to thrive in that environment: I got used to the meetings; the performance assessments, which used to take me a couple of days to write, I now wrote in a couple of hours; and I showed more interest in the people I worked with. I still couldn't connect with those who complained about the ice cream machine not working or the coffee machine being too far away. But instead of walls, I built boundaries and embraced only the people and the projects that would not take all my energy. The energy I needed to write.

This shift happened after I read an interview with the American poet Mary Oliver, in which she mentioned she could only write because she gave her employers her second effort of the day. The first one was to get up early and write. I wrote that on a sticky note and put it on the wall above my writing desk. I wasn't getting up earlier, but I started writing every day during breaks, in the evenings and on weekends.

That interview made me want to learn more about Mary and her work, so I read a collection of essays called *Upstream* and fell in love with how she described losing herself within the beauty and mysteries of both the natural world and the world of literature. After that, I read about her personal life and learned that she and her partner of forty years, the photographer Molly Malone Cook, had no children and had met in the house of poet and playwright Edna St. Vincent Millay, who also had no children.

What was left of my downtime that year I spent in the

UK, visiting the houses of local famous writers who had not become mothers: Jane Austen's cottage in Hampshire, Virginia Woolf's home in East Sussex and Beatrix Potter's Hill Top Farm in the Lake District. I stepped on their doorsteps, touched their chairs and desks, walked the streets they walked, wept where they drowned and took a deep breath where they coughed last. And every time I left, I carried the certainty that it was in these places, their places, that I saw the whole world open up to me again. My brain was bubbling up with ideas, and my body was healthy and willing to take me anywhere I wished to go. Life was bountiful, and I was back in orbit.

*

Every time I tried to transcribe the recorded interviews, I'd stop soon after, my fingers struggling to manage the continuous play, pause, type routine. Succumbing to the realisation that I was probably not cut out for the strand of linguistic work that converts speech to text, I placed an ad for a professional transcriber. Daniela replied the next day, expressing her interest in the task. She asked me what the audio files were about, and I told her they were interviews with women without children. Daniela didn't have children, and over the next three years, not only did she transcribe every single story in this book, but she chose to also add her story to it. I can't thank her enough.

Daniela, 43, American, non-profit administrator in arts education

Stevens Point is my hometown. It's in the middle of Wisconsin, in the United States. I have a bachelor's and a master's degree in jazz performance. I was a jazz singer for ten years, but being a jazz singer is an American art form, and I always had such a huge love of languages. Early on, I discovered that Brazilian music satisfied both things in me: I could do all the improvisation that I love about jazz, but I could also sing in Portuguese and learn about another culture. Eventually it led me to start a PhD in ethnomusicology and Latin American studies and to spend 2011 and 2012 living in Belo Horizonte so that I could research and understand the music I was singing.

In 2013, my husband started work as a professor of music at the University of Chester in north-west England, and I moved there to join him. Soon afterwards I noticed that my periods were getting heavier and heavier, but not to the point where I gave it much thought. I dealt with the inconvenience and went on with my life. In January 2014, I had heard about a translation course in London that was going to take place once a week for a year. As I was writing my dissertation, I fell more and more in love with Portuguese so I signed up.

In my second week travelling to London for this course, I got there an hour early. I had dinner in a little café and I stood up after finishing my meal only to look down and notice that my trousers were covered in blood. I thought, *I'm really in trouble here*. I was absolutely mortified, so I wrapped a jacket around myself to hide the stain on my trousers and walked a few blocks to the university where I was taking classes. In the bathroom, I realised I was haemorrhaging and starting to feel faint and dizzy. Worried I might pass out, I asked a stranger to call an ambulance.

They took me to a hospital and that was the first time that I had full scans, which revealed my diagnosis of uterine fibroids, non-cancerous tumours that grow inside the uterus, within the muscles of the uterus and also outside the uterus. I was unlucky enough to have all three types. I had lost so much blood that I was considered profoundly anaemic and had to stay overnight for two transfusions. And the crazy thing about it is that I knew that my mother had had a hysterectomy when I was five or six years old. So I spoke to her about it and it turns out that not only her, but also my grandmother had a hysterectomy. I thought, *Well, geez! Thanks for telling me that I might get this, Mom!* I wish I could have been more prepared. My sister always had heavy periods growing up, and she had to be medicated for it, so I never complained about my own periods because I knew how much pain my sister had. That belief contributed to me not taking my own worsening symptoms seriously.

I could tell that my mother regretted not talking about this earlier, but it's just her nature. She is very private and there are a lot of things about her life that she doesn't find easy to share. It's not her fault.

Uterine fibroids cause serious bleeding, and at my worst, my periods were between twelve to fifteen days long, and so heavy that there would be many days when I couldn't leave the house. There was a lot of clotting and the heaviness would actually push tampons right out of me. When you lose control of your body like that, the feeling of helplessness is debilitating. It was a really difficult time. My husband's university had also hired me to fill in for his colleague. But when the temporary position ended, I didn't pursue additional work with them, because I couldn't imagine having an incident in front of a classroom. So I stepped away from teaching music and performing was definitely off the table. My last time on stage was in 2014; I enjoyed it, but I also remember being worried about the short dress I was wearing and stressed about getting a heavy period. It was devastating.

But after falling so ill, not even teaching music at a university seemed possible, and what had once felt like a job for life suddenly felt like a dead end. How would I explain my time off from work on my CV? So, I did my translation certificate and started getting my own business off the ground.

My husband, Will, is a guitarist. We've been married for fifteen years and lived apart quite often throughout our marriage due to various visa issues related to our moves to Brazil and England. When I was thirty-seven, I was told by my consulting gynaecologist in the UK that my options for dealing with fibroids were either to get pregnant or to have a hysterectomy. If I did nothing, these terrible bleeding symptoms would continue to keep me from working.

Will and I sat down and thought, is this something we want? We had never had a strong urge for children. Even as a child, I never really dreamed about what it would be like to have a family. Faced with this ultimatum, we thought, maybe? It wasn't even a full yes, but we had a limited amount of time to choose between getting pregnant or having a hysterectomy. So we thought, *We could be good parents, let's do this.* And soon after, I got pregnant on the advice of a doctor, mostly because I thought that it was my last opportunity to do so. It was an optimistic time. We were suddenly on a new adventure. But when I think back on it, I still never really imagined what an actual baby or child would be like. It was more about a new dimension to my relationship with Will. I was pregnant for nine weeks and then I had a miscarriage.

Looking back, the thing that upsets me the most is that the doctor gave me this ultimatum. As I discovered later, there were many other solutions that were not presented to us. I think he made some faulty assumptions. First, that most women want to become pregnant, and second, that because pregnancy often causes fibroids to shrink, that pregnancy is a suitable solution for all women. It's true, I had said that I wasn't sure about the hysterectomy since my husband and I hadn't ruled out having kids. As a doctor, shouldn't it be his business to encourage anyone who isn't sure about having kids to really think about it seriously before getting pregnant? Our uncertainty just reinforced his assumption that as a woman, I wanted to get pregnant.

I read about his background later, and realised that this

doctor apparently wasn't trained to do other types of fibroid surgeries in which the priority is to maintain the health of the uterus. His specialty was hysterectomy, so he presented it as the only option: get pregnant soon or remove your uterus. I remember not feeling comfortable with that and asking him if there were other doctors in his field nearby that I might be able to contact for a second opinion. He said no. When in fact, the wonderful doctor that performed my myomectomy a year later was less than thirty miles away. I still feel furious with this man. That's a really ridiculous choice to give somebody, when as a doctor you know there's more out there. It's irresponsible. If he doesn't do those surgeries, then he should tell you that they exist, and that you can find another doctor that does them to learn more. But he didn't educate me at all.

Because we didn't want to go through a second miscarriage, Will and I talked a lot more about it until we realised it was the pressure that had made us decide to get pregnant, not the true prospect of having a child for our whole lives. I was so desperate to get rid of the symptoms and the feeling of uselessness that unemployment gave me, that I made a terrible choice. That's when it became obvious that having kids was never going to happen. We would not become biological parents, and more than that, we didn't have the desire. Even before I was diagnosed, when we talked about potentially having kids, we had always felt that neither of us was excited about an infant. A five-year-old we could actually talk to is much more enticing. I love interacting with my nieces and nephews.

Also, it had been such a difficult pregnancy. It never seemed to be going well. There's always that image out there in the world of glowing women. Their hair is vibrant and their faces are beaming and people pass them in the street and say, 'Oh, you're such a beautiful pregnant woman!' That was not my experience. I was hiding at home carrying an extra set of trousers around in case I bled through the pair I was wearing. I could barely climb the stairs. I couldn't think straight, and yet I was still dutifully writing my dissertation, running from the room five or six times per hour some days to pass blood clots. It was a nightmare from start to finish. And I was going through that when we weren't even particularly excited to have a baby; it was just purposeless. It made no sense.

When the miscarriage was confirmed, we were both sad, of course. But the overwhelming emotion was of relief. I remember sitting in the ultrasound room, and I could tell by the woman's face that she was trying to decide how to give me the 'bad news'. She finally said, 'I know this isn't the result that you wanted, but I'm afraid that I don't have a heartbeat.' And I didn't reply because my immediate thought was, 'No, you really don't know how I feel, because I'm actually really relieved. This was a terrible experience!' My body not coping, not being emotionally committed, not trusting my doctor while going through it. I had mixed feelings all along. And it's hard to be open about this because I think about the women who have suffered miscarriages and who truly wanted a child and all the pain they went through. In fact, my ER doctor told me her whole life story about having five miscarriages before her son was born. She told me my dream would come true soon. And I had to just lie there knowing I wouldn't be trying ever again. I just didn't feel that kind of grief. My grief was for myself, for the torture some doctor had put me through for an outcome I didn't want in the first place. I just wanted to be healthy.

It took a year for me to get the myomectomy once they told me I needed it following the miscarriage. A year of waiting with these awful symptoms. The tumours were at a size where I still had a lot of physical discomforts. One tumour was growing on the outside of my uterus and pressed down on my bladder, so I had to pee all the time. There was another one that pushed on my intestines, so my evacuation was difficult. It was inhumane. My life stopped. Finally, in September 2015, I had the myomectomy in the UK and everything started to get better.

Will and I had decided to return to the US. So I was slowly packing, taking short walks and getting back to my regular weight again. I was so relieved I could take a walk without worrying, and it felt amazing. My periods were the lightest I'd ever had in my life. I can't believe women have periods that light all the time! I felt human again.

This whole experience made us be more honest with ourselves and with each other. We've continued to talk about it and realised that if we felt a strong urge to become parents in the future, we could adopt. As we've always been more enthusiastic about the education of the child, the activities and the conversations, we could be a really great adoptive family. We are content with how we feel about this now.

We moved to Tucson, Arizona, and when I first arrived I thought I might want to go through the experience of becoming someone's mother one day. But having a career was always a higher priority for me. Circumstances had switched me from this to that and from here to there so often that I just wanted to have several years under my belt of one profession before I could think about a third person. And then there's money. Because both Will and I are creative types, we gave so much to paying off our student loans, and only now are we getting on our feet financially, in our early forties.

One of the phrases that we've always batted about is 'Once this happens, then I'll feel this,' or 'Once that other thing happens, then we'll be able to do that.' So we decided to break that pattern by settling in one place and not moving around to different countries anymore.

We've adopted two beautiful dogs and we spend a lot of time hiking with them. It feels good to get out into nature with them and get out of my own head. I also started working for a non-profit organisation that provides music education in disadvantaged schools. In that capacity I'm not working as a musician, but my musical experiences help me to run a team of teaching artists, while my research experience has been critical in writing grants to support our work. So that's a passion project that pays, and that feels good.

With all of this happening, we're slowly putting down more and more roots and trying to stay in the present. The house, the steadier jobs, the friends, our parents being able to visit twice a year: these are all important to us. As we've grown into these roots, Will and I realise that we're enjoying our journey together as a couple, and kids just don't fit into that journey.

I think about my brother's little girls. I wonder genetically how that works for them, and if my mother's genes would pass through my brother into my nieces. I need to research that and, in the future, when they are old enough, I'd like to have a conversation with them about uterine fibroids, because I want them to have a better consciousness about their bodies than I did. I'd like to think I could share my experience to educate others – that's a good legacy.

2018

Deep Cuts

The new office was in London, but the design was the same: the canteen on the rooftop. I was having lunch when my phone beeped. I unlocked the screen and saw a message from my mother. She'd sent a picture I couldn't make sense of at first.

'What's that? Is that your arm? What's the white thing?' She sent another less zoomed-in picture where I could see bandages. 'Oh my god! What happened? Is that a hospital?' A minute later, WhatsApp delivered an audio file. I listened to it and then ran to Ben's desk on the third floor.

'What happened?'

'I have to go to Brazil.'

'Why?'

'My mother got stabbed.'

'What?!'

Thirty-six hours later, I landed in Brasília.

Day 1

Davi picked me up at the airport.

'How did this happen? I still can't understand it,' I said.

'They were in the countryside house, and Mom heard the neighbour beating his wife up, so she went there. You know how she is.'

'How she is? Wouldn't you have gone there to help?'

'Yes, but we had heard stories about the guy being violent, so it wasn't like she had no clue it could be dangerous. She should have called the police.'

'Is she in hospital?'

'No. They discharged her three days ago.'

'Three days ago? What the hell? Why didn't anyone tell me?'

'I tried to, but you know how she is.'

'Yes, still, you could have told me.'

He parked in front of a modern white two-storey house. Not the one where Ben and I had stayed when we'd visited them only eight months before.

'Thought they liked the other house?'

'Yes, but ...'

'If you say "you know how she is" one more time, I'll smack you.'

He smirked while taking my luggage from the back of his silver Toyota. A dark-haired, heavily built man, maybe in his late thirties, opened the main gate to the house.

'Who is that?'

'The security guard.'

'The what? Wait, is that a gun?'

'Yes, miss,' the tall, dark-haired man said.

'Jesus Christ, what's going on?'

'She is in her office. Second door on the right. I'll be back later,' Davi said, returning to his car and honking twice before driving away.

'Mom?' I said, opening the door slowly.

'Here, fifi.' Our eyes met and she smiled. She was sitting still on her office chair while a young lady changed the bandages on her face and shoulder. A pile of gauze was on her desk, and a bucket filled with old ones soaked in blood was next to the chair. I got on my knees in front of her, wrapped my arms around her hips, and rested my jet-lagged head on her thighs, the stream of my tears wetting her purple cotton dress. She caressed my hair.

'It's all right, my love. Look, I'm alive. All good, see?' I started wiping the tears away. 'Fifi, this is Milena, the angel who has been caring for me.'

'Hi, Milena, nice to meet you.' I managed a smile. Was she a nurse? Milena gave me a half-smile back.

'Did you have breakfast yet?' Mom asked.

'I ate some on the plane, but that was a while ago,' I said.

'I asked the maid, Dulce, to make you rice milk pudding. Go to the kitchen; it's in the fridge.'

'You're not coming?'

'I need to finish a petition first,' she said, reaching for the laptop on the desk.

'A petition?'

'Yes. You go, I'll be there soon.' She started typing. 'Milena, my daughter, can you find the template so you don't have to type the whole thing?' was the last thing I heard before carrying my suitcase upstairs, now sure that Milena was not a nurse but her new 'assistant-daughter'.

Day 2

Yara's doctor checked on the progress of the scar tissue healing. His white-gloved hands removed the bandage on the left side of her face. When I saw her teeth through the ripped skin, I gasped.

'This wound is opening up, Yara. I'm afraid I'll have to stitch it again. I'm sorry.'

'You do what you've got to do, doctor.' With his stitching came her wincing, but she didn't make a sound. She gripped the edges of the stretcher and I rubbed her right shoulder, the one without a stab wound. She had been stabbed inches from her heart and medulla.

'The shoulder is healing well; I like the look of it. Now, the cheek needs more time. Can you open your jaw for me? Good, thanks. This is a tricky angle, but it will heal. We just have to be patient. Lots of rest and no sun. Keep it covered at all times,' the doctor said.

'Understood. Thank you, doctor,' said Mom as I buttoned up her blouse.

We went back to the car. I was carrying her purse, a summer hat, a bottle of water, a bag full of new bandages and the hope that she'd go to bed when we got home.

'Let's head to the notary. If you see any pharmacy on the way, please stop,' she instructed the driver.

'Mom, shouldn't you be resting?'

'It will be quick. Then we go home to eat the *feijoada* Dulce made. Did you sleep well?'

'Yes, but you should be the one sleeping.'

'I will fifi, I will.'

It took us hours to get back to the house. Then she was either reading courtroom procedures or dictating words for Milena to type. I sat on the sofa of her home office and offered to help so she could rest, but she refused. We had fragments of conversations that stopped abruptly for various reasons. The last one stopped soon after she told me my chin-length bob hairstyle made me look like an old woman and that I needed to try 'something edgier'. She said that from under a veil of fake mega hair with blue streaks layering her black curls.

Day 3

Barking dogs woke me up at 7 a.m. and I zombie-walked downstairs.

'Sorry, Nicole. Sometimes Chico decides he hates Baboo, and we can do nothing. He goes straight for the neck,' Dulce said by the metal bars that separate the kitchen from the backyard.

'I can't believe Baboo is still alive. We got this dog I don't even know when.' Baboo ran to me. I let him in to check for wounds. 'Only a few scratches, buddy. You'll be fine,' I said, petting his ears. He licked my face and rested his front paws on my knees.

'Is Mom up yet, Dulce?'

'She's out.'

'Already?'

'Yes. She asked me to tell you there's papaya in the fridge.'

'That's nice. Thank you. Do you know if Davi is coming today?'

'He hasn't visited much lately. They had a spat, and he moved in with his girlfriend.'

'He did? Who sleeps in the other suite upstairs, then?'

'Milena.'

'Oh, she lives here?'

Day 4

I had changed my mother's bandages every morning since I arrived. Milena wasn't pleased.

'Let's go to the beach so you can get a tan,' Mom said as I put micropore tape on her face.

'I didn't come for the beach. I came for you. And the doctor said you should avoid the sun.'

'What is it now? 8 a.m.? It's fine. I'll stay under the parasol. Milena, my daughter, why don't you change into a bikini?' Milena stood up and took her unfinished cup of coffee upstairs.

'I thought we could spend some time together today?' I said.

'We are. I blocked my morning for you.'

'I meant alone, Mom.'

'Are you jealous of Milena?'

'No. I'm not jealous of Milena. I'm your daughter; she is not. Although you call her daughter, and she lives in your house.'

'Yes, Nicole. She lives in my house. You don't. You left. So you can't expect me to put the people here aside when you decide to come.'

'You got stabbed! Of course I'd come!'

'I told you I was fine.'

'Yes, but you are not. I wanted to come.'

'Exactly, so you have to accept how things are here.'

'I accept how things are here. I don't understand why we can't spend a minute alone. It's always you and your husband, driver or new secretary-daughter.'

'As I said, I won't hurt their feelings.'

'No, Mom. You won't. You never do. Only mine.' I went upstairs.

A few minutes later, I heard a car driving away from the house. Then Tácio knocked on the bedroom door.

'May I come in?'

'Yes.'

He sat on the maroon armchair next to the bed. His hair was greyer, and his body fuller than the last time I had seen him. 'Listen, daughter. I may not be your father, but I love you as if you were mine. And your mother . . . I wish you could see how she talks about you when people ask about her children. She always tells them that you're a comet. That there's no stopping you. She is so proud of you.'

'Then why won't she tell me that?'

'Your mom has her way of doing things.'

I kept shaking my head. He stood up and said, 'How about we play dominoes? It's been ages.'

'Yeah, okay. We can do that. Just give me a minute,' I said.

'I'll be downstairs,' he said, putting his hand on my shoulder before leaving the bedroom.

It warmed my heart to see Tácio trying to patch things up, but I couldn't get rid of the old pulsing anger that had increased by the hour since I arrived at their house. The new house with the new dog attacking our old dog, the man guarding it with a gun, the newly adopted errand girl, my mother working tirelessly less than one week after having her flesh ripped by a kitchen knife, Davi not coming to visit, Tácio giving her more work to do. But it was their house, their life. There was no place for me there. That's why I had left before. That's why I'd leave again. I opened my laptop and changed my return ticket to the next day.

Day 5

At the airport, I hugged Tácio first. Davi hadn't come. Then Yara gave me a quick but tight hug. 'May God always protect you, my daughter.' Her voice cracking ripped my heart.

I sat beside a young mother and her two children on the flight back. Being such a light sleeper, I rarely get to rest on planes. Even more so when next to a baby and a toddler. I was preparing myself for resorting to a lot of movies for the next nine hours, but a blinding headache made it hard to handle the cabin lights, so I put the sleep mask on and covered my chest with the small grey blanket provided by the airline. Then everything went black.

I woke up to a tap on my shoulder. The stewardess said we were about to land and asked me to put my seat back in the vertical position. About to land?! I looked down and noticed an extra blanket covering my arms and legs. 'I hope you don't mind. You were shivering,' said the young mother sitting beside me. 'You didn't get up or eat during the whole flight.

I was worried,' I thanked her with a hug while trying not to crush the baby on her lap.

Ben picked me up at the airport, and we went straight to our place. After showering, he brought me food and offered me a massage.

'That would be nice, but I don't think my body can take it now. Everything hurts.'

'I can imagine ...' Sitting at the edge of the bed, he held my hand.

'Are you coming to bed too?' I asked. My eyelids felt so heavy I couldn't keep them open.

'Not yet, not sleepy. It's not even 8 p.m.'

'Off you go then.'

'I'll stay here until you fall asleep,' he said.

'All right,' I said, closing my eyes. Then I felt his fingers run through my hair, and everything went black again.

After that, I started having nightmares. They were variations of the same theme: someone breaking into my mother's house. At first, I arrived at her house before it got broken into, so I could hide her somewhere. Then time ran out, and the dreams changed to me watching her neighbour approach and begging him not to stab her. I'd tell him to stab me instead, but he wouldn't. Night after night, he'd go after her. The dreams then split into different versions of her being stabbed before me until I saw pieces of dogs scattered all over my street in Islington.

It takes touching our scars to recognise other people's brokenness. Now, whenever I'm too hard on my mother, I try to remember that she too is broken and that, in all her brokenness, she came a long way. The youngest of six children, Yara had just turned fourteen when she left her mother's house in Fortaleza with a little bag and got on a bus to start a new life in São Paulo. She then suffered unspeakable violence in the streets and in the houses she shared with people from all walks of life. One day, after returning home from one of her two jobs and finding that all her belongings had been stolen, she went to the police station. There she met my father, who had given a ride to a friend who had just had his car stolen. Yara and Afonso started dating. She got pregnant. They got married. She was eighteen. He was twenty-four. They divorced when she was twenty-four; she married Tácio and had Davi at twenty-nine. She finished her high school education at thirty-two and completed a law degree at thirty-eight. Along the way, she learned how to make flip-flops, drive trucks and restore old furniture. At different points in her life, she was the owner of a grocery shop, a clothes shop and a hotel. Then, she opened a law firm with Tácio.

Growing up, I remember not understanding how she could always be so tired. As an adult who constantly feels tired, I feel closer to her. I also force myself to remember that she was never mothered. Not the way fourteen-year-old girls are supposed to be. Her father died of lung cancer the year I was born. By then, he had long left my grandmother and their children behind for other women. My grandmother opened a bar in the living room of her house. That's how she sent her kids to school, by selling drinks to the football players who practised on the field next to our house. Because Yara didn't want to burden her mother, she left as soon as she could. I don't know what else she carried in her bag apart from courage, but I know that she hasn't only survived but succeeded in paving a better existence than the one available to her had she stayed.

Then she met Tácio and he became her protector. Somehow, they made it work for three decades that I perceived as relentless but that were probably better than the ones they had had before they became a couple. I try to understand her unlimited gratitude towards him. The infinite debt that extends from her to her children. For our education, Davi's health and her career. And while I share the appreciation for having Tácio in our lives, I believe that gratitude too, just like everything else in life, needs boundaries. Otherwise it's a curse, and I don't think my mother knows boundaries. She crossed so many to get this far that she might not be aware they exist. I also don't think she knows how to stop running away from whatever she still runs away from.

Who is that tiger chasing you, Mom?

Because of all that, I have her picture on my bookshelf wherever I am in the world. It's a faded 5×7 photograph of us. She is lying on a white sofa, and the one-year-old version of me is sitting on a cheap-looking baby pram. She is smiling at the camera. I'm smiling at her. The wood frame I chose is painted lilac. Her favourite colour.

*

Ben organised a pub crawl with a couple of new friends to get my head back to what used to be our fun times in London. One of his Italian colleagues brought her fiancé, an Irish architect, who brought his best friend, whose godmother is childless. I was on a train to Reading a week later to meet Nannette, who fed me the tastiest scones I've ever had and let her dog sleep on my feet as I listened to her contagious laughter and recorded her story.

Nannette, 64, British, nurse

Born and bred in Reading, I've travelled abroad quite a lot. I've been to China, Hong Kong, Australia, New Zealand, Peru, Sweden, Italy and the United States. My favourite is Italy. I love the scenery, and I love the people there. But I have never lived outside of my own country.

At sixteen I got a nursing qualification from the Royal Berkshire Hospital. You could see whether or not nursing was a career you wanted to pursue. The hospital gave you two years as a trial period. In the end, I was a sister on the ear, nose and throat ward. Then I left and went into the nursing-home sector, which is elderly and dementia care. That's what I'm doing now. Being a nurse is all I ever wanted to do.

My plan was to go to Australia to work, but being an only child, and my mother having died when she was only forty-six and I was seventeen, it was difficult. My father didn't want me to go. He was on his own, so I felt responsible for him. That's when I started working in nursing homes.

Four years ago, I had a mastectomy, and at sixty I went part-time and began caring for people in their own homes. I enjoyed the nursing-home sector because you had to maintain standards. But now I like the fact that I've got time to work one-to-one with people, and there's less rush than there is in nursing homes. You've got time to be with them and you get to know their relatives and all their lives. So you know them better. I do all sorts of home-care things; it's not just washing and dressing and giving them drugs. You do some housework for them and cook for them. Now I am doing what I was trained to do, to care for people and look after people.

Mum worked for Huntley and Palmers. I think she worked on the biscuit line. In those days, you looked after your children, and not many women went to work. So she didn't work after I was born. Only my father did. He was a personnel manager for Hacker Radio in Maidenhead. He did that for years, but then they were taken over by an American company, and he was made redundant. It was not long after my mother died so he sort of lost the plot. He got depressed and took a job as a porter.

If I had got married, I think I would've divorced. So I'm single. Many years ago I was in a relationship with a man called Trevor for several years and thought that was it, we would marry, but then the usual happened and I found out he was cheating. So that all finished and it was terribly upsetting. I've had various others, but I haven't found the right person. I've got a very good friend whom I go on holiday with, Steve – I nursed his mother and I've known him for thirty years – it was romantic to start with but there's no way that we could ever get married.

For me, the right person is someone who can cook, who is fun, not moody. Someone who likes to travel, is handy, intelligent, doesn't get in the way and lets you do what you want. Basically, they don't exist.

When I was about twenty, the normality was that you got married and you had two children. After I split up with Trevor, I thought, oh, I'm going to be the odd one out among my friends. But they didn't bat an eyelid. Nobody seemed to care about my status.

And really, what does it matter? I didn't care either. I think it would be quite ghastly to be married now because I'm not used to having to consider anyone else. I can have who I want here, I can go out when and where I want to. So the relationship I've got with Steve is absolutely perfect because he lives fifteen miles away. Most of my holidays are with Steve, and it's good fun. I find it's very important to have opposite-sex friendships because it puts a different perspective on life.

Living with three cats and a dog keeps me busy. I just adore my animals. They are always here and are the most fantastic company. I don't have any nieces or nephews, only second cousins. I've got three godchildren – two girls and a boy. I met two of the parents of my godchildren through work. Nursing can be quite an emotional job because everybody bares their soul and there's nothing to hide. You can become quite close to your patients. I really think that if you do take on the role of a godparent, you should actually do what it says and look after them. Keep an eye out on them. Not just say, oh yeah, fine, a pretty little baby and their nice dress or jumpsuit.

Because I won't get my state pension until I'm sixty-six, I still have to work. I've got a private pension too. I'm not sure if I will want to retire when I'm sixty-six because I enjoy this job that I've been doing for the past five years. It's not stressful and I get to meet some really interesting people. The only thing I might change is that I wouldn't do as many hours a week – maybe only twenty.

There's an awful lot of dementia out there because there is a huge ageing population. Our elders never used to live beyond eighty. Seventy was really old! Now they live to be ninety or one hundred. It's incredible. Quite a lot of people have live-in carers, and it's expensive. It's cheaper to pop somebody into a care home. So many end up there. It's the culture over here that people are looked after by a care home, but the problem is finding a good one.

The thought of having children changed for me when that long relationship went wrong. I was besotted with Trevor, but, to be honest, I don't think he would have made a good father, and I believe I would have been divorced very quickly. So I suppose I just didn't meet the right person.

When I was in my twenties I had other things to occupy myself with and I enjoyed people, so I simply didn't focus on having a baby. And because I've got friends who have got these lovely little pretty things that you can give a cuddle to, and when they start screaming, you can give them back to mummy, I borrowed them, really. I borrowed my godchildren.

Maybe IVF was a possibility or I could have just asked somebody, but I've never had that desire. What would I do with it? How would I cope? If I had a partner, it would be slightly different, but how as a single parent would I manage to financially and psychologically support a child?

By the time I was thirty, I knew I would not become a mother and I didn't feel anything. I was lucky with the people I mix with, because nobody asked me questions about it.

Two of my close friends couldn't have children either. The difference between us is that they're married, and they always wanted a baby. Whereas I've been single for most of my life and have never had a desire to have my own child.

At one point I told them, if you want to put your eggs into my body, I'll be a surrogate mother. But they said no. Adopting is a good option and I think it's marvellous to think this way.

Many years ago Steve and I went to Guilin, in China, and it was terrible. There were little kids running around, and we were on a bus and the windows were open and they were saying, take my baby, take my baby. They wanted us to take their babies home because they didn't have the means to care for them.

Being childless is not something that comes to my mind. If I have to introduce myself, I say, 'I'm Nannette, I'm single and I've got a dog and three cats.' I don't mention that I don't have children because I just don't think about it.

It's becoming very normal to be a spinster and not to have a child. My mother had quite a few spinster friends, and they always used to come in in fur coats and speak to me, but I used to hide behind the sofa because they frightened me. I wasn't sociable when I was young, and I was scared by their booming voices.

A friend of mine tends to ask people why they don't have children, but I don't think I would ask anyone, because I know people who couldn't have them, and it's still quite an open wound for them. If people ask me about my situation, I'm quite happy to talk about it because it's never been a problem for me. It's easy to say I just had no desire.

When I was young, we studied human biology, which showed you all of the bits, but motherhood or anything like that just wasn't talked about, either at school or at home. Nowadays there is more sex education and I think children should be taught about the reality and consequences of getting pregnant. Unfortunately, abortions are still common. Here in the UK, they are legal for pregnancies under twenty-four weeks.

In addition to taking care of the elderly, I spend some of my free time volunteering for the homeless and the vulnerable. We serve them meals and chat with them and give them clothes if they want them. I do it every Wednesday. It's really interesting to get to know them. Some are very intelligent, some are dyslexic, some are not as intelligent, some are on drugs, some are in a bad way, some are in a good way. Some homeless people have jobs, but occasionally they're unemployable because they can't get references or they might have a police record. And if they've got no fixed abode, it's difficult to find employment. And they need help, they need guidance. There are experts who can help them. One person was taken to rehab this week; it's good to see lives improve.

I love good food, and I loathe cooking. So it's me and the microwave. Or I eat out. I've also got lovely neighbours from India and Malaysia who bring me takeaways. I guess I just got used to being on my own and I think I'm very lucky. I *am* very lucky; I don't have any family, but I have these wonderful people around me. I get the love, attention and support I need from them. And I have my godchildren and some friends who look after me very well, so I've distributed some of my money between them because, at the end of the day, I'd rather give it to them while I'm alive than when I'm dead. Until then, my goal is to care for myself and a thousand others like me. As the good old saying goes, 'Live for today, for tomorrow never comes.'

Retortus

The hair salon on Caledonian Road was open on a bank holiday. I booked an appointment, not to make my hair edgier but to shorten it so I'd think about it even less. The owner said he would take care of me, so I sat on one of the chairs with chrome finishing under a striking chandelier, and he threw a pink gown over me. There were black ones too, folded next to the mirror, but 'girls get the pink,' he said. He was very talkative, and I was still having nightmares about what had happened to my mother, so I was sleep-deprived and quieter than usual.

He asked many questions. I asked some back. He went on about how he had come to the country with his family in the '90s and built his hair salon from scratch and spent his days there, including weekends. I asked if it was hard not to spend time with his family. He said it was the price he paid to be a successful man. He asked what I did for a living. I told him. He asked if I was married. I told him. He asked if I had children. I told him. He asked me why not, point blank, inside his crowded hair salon. I told him, 'Because I don't want to.'

He went quiet and cut two of the three sections he had divided my hair into without saying a word. Then he said,

'I'm the proud father of four children. They are the most important thing to me because they give meaning to my life. Trust me, when you get promoted and open that bottle of champagne alone, you will realise you are missing something. And when you get older and nobody is there to look after you, you will understand that you made the wrong decision.'

I stared at his face in the mirror in dismay. A proud father of four children raised by his housewife while he was successful in his salon believed he had the right to predict my future and project his fears onto me based on one line I had said. Would he say that to another 'successful man'? Was choosing not to have a child for lacking the desire to have a child and saying it out loud so unacceptable that a stranger would think nothing of throwing a perpetual punishment scenario at me? There was so much wrong with what he said that I felt I could spend the rest of the day shouting at him. Instead, I froze as his scissors slashed the last section of my hair.

When I felt like pampering myself again, I found another hair salon. There was nothing shiny about this one. A woman with a hunched back sat behind a cabinet eating her lunch. I told her I could come later.

'It will only take a minute.'

'Please take your time. I can wait.' I had no book with me, so I sat there looking at nail polishes, bubble pop fidget toys and mobile phone cases for sale on the window display. Then I closed my eyes.

'Magazines over there.' She pointed to a basket on top of the noisy mini-fridge. Under a pile of tabloid crap were some old publications about horses, cooking and culture. I picked the last one. As I put my glasses on, the headline struck me: 'Why are so many successful women childless?'

Now completely alert, I scrutinised the cover. The image depicted four politicians – Nicola Sturgeon, Liz Kendall, Theresa May and Angela Merkel – standing around a ballot box in a cot. Their expressions were apathetic, contorted and dejected. The article examined why female MPs tend to have fewer children than men and argued for an end to the view that women without children are 'selfish'. Yet, the cover did nothing but reinforce the prejudices it claimed to wish to combat. It was hard to believe how crass the whole thing was.

Later that day, I googled 'female politicians no children' and what I found was an avalanche of instances of politicians fighting for leadership positions by claiming they had an advantage over others because they were mothers. 'As mothers,' they professed to understand the pressures on modern family life and to have a real stake in the future of their country. Many women who dedicated their lives to politics and occupied some of the most powerful seats in the world were being called 'deliberately barren' or belittled for 'not embodying the experiences of most women.'[15] Their qualifications, government plans and actual performances in the jobs they had been elected to were rarely given as much attention.

In 2016, Scotland's first minister, Nicola Sturgeon, was asked why she didn't have children. She spoke for the first time about the miscarriage she had suffered six years earlier. When the article was published, it featured an accompanying infographic with photos of six 'childless politicians'. All of them were women. The piece caused an online backlash for being sexist.[16]

Another aspect of the article criticised by readers was that in addition to having to justify themselves, female politicians without children are expected to declare their grief about not becoming a mother.[17] Privacy on the matter is not an option. And declaring it was a choice, when that was the case, is also out of the question. Why? Because it opens the door for people to wonder, and more often than not, the wondering happens within the tunnel vision of what Laura Carroll refers to in *The Baby Matrix* as the 'Normality Assumption': the pronatal assumption that there's something wrong with those who don't have children, women in particular.[18] This assumption can lead many to wonder, 'Why did she choose this?' 'What could be more important than children?' 'What is wrong with her if she thinks this way? She is deficient in some way. We can't trust her. Therefore, she can't lead us.'

In 2017, the UK's then prime minister, Theresa May, was asked by a radio show host, 'What has the impact been on you that you've not had children?' and 'How might Theresa May have been a different woman had she had children?'[19] The same year, she met the leaders of the top industrialised nations in the G7 summit. Five of the seven leaders had no biological children.[20] Japanese prime minister Shinzo Abe, Italian prime minister Paolo Gentiloni and French president Emmanuel Macron were not asked questions about not having children, nor was their professional capacity undermined by a personal choice or circumstance.

After a couple of hours of stupefying clicking and reading, it was impossible to miss the gender double standard that permeated everything from everyday conversations in hair salons to national and international debates in the media, which seemed particularly prevalent in the UK.

I had started feeling like I was in the wrong place again. I wanted to build the life I truly wanted elsewhere. But where? The world was going through a rough patch.

Trump and his punchable face had been elected president in 2016, and he seemed to split his time between tweeting and golfing. Brazil was following suit – the polls for the October 2018 election indicated that Jair Bolsonaro, an ultra-conservative right-wing former army officer, was likely to become the next president of Brazil, only thirty-three years after the bloody military ruling of the country came to an end in 1985. The UK had started proceedings to leave the European Union with a vehement refusal to pay the divorce bill, and London had just reached an all-time-high rate of acid attacks and knife crimes, and suffered several terrorist attacks. It was hard to imagine things getting any grimmer. But they did.

On a balmy day in July 2018, Ben and I were on our way to work when we realised that the red tinge on our soles was blood from a fresh puddle only two hundred metres away from our building. A neighbour had been stabbed at the bus stop.

What's deep down, where no blade can reach us?

It had been only a year since I moved to London, but it didn't feel right. I was always startled. The ambulance sirens and police cars everywhere were maddening, the smog in the streets boosting my asthma, the buses and bikes fighting for lanes, the drunk crowd of football chanters cutting off conversations and muttering thoughts, the national desire to send immigrants 'back from where they came from' becoming more and more tangible.

Did I miss a yellow arrow?

Meanwhile, Ireland had elected its first openly gay prime minister, legalised abortion during the first twelve weeks of pregnancy, and continued welcoming immigrants and giving them a fair chance to become citizens. To become citizens – a world apart from only being granted passage to their kingdom.

Dr Una, are you still there?

*

Lucy and I met in London after a long time apart. She had visited her family on the Isle of Man and was about to return to Sweden. We met for dinner in an Australian restaurant where she told me about her shift to translating literary work and that she was learning Manx. I was delighted to see her again. Before walking back to her hotel, she asked me for my phone and added someone called 'Cecilie' as a new contact. 'Text her. I've already told her about you.' She hugged me goodbye.

Cecilie, 45, Norwegian, head of development at a film centre

Nine years ago I got pregnant and had an abortion. I had it done in Sweden and the experience was as good as something like that can be, all things considered. Nobody was intrusive with questions, which I appreciated. I'm very happy about my choice now, but for a while I felt as if I was in *Sliding Doors*. I kept thinking about this other life I was not living: *So, if I'd have kept that baby, I would now be pregnant, and going into labour. Now the baby would be three months old*, etc. And then after a year, it just stopped.

Being pregnant and having an abortion is such an either/or situation. Very seldom do you have choices that are so absolute. So I think it was natural to spend time wondering about that other possible existence that presented itself to me in such a clear way. It felt as if my brain had to work through that timeline to be able to move on.

I didn't like the guy I was with very much, and I had no interest in having a relationship with him, so the moment I saw the test and knew that I was pregnant, I knew what I had to do. Still, it wasn't easy and I decided that I probably wouldn't do it again. It's not that I'm actively trying to get pregnant, but it is harder to think about going through it one more time.

I was born outside of Oslo, in a city called Drøbak. My parents moved back and forth from Norway to Sweden when I was small. So before I was eight, I had already lived in four different cities, but always in Scandinavia.

Because I grew up in this very small and extremely religious place on the west coast of Norway where there was nothing to do except go to church or join the track team, and I wasn't up for any of that, the library was my refuge. So, as a child, I became obsessed with books, television and theatre. And I pursued an education in art in media and communications. Now I work with innovation in the creative field where I focus on development funds for filmmakers who want to experiment in new ways and formats.

My marital status is divorced, formally, but it's been such a long time since I got divorced, that I usually think of myself as single. We met when I was only eighteen and broke up when I was twenty-eight. Since then, I've been in love with one person and kind of living together with another person. Now I'm forty-five, so I don't think it will happen, but in my thirties I was very much the person who wanted to make decisions. I'd say yes or no to everything in my life, but, in some sense, I've kind of mellowed. And I came to realise that we can't always figure out the effects that our decisions will have on us long-term. Things are simply not as clear-cut to me anymore.

I have chosen by being passive or active not to have kids, which is probably my answer to the fact that I've never truly wished to become a mother. I have systematically navigated my life in another direction – probably a lot more than I'm ready to admit. And maybe that's because while I don't identify with wanting to have children, I also don't identify with someone who from an early age decided to never have children. Those two certainties are equally strange to me. Getting to where I am at the moment was not really governed by a strong conviction of either this or that.

In this sense, I object to the wording and I don't define myself as childless. I simply live my life, and it's only when I'm confronted with society's demands for my life that I become aware of the labels being placed on me. I find that it's important for me to hold on to this middle ground.

My marriage broke up for a myriad of different reasons, but one of the main things that contributed to it was that, as we had talked about having children previously, one day my husband, Hanz, said something along the lines of, 'So, within the next two years, we're going to think about having a family.' Back then, two years felt like a long time, and I was completely with him on that, as it felt like the next natural step. Then one day he said, 'I think I'm ready to have children now', and I thought, *I have a child, I have you*, as it often felt very much like he was my child. So it wasn't so much the thought of having a child that tore us apart, but that I realised that I really didn't want to have kids with someone that I felt I could not lean on, as I was driving everything in that relationship. That was a very depressing feeling and the one that led to the break-up.

After that, I met Erik and we lived together. That was a very weird relationship, and the most actively I've ever pursued having a family. I couldn't help but feel that I was running out of time. I hated my job, but I'd taken it so that we could buy a big apartment, and the whole thing was just one bad choice on another bad choice. Upon feeling that we didn't have a good dynamic, I tried to use the question of having children to lock him down by repeatedly asking if he was committed. So there I was again, with the train on the tracks, driving us to the next thing, then to the one after that ... I had this need for my life to move forward, and in-cidentally, I think many people have children for the exact same reason – to feel that they are advancing.

A ten-year failed relationship made me feel as if I had lost too much time, so I picked a guy who I thought was never going to break my heart, because I was not that in love with him, and ran with him by telling myself that he was stable and that we were good friends, which was true. But it was also a small crisis. I'm so happy that we're friends today, and that he has three kids, but not with me.

Later on I met Terje, who was much older than me, and who already had two kids, so he was adamant about not want-ing any more. That caused friction because the pre-defined slot in his life he wanted me to fit into was not very attractive to me. So I backed out of it. That was eleven years ago and I regretted that for a long time because I was very much in love with him.

My last relationship was three years ago with Kristian, and he wanted kids. Just as I had in the two previous ones. But I was forty-two by then, and my sister had just had a child and I was loving being an aunt, while he was also an uncle. So part of me thought it was not realistic to have a child now, at this age. Instead of focusing on having children ourselves, why don't we focus on giving time and attention to the kids already in our lives? But he was uninterested in that. So that was that.

Looking back, it's clear that all my relationships have culminated with this idea of having kids or not, and it has always been me backtracking from it and going against what my current partner wished to do. Getting married again is a possibility for sure, and there's a fair chance that if I have a new partner, he will come with some kind of family of his own. I'm not averse to being part of different family constellations and I like this set-up that is different from motherhood, which is a committed state that can be incredibly stressful.

There's this tendency that I have to find friends who are younger than me because people at my age tend to already have kids. I'm drawn to people who don't have kids like a magnet because, usually, they have time and make a point to go into their hobbies. They are not afraid to explore themselves and experiment with new things.

I have great friends who have children too and I'm always open to the idea that they will go back to being interesting, but I think it's like working out. It's like a muscle, you have to exercise it. And I do think that the focus you have to put on raising someone else means you stop focusing on yourself or on parts of your own existence.

Not having kids is a circumstance and an aspect of my life, not my identity. It's like being an atheist. It's very clear to me that I am, but I don't go around thinking I am not religious. Just as I don't go around proclaiming myself as childless or even childfree.

The fact that I chose not to have kids does not mean that I think it would be horrible to have kids. I think it's important to know the difference and to keep a flexible and open mind, especially for those who haven't made that choice yet. Because, unlike the abortion scenario, which is very black and white when it comes to having children – as in you have to decide if you're going to keep that baby or not – for the rest of your life the colours can get quite blended. You might find yourself saying one day, 'Yeah, then I was forty-five, I met this guy who made me see all these other possibilities and I changed my mind.'

I don't think I would've got into a relationship with someone who was that convinced of having kids. So it was more something that we grew into and then I left before they could propose an ultimatum. I think it's a conversation that kind of pushes itself to the forefront. Now that I'm older, this conversation happens much earlier in a relationship. Sometimes it happens *too* early. I went on a blind date once where the guy asked, 'Why don't you have any kids?' I thought, *That's a weird question to ask on a first date.* I've never screened people on the basis of whether they have kids or not or tried to assess if they are a bad person, this or that, based on their parental status.

Being between thirty-five and forty was by far the hardest time in this regard because it was just full-on questions. Now that I'm over forty people assume my time for babies is over. I meet friends or acquaintances and I ask about their kids, because I understand they're an important part of their lives. We talk about their kids for a while and then they stop themselves, assuming I'm not really interested.

They ask, 'How's your cat?' But the thing is, children and cats don't mean the same thing. I understand that they are trying to be nice, but the pets are just fine. We don't have to talk about them. So their interpretation is that, because I don't have children, the next important thing in my life is my pet. And don't get me wrong, I love my cats, but I didn't get them because I thought they were going to be my babies. So it can get awkward socially, as it requires a lot of manoeuvring around it, but it's nothing that makes me feel that I wish I had some kids to push around so that I can feel that I'm part of society.

The fact that I have cats doesn't really help as it means I get stereotyped even by the people who are close to me. For example, because many of my friends are very LGBTQ+ friendly, they tend to be quite aware and open about many things in life, but when they used to call me the crazy cat lady, I'd call it out by saying, 'Don't you think it's a dilemma to be very socially aware of stereotypes and then use the cat lady as a stereotype on other people just because they don't have kids?' Over time they stopped calling me that, so I guess it helped.

I've been involved with an organisation that coaches young girls. It's like a big sister programme; the girls get someone to talk to for a year about anything they want, or someone to hang out with. When I look at this shift from my thirties to my forties, I realise it's been influenced by this coaching mentality, because I have learned to become less judgemental about myself and other people, and to be more open to the many possibilities that are out there. We learn not to ask leading questions and to avoid wanting to help someone by taking over. It's important that the young girls set the pace themselves and that they are always the ones making the decision about what they want to do.

In a way, it's the same with my parents and the way they raised me. They were very insistent on freedom and I think that has certainly impacted the way I think about motherhood.

In the end, we are biological beings. I'm a progressive and a liberal, but I do react to a lot of the Swedish philosophy. For example, the notion that if you take away gender-specific names, then all humans will be equal. I don't think that you can do social constructivism in that sense. It's an unsolvable dilemma. And the same goes for concepts around parent-hood. All of us are born into a family, whether it's functional or not, or still existent or not, so it's programmed into us to see ourselves as part of a family structure. And I don't think you can unlearn that. It hasn't been all that long that women have had the choice to live the way we want to, but my hope would be that with our practices and with our lives, we can start illustrating and being good examples to each other that there are different ways of doing things, so that we will be influenced by the stories around us.

One thing that I feel conscious about when I think of my life without children is the decreased focus. I think kids keep you alert; they challenge you in a different way and make you sharper. When I talk to my friends who have kids, their stories often contain specific dates and years as they say things like, 'That must have been in 2014 because she had just started school.' They have a very active relationship with time be-cause things are always changing around them; their kids are changing all the time. Whereas for me, in my forties, time is more mushy. Everything just rolls on.

But then I look at my life now, and I have time on my hands. I have time for myself, to do whatever I want. Like sleeping in in the morning, knitting, reading, watching TV, cooking, pottering about, and having head space that's not disturbed, which I truly appreciate, because I recharge when I'm by myself.

Still, despite being kind of a loner, I have to think about having an active relationship with and being part of other families as a strategy for growing old well. So I've talked to some of my friends, some with kids and some without kids, about us trying to have a communal house after we turn sixty.

There's a famous Swedish children's book called *Aunt Green, Aunt Brown and Aunt Lavender* about three old ladies who live together; one likes to do the gardening, one likes to do the baking, one likes to hatch silly schemes and then Uncle Blue comes and visits them. So we have this standing joke, that we should live in a communal house with a guy who comes and visits.

Wherever I end up, I would love my last home to be near the sea. I've learned that it is easy to imagine all the negative things that may happen but it's much harder to imagine all the wonderful things that can happen in the future. So I am preparing to be amazed by all that I don't yet know.

PART III

Looking Ahead

Puppet Master

The hairdresser was right about one thing: I did get promoted. And that's because I loved my job. As a creative writer, I had to write thousands of human-like answers for a virtual assistant expected to understand and reply to anything someone could ask. When it came to job satisfaction, nothing came close to watching people trying to have a real conversation with this puppet that my colleagues and I had spent hours assembling.

My all-time favourite glimpse into the alchemy of automatic answers from our database was in a YouTube video of a nine-year-old Brazilian girl who, alleging she couldn't sleep, recorded herself talking to the virtual assistant in the middle of the night.

'What do you do when you can't sleep?' She lay her head on a fluffy pink pillow.

'Can you see me?' She pulled the phone closer to her face.

'Are you my friend?' she asked.

'Can you do my homework?' She opened her mouth, waiting excitedly for an answer.

'Do you have a boyfriend?' She laughed at the virtual assistant's joke about getting cold feet with an air conditioner.

'Do you have children?' She didn't like that the answer wasn't a simple yes or no.

Like a puppet master, I had to remain behind the curtain. I couldn't answer her questions the way I wanted. I couldn't tell her that I was sorry she couldn't sleep, that I'd love to be her friend, that it was important that she did her homework, and that I had a boyfriend but no children. I couldn't tell her that not all women will become mothers. And that they too can be happy. That was not my job. My job was to create enough answers to maintain the illusion that the puppet was alive for as long as she, or anyone with a computer or a smartphone, wished to play with this modern version of a Tamagotchi.

However gimmicky and, quite frankly, far removed this technology was from the world's real needs, I loved being part of the team that brought it to life. It was, by a long shot, the most fun job I had ever had. But I didn't want it to be the only manifestation of my writing. I wanted to tell stories, not jokes. I wanted to narrate something from beginning to end without worrying about the space constraints of text and audio bubbles. I wanted to open the curtains and show my face as I carried a stack of paper. What would these pages in my stack say, though? I knew many would be about the women I had interviewed, but would I be there too? And how would I feel once the spotlight was pointed at me? All those years I had spent immersed in the lives of women who had not defined themselves based on motherhood had shaped my days so completely that it had become a way of living for me. Was I ready to move on?

There was only one way to find out. I decided that Cecilie

would be the last person I'd interview for this book. It was time to write.

In the early autumn of 2018, I travelled for four hours on a bus that dropped me at the gates of the red-brick building of a residential library in Wales. I carried my one piece of luggage into a bedroom with only a bed, a bedside table, a silver lamp, a small writing desk and a big window looking out onto the garden, and unpacked slowly as I admired the walls covered in bookshelf-themed wallpaper. I wanted to live there for the rest of my life. But the plan was to stay for a week. The plan was also to find out what would happen once I went back to contemplating the emptiness in my womb.

It was 3 p.m. on a Saturday, and the pictures of the reading rooms had not left my mind since I first saw them on the library's website, so I decided to start there. On my way downstairs, the rays of light coming through the stained-glass window felt like an invitation to go outside, and before long, I was sitting in the sunniest part of the garden, accompanied by a journal and my favourite BIC pen. I started by fiddling with the journal that Lucy had given me, which was made out of elephant poop. The note she left on the first page read: 'Write that shit down.' That was very Lucy.

I looked around, impressed by the set-up of the place, and I saw a green butterfly, a patch of wildflowers, a vegetable garden and a family of four ordering afternoon tea. Before long, my pen started dancing on the page, choreographing words, lists and diagrams. It moved faster and faster until, about twenty pages in, I could barely read or make sense of what I'd written. When the kind lady told me that it was dinner time, I wondered where the sun and the past three hours had gone. After a bowl of leek and potato soup at the Food for Thought bistro and some short exchanges with other residents, I went back to my room.

Strange things happen in enchanted places. Longer versions of this routine unfolded over the next few days. By the end of that week, I had covered all the elephant poop pages with thoughts, doodles and coffee stains. It was almost Saturday again when I turned my phone back on and found two new messages on WhatsApp. The first one was from Ben: 'I hope the place is everything you hoped for. Love you. x'

The second was from Gabriela: 'He's here! His name is Rafael. He took his time but finally came to my arms today. I'm exhausted, and everything hurts, and I want to cry all the time, but then I look at him and I smile. We can't wait for you to come and visit us,' followed by a heart emoji and a picture of Rafael sleeping on his back in a brown bear onesie.

He had his mother's tiny nose and thin, light-brown hair. I couldn't believe any of it. I couldn't believe Gabriela had given birth to her baby the same week I had started drafting my book. Still, it happened. In September 2018, in different hemispheres, we were both giving birth to something; only hers came out of her vagina. I wrote back: 'He *is* perfect, Gabi. And I can't wait to hold him.'

He *was* perfect. He was perfect to her because he had been wanted. So wanted. Since Gabi and I were little girls, she had names ready for him and his brother. She had always said she would have two kids one day and that becoming a mother was her biggest dream. He was perfect to me because he had made my best friend's wish come true. And I hoped that one day he and I would become friends too.

2019

Fight or Flight

Two years into the puppet-master job, my manager informed me that a dozen fellow writers had been laid off and would leave the team in thirty days. He dodged all my questions about why they had been fired and given such short notice. I then asked when it would be my turn.

'Leadership has decided it's best if the whole team works in one place, so you'll have to consider moving to New York,' he said.

'New York? I'm not moving to New York!'

'Why don't you take some time to think about it?'

'Because I'm not going to move to the other side of the world because someone decided our team should sit in the same building in Manhattan.'

'Look, Nicole. I understand you're upset, but there's nothing we can do. It will be easier for the team to spend more time together,' said my manager from the Tokyo office.

'But we've been doing it all this time. Why change it now?'

'As I said, it's a leadership decision.'

'And how long will this leadership give me before I'm made redundant?'

'You don't have to worry about that. You have time.'

'I do have to worry. My stay in the UK is tied to a work permit. How long do I have?'

'Six months.'

'There we go. Transparency. Thank you.'

I left the meeting room, exited the building and walked by the canal, feeling ejected from my life in the UK.

That night, while we watched *The Great British Bake Off*, I told Ben that my time in that country and company had ended. I wanted to build a home again, this time with him, but I wanted to do it in Ireland. Like most conversations we had had before, that one, too, was easy. 'Ireland it is,' he said.

'Are you going to quit soon?'

'Not until I find a new job.'

'Thought so. But I understand why you want to go back. When you're ready, start looking for a new job, and once you get it, I'll do the same. If need be, we go back to getting on planes for a while until everything falls into place. Don't you worry. We got this.'

Six weeks and thirteen interviews later, I received a job offer from a company in Dublin.

When we hit Irish ground, we were elated. Arriving at the peak of the summer, our mission was to find two places: one to rent for a short time and one to buy. For the former, we chose Howth, a lively fishing village on a peninsula thirteen kilometres north-east of Dublin, where I had wanted to live since my first visit in 2014.

The day after signing the tenancy agreement, we started moving our things into the house. Considering the first phase of our mission complete, I picked *Motherhood* by Sheila Heti from one of the boxes and crossed the street to a high view-point looking over the harbour.

Sitting on a memorial bench, I felt so transfixed by the sea that my eyes didn't land on a single page. Instead, I stared at the pale horizon contrasting with the brightly coloured boats and smiled at the little seals' heads popping up in various spots from the teal-tinted waters. Time stood still until a man, who looked to be in his late sixties, parked his bike next to the stone wall and sat on the opposite side of the same bench. Not too close as to startle me, but close enough to remind me I was no longer alone.

'Glorious day, isn't it?' he said, looking at the sea.

''Tis, indeed,' I replied, continuing to look straight ahead.

He then unzipped a small backpack he had placed on the ground. 'Which one do you want?' he asked, holding a banana and a plum.

'Err ... I'm good, but thanks,' I said, putting both hands between my knees.

'It's not poisoned or anything.'

'Oh no, I didn't think it was. It's just that—'

'It's all good. No worries.'

I nodded with a relieved smile but was unsure what to do or say next.

'Whereabouts are you from?'

'Brazil.'

'Now that's far away.'

'Tell me about it.'

'Do you miss it?'

'I miss parts of it. The people, the sun, the food ...'

'That is a lot to miss.'

'It is. But my heart is here now. I love your country.'

'You do, yeah. I can tell.'

'Yeah?'

'Yeah. You're not here for the fish 'n' chips; you're here to talk to the sea. That's what we Irish do. We talk to the sea.'

I turned to my left and looked him straight in the eye for the first time. He looked right back with smiley cobalt blue eyes. I could feel the tears coming to mine.

'All right, lady. I'll leave you to it. Lovely meeting you.'

'You too. Thank you for the chat.'

'No bother. Take care of yourself now.'

'Same to you.'

2020

The Next Mountain

We chose an apartment in a less touristy neighbourhood for our permanent home. No longer by the sea, but next to a park destined to become our haven. We got the keys in time to celebrate another Valentine's Day by cleaning the whole place before two men and a van arrived with our belongings. The sun was long gone when we surrendered to our uncarpeted floor and curtainless bedroom. We used a few bags and boxes as a privacy screen, ordered Thai food, and sat grinning on the newly bought mattress. Just three weeks before, we had stood in that spot as we said to each other: 'I think we've found it.'

'How much do you like it?' he asked, testing the double-glazed windows.

'A lot,' I said, touching the walls.

'Yeah, me too. Anything that you don't like?'

'Not really. I like everything. The ceiling is not too high, which is good, so we won't spend a fortune to heat it, and the balcony is south facing!'

'I know. Perfect for my lizard woman,' he said, clapping twice. 'I wonder if I can drum here.'

'I'm sure I can write here.'

'Any concerns?' he asked.

'Just one,' I said.

He walked back to the hall and met me in the main bedroom.

'Tell me.'

'Still no babies?' I asked.

'Oh. That. No. Not for me. You?'

'No. I don't think so. Just checking, 'cause this is a big deal.'

'Yeah, it's probably too big for us . . . '

'No, I meant buying a place.'

'Just joking. I know getting this place is a big deal. But I'm ready for it if you are.'

'I'm ready.'

On our first weekend there, I woke up early, made a bowl of porridge and entered the second bedroom down the hall, where I had stored most of my belongings. I hung a cork memo board and the large portrait of Frida Kahlo that Ben had given me for my thirty-sixth birthday above the standing desk, unrolled a rug in shades of green and lilac and hung matching curtains on the window with a view of a walnut tree, an all-boys primary school, and the gardens of a retirement home. I wanted the room to resemble a lavender field, and I was getting there.

Standing in the corner that turns gold on sunny days, I kneeled in front of the bookcase and plucked journals, newspapers and magazine clippings accumulated over the years from various folders. Then I made a pile of the books about childlessness I had read, dug a family album from a storage box and stacked them all on one side of the desk. A water bottle, reading glasses and earplugs were on the other side. I turned the laptop on, opened a file where I had dumped loose thoughts and fragments of dreams, renamed it 'Manuscript' and started typing.

With all sorts of mirrors reflected at me, I thought about my childhood and let the memories rest one after the other on the pages, adding flesh to the bones of a book I had started to arrange in the garden of the residential library. The flow continued through that whole weekend. It went dormant while I worked eight hours a day from Monday to Friday and returned in the evenings, after dinner, compelling me to capture more snapshots of my life for three weeks straight. Hand cramps aside, I pushed through the fifty-page mark. And just when I started to think I was flying, I hit a wall.

Erik. How was I to write about Erik? Which parts should I reveal or conceal?

I had to think this through with the laptop closed before typing more things down. I pondered whether I should call, send a letter, an email, or anything. Our last contact had been in November 2018, when he wrote to say he wished to sell our apartment in Lund, and I sent him the paperwork. A brief and practical interaction, more like a transaction. How was I to start a conversation with him after a year and a half without contact? Not knowing what else to do, I returned to his Instagram account, shame and all. The only window left open to his life. A picture posted three weeks earlier showed him sitting on the grass next to the most heavenly baby girl. And she looked a lot like him.

A father. He was a father of a baby girl now. He always wanted a girl.

My legs weakened.

Lying down in my imaginary lavender field, I surrendered to a dizzying range of emotions – I was rejoicing and grieving, not only for Erik but for Joanne too. The family that had been my family for eight years. I was happy for them, and I was sad I had lost them. There was space for it all in me. Happiness and sadness. I didn't have to choose or censor what to feel. So I stayed there. Very still. Unwinding. Feeling each emotion leave my body and, eventually, my writing room. Ultimately, what stayed was an enormous sense of relief. My instincts were right: he wished for a baby, and setting him free to make his wish come true was the right thing to do.

In all my agnosticism, right there and only then, I felt as if God herself had squeezed my hand and blessed our separate journeys to the next mountain. His journey was becoming a father; mine was becoming a writer.

In the Lodge

The bookshop is in an old chalet.

Before I say a word, the little girl behind the counter tells me, 'It's on the second floor.'

I climb the curved stairs to the mezzanine, and the building resembles a horseshoe-shaped opera house with many tiers stacked like a layer cake.

The orchestra pit and the arena seats are empty. Scanning the other elevated floors, I see the head of someone sitting in an aisle seat. I look through binoculars at it, notice the polka dot pattern that resembles Joanne's armchair and quicken my pace. Upon stepping into the occupied lodge, the floor makes a squeaky sound that bounces back and forth against the walls.

'Sorry. I didn't mean to disturb you,' I whisper, mortified, standing behind the armchair.

'You didn't,' the voice says, without the head looking up or turning back.

Her hair is silver. Her wrists gleam with bracelets. Her hands are full of rings. Those are not Joanne's fingers. Those are the tapering fingers I inherited from my Grandma.

I can't think of another thing to say. I don't want to stare at her, but I don't want to move away either. So I stay there, looking above her shoulders at the shining strands of her hair while trying not to make more squeaky sounds.

Still sensing my presence, she says, 'It's on the third floor.'

I look around but can't find another flight of stairs up.

'Is there a third floor?'

'Yes. You can go up now.'

She turns a page and continues reading the book on her lap.

I woke up.

Lockdown

Some walls were personal; others were universal.

27 March 2020 hit everyone in Ireland with the first of three stay-at-home orders issued by the government and enforced by the police over the year. We were in lockdown.

Mentally blocked and physically constrained that spring, I avoided the manuscript so thoroughly that I worried I'd never be done with it. In all my restlessness, my attention turned to work. If I wasn't in a meeting, I reviewed translations or delivered training to translators. When I wasn't doing one of these things, I was stretching my lunch hours by eating quickly and reading slowly in the park within the two-kilometre radius where we were allowed to exercise.

With libraries and bookshops out of reach, I returned to my archive of books on biological determinism, reproductive autonomy, women's subjugation, social expectations, purpose, vocation and craft. Searching for the ones with the most Post-it flags, I chose *Paradise, Piece by Piece* as the book for the day. That, plus an egg sandwich, was all I needed to head to the Rose Garden in the park near my apartment, where I sat on a bench next to a bed of orange flowers with white edges I first thought were called 'Mating' until I put my reading glasses on, looked back at the name tag, and saw the name was 'Matangi'. *That's better,* I thought.

Deciding that scented spot would do, I entered the portal I hoped would take me back to my manuscript. The book in which poet Molly Peacock tells the story of her dysfunctional childhood, her decision not to have children and her search for fulfilment through creativity. The one I first found in 2013 at the Malmö library and returned only after shipping a copy from the US to Sweden. The one I had carried on trains and planes as if it were my emotional support animal.

I stared at the painting and the open door on the cover and wondered: was that Molly's house? Her childhood home? Why had I never attempted to contact Molly when her book continued to mean so much to me? A jolt of exhilaration ran through my body when I found her Twitter profile. Her last tweet, only a couple of hours old, was about seeing the opportunity to let creativity bloom in those weeks of involuntary isolation. Her words soothed me. I liked the tweet and started following her.

The next day, I was awestruck by the little red hearts Molly had placed under several of my tweets. At the time of her visit to my feed, I had written tributes to more than three hundred female writers, painters, sculptors, musicians, politicians and athletes who had no children – including one in homage to her that dated back to 2017 and included a photo of her smiling straight at the camera, with her right hand partially covering her chin and a quote from one of her events:

We live in a pronatalist culture, so when you decide not to have children, you find yourself at the far edge of the bell curve. How do you live happily there? Well, you live happily there if you are comfortable with your own nature. And that requires talking about how to separate motherhood from female identity. It's still a taboo subject – not even discussed in women's studies programs. And endlessly fascinating to me, especially as the Census Bureau tells us we will be seeing increasing numbers of people making this decision.

I sent her a message telling her how much reading such a personal and detailed account of the life of a childfree writer had meant to me. I explained that reading her examine her past with curiosity and eagerness to learn how she had become the person she was had inspired me to do the same. And how, in a time of extreme isolation, I often felt she spoke directly to me in her memoir.

It wasn't long before she replied, asking me more about the 'book in the making about women without children' I mentioned in my profile. I then asked her permission to email her and write more freely outside the apps. We started corresponding, and over the following weeks, I learned more about her: although she was American, she lived in Canada. She had been to the UK and Ireland in the years I lived in each country doing research for a biography about Mary Delany (an English artist known for her paper-mosaics and botanic drawings) and another biography about Mary Hiester Reid (an American-born Canadian painter). Both her subjects had no children. As my admiration for her multiplied exponentially with each email, I mustered the courage to ask if she could mentor me. To my complete delight, she said yes.

We bridged the gap between Ireland and Canada with regular Zoom calls. And it was in those calls that I noticed her hair was silver, and she spoke with animated hands adorned with bracelets and rings. The fingers were not the same as the ones in my dream – those were mine – but everything else I had seen was hers. Molly had lived in both my conscious and subconscious mind for a while. And now she was on my computer screen.

I remember most things about our conversations. Above all, I remember her saying, 'In your last email, you said you felt paralysed by concerns about portraying the people in your life.'

'That's right.'

'Distorted – I think that's the word you used, wasn't it?'

'Yes. Distorted reality.'

'There. You were afraid of portraying them or events involving them in a distorted way.'

'Still am.'

'I get the concern. I've been there too. But I suggest you think about it this way: what you remember about events and people is all you have. However distorted it may be, it's *your version* of it, and that's the story you tell. That's the only story you can tell, Nicole.'

It was a simple way of thinking about the maddening idea of writing about the ones we love – one that rang possible and true. And by the end of that call, as if a character in a cartoon, I watched the big monster disintegrate before me.

I loved her for making me feel able to write again, and I have loved her since. Her generosity in sharing her wisdom and planting the next yellow arrows ahead in my writing path allowed me to sprint to this book's middle section by December. And I had every hope of crossing the finish line by the summer of 2021. But other things were on the cards for me.

2021

Pandemonium

In that first week of the new year, I felt discomfort in my right hand, which I dismissed as too much time in a dinosaur pose in front of the computer. Then the pain lodged on my right elbow expanded to my right hip and snaked into my right foot. Less than a month after the first sign that something was off, a sharp pain struck in the middle of the night, making me toss and turn in bed, thinking it was first indigestion, then period pain, then that I was given birth without being pregnant. I walked to the bathroom and felt my legs buckle and I collapsed on the tiles. My scream woke Ben, and within seconds, he was on his knees holding my head, trying to understand what had happened as I lay in a foetal position on the floor, covered in sweat, then in vomit.

He took me to hospital. Once we arrived, we joined the long line of people standing outside, waiting for a spot in the reception area to avoid the raindrops that plonked our heads. One hour later, one of the admission staff with a blurred badge that read 'Mark', asked, 'Any cough, shortness of breath, difficulty breathing, fever or body pain?'

'Body pain,' I said.

'Where?'

'Here,' I said, touching the right side of my pelvis.

'Probably not Covid then. But we will do a test anyway. When did it start?'

'About 5 a.m. I thought it was period cramps, then I got up, and something snapped—'

'Snapped?' Mark quizzed.

'Yes, it felt like a rupture.'

'Are you pregnant?'

'No.'

'Could you be pregnant?'

'No.'

Mark glanced at Ben, looking for confirmation. I sighed. Ben placed his palm gently on my back. 'No baby then. Okay. I'll pass this information to the consultant, and we will investigate. For now, please have a seat there,' he said, pointing to a chair at the back of the reception area. Ben handed me the duffel bag with clothes and toiletries, and that's when he saw my dilated pupils and felt the sweat on my palms. He knew why. I had been to hospitals many times before – with Davi due to his numerous bone injuries and as an overnight companion to Grandpa after his pacemaker surgery – but I had never been the patient. And I could hear my heart thumping inside my chest.

'It's going to be okay. You'll be home very soon. Please let me know once you're in a room,' he said, pulling me closer.

I nodded. Before turning my back, I let out a breathy 'I love you'.

The room was in the oncology department. I wanted to know if that indicated a potential diagnosis or if it was just the first bed available that Thursday morning. My bed was the one furthest away from the sunlight. Still, I insisted on staring at the window after changing into pyjamas and putting the rest of my things in a little cupboard. A phone rang. It wasn't mine. I watched Vera (the seventy-year-old stage-IV cancer patient who had had a procedure to remove fluids from her lungs) struggle to grab the phone from her handbag, so I asked if she wanted me to pick it up for her. She made a thumbs-up sign. I squatted by the bed parallel to mine and held the phone next to her ear so she could talk to her daughter. It had been ten days since Vera had entered that ward. When she was not sleeping, she killed time getting acquainted with Margaret (a fifty-eight-year-old stage-III leukaemia patient going through her latest round of chemotherapy), who occupied the third bed in the room closer to the toilets. Margaret had been there for a couple of days. She stopped by my bed for a little chat on her way back from throwing up and told me her prognosis was starting not to look so good and asked what I had. I said I wasn't sure. She patted my ankle over the bed-sheet.

Unlike Vera's, Margaret's phone didn't ring much. And when it did, it was always her husband. They had two children: one lived in Australia and the other lived with them still but was 'emotionally distant'. That confirmed my suspicion that, in the end, children are no guarantee of companionship or care. There will always be trying moments we must go through alone, no matter how much love we feel or give. And so, there we were, Vera, Margaret and me, going through some of it alone. With no mother, partner or children to nurse us, we nursed each other.

Next thing I know, I'm fasting and drinking four litres of laxative in preparation for tests booked for early in the morning of my second day in hospital, which I spent going in and coming out of a sedated state. Day three had me pushing an IV apparatus as I walked back and forth in the corridors where the stark lighting spotlit the purple patterns forming on my arms after needle-pricking sessions in search of veins. By day four, I could eat a full meal again, and the bruises had turned green. On the fifth day, a doctor who looked like a rugby player stood by my bed. Surely he would tell me what was going on. And that it was not cancer. And that I could go home. Oh, please, *please*!

'Hi. I'm Doctor Murphy, the gynaecologist on call. The nurse told me you want to discharge yourself?'

'That's correct. It's been almost a week and nobody knows what I have. I feel better now, so unless you tell me my life is at risk, I'd rather go home. It's a pandemic. I'm sure other people need this bed.'

'Well, PCOS is not life-threatening.'

'I'm sorry, doctor, PC what?'

'Polycystic ovary syndrome. It's common for women to have it after the first menstrual period, but it can also develop in the twenties or thirties. In your case,' he looked at the chart, 'at thirty-seven, it's a bit late for that. So I don't know what we are dealing with, but I could suggest your discharge and arrange an appointment at my clinic in Blackrock.'

'I don't understand: ovarian cysts caused the pain I felt?'

'I don't know what that pain was. Maybe a cyst burst, but we found no fluid in the ultrasound.'

'So the pain was from my ovary being swollen?'

'No. It wouldn't be that. Ovaries don't hurt.'

'I'm sure they do, doctor.'

'Not according to my years of experience as a gynaecologist. Your right ovary is quite swollen, and there may be cysts, but that doesn't explain the pain you claim to have felt.'

The pain I claimed to have felt. I was dumbfounded. During my stay in that hospital, I had been asked if I was pregnant four times; I'd had a pelvic MRI, an abdominal ultrasound, an endoscopy, a colonoscopy, a urine test, a faeces test, three blood tests and four X-rays. Only to be told in passing by a rheumatologist that I had inflammation in my right limbs and, in the most condescending way by a gynaecologist, that I had cysts in my right ovary and that ovaries don't hurt. Oh yeah, and that these things were not connected.

I wanted to strangle him. I wanted my arms to stretch in his direction and knock the stupid patient chart out of his hands, my knuckles to hit his long, pointed nose, my swollen fingers that had not bent in days to find their strength again and wrap themselves around his neck. I wanted to maul his face and shout that I'd had thirty-seven years of experience having a female body and had never felt pain like that before. The stabbing pain that made me leave the safety of my home, where I had been sheltering for almost a year, to go to hospital and expose myself and others to a highly transmissible virus. The stabbing pain that made me think I was going to die in that bathroom. The stabbing pain in my right ovary which was twice as big as it should be. But I didn't say that. I had no energy or confidence left in me. With watery eyes, sallow skin, greasy black hair and body parts that didn't seem to go together, I looked more and more like a monster, and what I said was, 'Thank you, doctor, but there's no need for an appointment at your clinic.'

'Nicole, my job is to tell you what I think your condition is based on your test results. And if you have PCOS, it might diminish your ability to get pregnant, so whether it's with another doctor or me, I'd advise you to follow up on this.'

'My ability to get pregnant . . .' I could hear my blood boiling up as it ran under my bruises.

'Thank you, Dr Murphy,' was all I managed to say as I lunged for the duffel bag in the cupboard.

After saying goodbye to Vera and Margaret, I went home.

Panic of the Closing Gate

As the Earth completed its first orbit around the Sun since the beginning of the pandemic, I noticed that something other than a virus was also spreading: many women in my life had become or were on their way to becoming mothers in between lockdowns: Gabriela had just given birth to another boy; Marcele, Davi's girlfriend, was about to give birth to my nephew; Yasmin, a work colleague, had started her maternity leave; and Elisa, a neighbour-turned-friend, was on her way to having Irish twins.

That second year of the pandemic brought many pictures and videos of babies to my phone. When not sent directly, the detailed reports on the evolution of miniature humans were uploaded in stories on social media or groups on WhatsApp, forming a steady torrent I often found myself caught in. There they were, growing hair and teeth; babbling first words and taking first steps; playing with cats, ducks and dogs; wearing hats, caps and bows.

I'd walk to the bedroom next door, to Ben's office cave, pointing at my phone screen, saying, 'Look at that face!' And he would go, 'Oh-oh. Should I be worried?' No, I'd tell him. There was nothing to be worried about. There was also nothing strange about it. I liked kids. I enjoyed playing with the ones who lived close to me and watching the ones who lived far away climb onto their parents' laps like little chimps in Zoom calls. That wasn't me getting broody. That was me keen to get to know and bond with my friends' children. But that seemed confusing to some.

A couple of friends withdrew from most forms of contact soon after announcing they were pregnant; one skipped the announcement altogether, and I found out by bumping into her pushing a pram somewhere in town. I didn't know how to ask them what had changed in our friendship since they had got pregnant and why I had been kept at bay without sounding incredibly clueless and self-centred. My way around it was to show genuine interest in their new routine and their kids. When they saw me making their babies and toddlers laugh or holding them in my arms in a way that didn't look like a potato sack, they'd tell me how 'I had a way with kids', 'would have been a wonderful mother' or call me Mary Poppins. I was not enchanting carousel horses or flying using my umbrella; I was simply smiling at the kids, holding their hands or caressing their cheeks. If they were older, I'd ask them questions and listen to what they had to say, but the social expectation on women without children is so low that any effort I made came across as repressed longing, and led to, 'Are you sure you don't want kids, Nic?'

Yes, some women (mothers or not) don't like, aren't interested in, or don't know how to interact with children. And no, they should not have to pretend to be any different to keep their friendships intact. But the assumption that women who are not mothers don't like children is, lo and behold, another widespread, baseless pronatalist belief. Think about it: so many teachers, nurses, paediatricians, social workers, childminders and babysitters have no kids and are entrusted with taking good care of them. Why would it be different for women in other professions?

Many female writers who aren't mothers have written books for children, preteens and teens, increasing their language, emotional and cognitive skills and encouraging them to overcome fears and inner conflicts.[21] The list includes Eleanor H. Porter (*Pollyanna*), Beatrix Potter (*The Tale of Peter Rabbit*), Dodie Smith (*The Hundred and One Dalmatians*), Tove Jansson (*Moomins*), Margaret Wise Brown (*Goodnight Moon* and *The Runaway Bunny*), Louise Fitzhugh (*Harriet the Spy*) and Thalita Rebouças (*Confessions of an Invisible Girl*). They may not have had children, but they cared about them. And so do I. Somewhere in my computer, there's a draft of an unfolding adventure featuring a hedgehog and an ostrich based on Gabi's sons.

I woke up to a message on Instagram from Carina, one of the people I enjoy interacting with the most online. We've never met in real life but have kept a personal and pleasant ping-pong of exchanges going for months. Earlier in our correspondence, she had confided the feeling of always knowing she didn't wish to become a mother but never being able to explain how she knew that. All was well until she turned thirty and her parents got frustrated and started demanding a more logical answer as to '*why* the hell not'. Her simply not wanting to have kids wouldn't do.

That morning, Carina sent me a link to a video in which a

linguist spoke about the literal meaning of the German word *Torschlusspanik*: 'The panic you get when you realise one day that you haven't done very much with your life, and if you don't act soon, then you may miss out on more opportunities as time passes.'[22] Being German, she confirmed the word's meaning was correct.

I watched the video to the end. The linguist explained that this word originated in medieval times when people had to rush to the city gates when under attack, and if they were too late, they'd simply be locked out. He finished the video by asking, 'Who already felt it?'

We were being attacked by a virus that kept mutating and that we had failed to contain or cure. A virus that had shown its capacity to decimate us. The gates *were* closing and people were making babies. How to make sense of human behaviour in times of crisis? Could it be that the collective grief on a global scale acted as a pressure valve that burst open the truest desires of many? Or was it that, when forced to face our mortality head-on, some of us chose to hold on to the little control we had left? Was making babies when we were fearful that life as we knew it could soon end a way to attribute meaning to the remaining days, or was it a way to launch ourselves into the future? Or to be launched into the future? After all, what reflects more the desire to continue to be alive than creating a new life from our cells and projecting it into the next century in the shape of someone likely to remember that we too were alive once?

By keeping up with the news, I was aware that domestic violence rates were going up exponentially[23] and that under troubling circumstances involving psychological coercion, withholding contraceptive measures or sexual assault by abusive partners, many women had got pregnant. These stories are infuriating, and it's clear that there was no choice in the matter. What puzzled me during that time of mandatory confinement were the many people who had *chosen* to have babies then. To me, that was simply staggering. What was moving them towards that path? Tradition? Fear of missing out? The genuine desire to experience parenthood? If so, did they know why? *Why* did they wish to become parents? Were more detailed and logical reasons only expected to be provided by those of us who chose not to or could not have children?

Like Carina, I struggled with the social expectation that if you are not going to have kids, you'd better have your life completely figured out. Think about all the aspects, all the scenarios, all that you will supposedly never be, feel or have if you have no kids. Oh, and one more thing! If you are a woman, you must do all of that by the time you are thirty. Okay, forty maximum. But that's it. Hush, hush, 'cause people *need to know* why you won't have children.

Now, do people who don't have children go about expecting or demanding parents to explain why they have become parents? It was looking more and more like having children in the middle of a pandemic was to be seen as a perfectly reasonable thing to do, something that would not and should not be questioned. No 'Have you thought about what happens to the kid if you get the virus and die? Or if you become chronically ill? Or how the hospitals are full and the nurseries closed? Or, beyond all of this, the possibility of obstetric violence, postpartum depression, or that the kid would grow not to like you, or you not to like them, and how expensive it is, and how tiring, and that maybe you shouldn't be having kids at all because you haven't really thought it through and don't even know why you are doing it?' No? Not allowed.

Questioning the logical skills and common sense of those who choose not to become parents is accepted as normal, reasonable and a sign of care. Yet the same question is not to be reversed and asked of parents. Because that would be rude or mean or insensitive or none of our business. It's a funny world we live in, is it not?

Two women I have not mentioned yet came to mind. Two women who got pregnant very soon after I interviewed them years ago. I was curious, so I replied to the pregnancy announcements they had sent me and asked if they would be willing to share what had made them change their minds.

The first reply (from a Spanish filmmaker) came via email:

I had never spoken for so long about forgoing motherhood with anyone before. Three to four hours of being asked questions about my personal life, career, hobbies, plans, goals and fears was a completely new experience. Hearing myself saying all those things out loud, some of which I had only thought to myself, if at all, was quite surprising. I realised I was not as comfortable with the idea of not becoming a mother as I had thought, so I decided to let fate decide. You know, whatever will be, will be. And I got pregnant right after.

The second reply (from a Danish interior designer) was sent via an audio note on WhatsApp:

For me, it was the part where I had to think about my future. You asked me what I wanted those last years of my life to look like. And however I looked at it, with a husband or not, in my own house or a retirement home, I saw a kid in my path. I couldn't understand why, as I could not see the kid whenever I thought about my present. That got me thinking, and I asked myself: Does that mean that, if the circumstances were right, I would want to experience motherhood? And what would these circumstances be? I went home and spoke to my husband about my feelings, his feelings, and those ideal circumstances, and then we put a plan together.

One woman let things happen; the other came up with a plan. Both became mothers. For the hundredth time, I wondered what it was like to want to become a mother. Whatever it was, I couldn't find it in me.

Even when doctors hinted at my fertility being at risk, wanting a child still felt like trying to grow a third arm.

A Severed Head

A ninety-minute biopic about Iris Murdoch that covered her student days in Oxford through her forty-year relationship with her husband and her battle with Alzheimer's made me decide that I needed more Iris in my life. Regrettably, her books were hard to find in Sweden in 2009.

When I moved to her home country five years later, I was sure I'd find her in every bookshop and that there would be a statue of her somewhere in Dublin. James Joyce has one, so does Patrick Kavanagh, and Oscar Wilde has two! But no Iris in sight. *The Sea, the Sea,* was all I could find.

One day, I took a wrong turn from where I needed to go near Grafton Street and came across a rare bookshop. I went inside.

'Do you have anything by Iris Murdoch?'

'Iris. Yes. Only one, though. But it's an early edition.'

'Really?'

'Yeah. It's *A Severed Head*. Let me get it for you.'

My heart skipped several beats while I waited.

'Here it is. And it's signed!'

I don't remember how much the book was. But I remember my first reaction being wide eyes darting at the woman's face.

I meandered around the shop with my treasure. I fondled the pages with care, saw her handwriting, and realised what was on offer was not the printing and the binding of old paper but the feeling of being closer to Iris Murdoch.

She was a brilliant novelist, and I enjoyed reading her fiction, but her most significant influence on me was through philosophy. Iris was the first female philosopher I could relate to. At university, I studied the discipline for a year, but Aristotle, Descartes, Kant and Sartre were the ones taught. Women were rare in my curriculum across the board.

Iris's contribution to philosophy includes a moral theory that stems from the idea of being attentive. Attention to reality would lead to increased knowledge of reality, which would allow the individual to see clearly. With clarity of vision, one would not be distracted by prejudices and biases and would be able to act simply in accord with reality instead of choosing more or less blindly.

Through Iris, I got to Simone Weil, from whom Iris borrowed the concept of 'attention'. To Weil, attention includes discerning what someone is going through in their suffering, and the fact that one is equally a subject of affliction.[24]

One led to another until I learned of the existence of other fascinating women moved by an undying wish to better understand and improve the world around them. They are Hannah Arendt, Simone de Beauvoir, bell hooks and Angela Davis. None of whom had children. Their bodies of work explore different viewpoints and span a range of themes encompassing freedom, religion, power, social justice, gender, race, class, sexuality and mass media. From where I stand, their intellectual contributions are a gateway that can expand

and deepen faculties of thought and judgement and spark hope and faith in the nature of mankind. And for all of that, which is an awful lot, I feel indebted to each of them.

Covid also shook our sense of normality at work. Most people worked from home, processes changed, new tools were introduced, new policies implemented, the need for flexibility in its many forms had increased, and all of this was understandable. The one thing that seemed to occur so starkly and repeatedly during that period that I had to wonder if they were pranks was the 'as a parent and 'cause kids' phenomenon. Not a week went by without me hearing a variation of it.

As a parent, I'm busier/I'm more tired/I'm more overwhelmed/I'm struggling more.

Okay ... Nobody asked about my circumstances, but they seemed pretty sure. Maybe I was working with clairvoyants and just didn't know. The comparing-and-assuming-without-asking game was not my thing, so I didn't play it, and I'd usually let these statements slip to avoid office drama. Then I'd say something along the lines of 'I hear you, I'm sorry it's been so tough,' and if the person was not a complete jackass, I'd ask if there was anything I could do to help. And I'd mean it. I did not mind helping. We were a team, and those were my colleagues. So, I'd do my best to support them or our operational routine by going beyond my responsibilities *if* I wanted to or could.

The issue about yet another assumption about my life based solely on my not having children was the expectation that I would *always* be able to pick up the slack where others (who had children) had left off. Sometimes, this would be expressed passive-aggressively: 'I won't be able to lead the meeting/complete the task/finish the project/attend the event because I have to (something, something) my kid.'

'Okay, no problem,' I'd say. But then . . .

'Maybe Nicole can do it?' they'd say, without warning, in front of other colleagues. That was not a question to me. That was a trap. Because if I dared to say no to a struggling parent, then I'd be the bad guy. Girl. Woman. Even though that parent did not bother to ask if I was readily available or in a situation that, while not equal to theirs, could also mean extra responsibilities (such as caring for a partner, a relative, or a friend; advancing my education by taking courses, or doing volunteer work in my community) or more distress in that moment (due to the loss of a loved one or dealing with a chronic illness or something else). Although the scenarios could go well beyond these, none seemed to cross anyone's mind. The one without children was always seen as the idle one who stayed at home in their pyjamas and had brunch all day, every day.

Other times, this myopic phenomenon would be kept active not by my colleagues but by the powers that be. My manager would let me know, usually at the very last minute, that I'd have to work late to cover for someone or be on call on Christmas Day because nobody else could.

'Nobody else can?' I'd ask.

'Well, people have kids, so they spend the holiday season with their family.'

People have kids, and they spend their holidays with *family*. Hold on a minute. Wasn't I a *person*? And didn't I come from a *family?* And, even if each of my relatives had been lined up and thrown off the Cliffs of Moher for some reason I can't think of, wouldn't it still be my right to spend my holiday season however I wanted if I had done all my work and still had days off to take that year? Yes. Yes, indeed! Okay, so what was going on?

I tried to point out some of the faults of the 'family' argument while also suggesting solutions: 'If an on-call operation for the translation team is needed (I mean, we are not doctors), could we maybe discuss a rotation for that week: a different person each day? Or, if that is not an option, could I cover this year and then someone else cover next year? Surely there were other ways to think about it?' My manager wasn't thrilled, but we settled for me covering for the team on the last week of the year with the prospect (not the promise) that someone else would do it afterwards. The other caveat was that it became my responsibility to organise the on-call plan next year. Did that make sense? No. *But these are desperate times. Try to be diplomatic*, I thought, giving in.

The last straw was when, in between lockdowns, my manager's manager started pushing for a summit. Like many colleagues, I had not seen my family for over a year, but now we'd have to rush to the US for a stupid summit to spend a week brainstorming and presenting slides to each other – all things we could do and had been doing online. Nobody was thrilled about it, but it wasn't optional. In my one-on-one with him, he suggested I go for two weeks. I told him the email said the summit would last a week. Why would I go for two? He said meeting more people in the broader team would be good for me. How about the others? I asked. The others couldn't "cause kids', but he'd ask someone else (and named a colleague who didn't have children) to go for two weeks too.

I could hear the shards of my polite mask hitting the floor.

I told him I'd not go to the US for two weeks and explained that I had a life outside of work – parents, a sibling, a partner, friends, a book I was writing in the evenings, hobbies that kept me sane, physiotherapy I had to do every week, and the need to rest on weekends as I had become chronically ill earlier that year, hence my many medical appointments lately. He told me I had to be careful not to develop a reputation for being hard to work with. I told him that sounded like a threat to me and that I'd report him to HR if he brought it up again.

He looked shocked. But that didn't stop me. This time, I continued: having no kids didn't mean having no rights. I (and I suspected my other colleagues without children) didn't want equality but equity in the working place, which allocates the same resources and opportunities to everyone, regardless of their circumstances.[25] I wanted to be treated fairly, impartially, beyond my parenthood status. I didn't want parents to lose rights or to make their lives harder in any way; I wanted some of those rights to also apply to me. I didn't need maternity leave, legal support adopting a baby or financial support for IVF, but I didn't want to be expected to have to work extra hours by default; I wanted flexibility in my working hours if I had a reasonable need for it, I wanted to be able to book time off when I needed it and not always after parents had sorted their calendar around school holidays, and I wanted my reasons for being absent from work to be deemed as critical as child-related ones. There, the whole speech.

He said he better understood where I was coming from

now and that he'd keep it in mind. I thanked him, thinking we had made progress. In my following performance review, he volunteered an unsolicited assessment of me, stating that I 'had been disrespectful to my work colleagues'. The guidelines of the performance review process clearly instructed that any feedback (be it positive or negative) should contain clear examples of when and how it happened, as well as its impact and who was involved. He didn't bother writing any of that. I asked my manager if he knew what it was about. He said he didn't. The other five colleagues who assessed me for previous months didn't seem to be among the ones I had disrespected, as they mentioned no such thing in their reports. As HR had not contacted me with a complaint, it wasn't hard to see what was going on. That's what retaliation looked like in the workplace.

But the phenomenon happened outside of work too. When people preface their sympathies to tragedy with 'as a mother' or 'as a father', they may think they are enhancing their feelings, but what they are doing is reinforcing the belief that there is less compassion in those who are not parents, which is not true. Becoming a parent is no guarantee of becoming a paragon of humanity. If it were, there would not be as many orphans or so many cases of child abuse and neglect by parents. So affirmations starting with 'as a parent' are nothing but biased generalisations that perpetuate prejudices against people without children. This is also the type of discourse that leads clueless pronatalist demographers to suggest that childless couples should pay more tax[26] and megalomaniac entrepreneurs to support the idea of eliminating voting rights for people without children based on the lunatic notion that those who don't have children don't have a say in the future of humanity.[27]

Whichever way I look at these occurrences, they seem like attempted punishment to me. The right to decide not to have a child (for philosophical, professional or environmental reasons, or simply as a lifestyle choice) is not respected. The many reasons why a person may not have a child even if they wish to are not considered (infertility, physical or mental illness, financial difficulties, difficulty in finding a partner, having had a partner die, being a caretaker for others etc.). Other common scenarios are discarded, such as someone having had a child but losing them or still deciding whether or not to have one. Are all of these people supposed to lose their right to vote for those who would govern them and pay more taxes for not being parents?

Sayaka Murata, a Japanese writer whose heroines find themselves in asexual relationships, uses her works of fiction as a platform to question the standards society expects from citizens and explore her character's fears of being expelled from the village for non-conformity and failure to be a 'normal cog in society'. Her first two books translated into English, *Convenience Store Woman* and *Earthlings*, were just what I needed to start speaking up at work.

Body Maps

In the maternity hospital for another gynaecological appointment, I crouched over a toilet seat and tried to stop the pee droplets from wetting the elastic-waist beige trousers I had purchased the week before to accommodate my increasingly inflated midriff. As I tucked my blouse in, I gazed at the poster on the cubicle door, where three pregnant women smiled at a fourth woman who was dressed like a doctor. Squiggly pink letters advertised breastfeeding workshops.

Another poster, above the hand dryer, gave baby feeding cues, illustrated by photos of the same baby with facial expressions that escalated from 1 (stirring) to 9 (colour turning red). Mothers were advised to calm the crying baby by cuddling, placing them skin-to-skin on their chest, talking or stroking. At the bottom, a smiling woman in a blue gown held her soothed baby close to her chest.

It had been three months since my hospital stay, and over the course of several follow-up medical appointments, I had become familiar with the visual and textual language of the educational posters in women's health clinics that never addressed women who didn't have a baby.

Back in the reception area, I ignored the parents' leaflets

piled on the side table and took a book from my backpack. Before I could finish reading a paragraph, a feathery voice from across the waiting room asked, 'How far along are you?' Struck by how certain she was that I was pregnant, I said, almost giggling, 'I'm not sure.' 'Oh, you'll know soon,' she said, tracking the curve of her pronounced baby bump with both hands.

How far along was I in knowing what ailed me? I meant it when I said I wasn't sure. In all the recent appointments, words like 'polyp', 'cyst', 'endometriosis' and 'perimenopause' had been thrown around when test results showed nothing conclusive, only to be forgotten the minute they asked if I was planning to have children, and my answer was 'no'. That's when they would move to bomb-dropping fertility rates in my age group in a way that never felt like an educational tool but as a coercive measure. When I showed no signs of bending to the pressure to 'decide soon if I wished to get pregnant', they'd lose interest in me.

Where to start with them? By saying that anything that made a woman swell, ache and surrender to the floor should be taken seriously and treated regardless of whether the issue at hand could cause infertility or the woman in question didn't wish to become a mother? The answer was yes, but I felt so out of my depth having to scold doctors in my second language when I could barely find the words to speak or the energy to keep my eyes open that I said nothing.

A door opened, and I heard Dr Maeve call my name.

That summer, I expanded the search for answers by visiting a rheumatologist and a nutritionist to investigate the symptoms observed beyond the borders of my reproductive system. The guessing game continued. *Inflammatory arthritis, irritable bowel syndrome, chronic fatigue, fibromyalgia* ... The consultants took turns poking my flesh, digging into my womb, limbs, throat, intestines and anus, and furrowing their brows as they read each other's reports on me until there was nothing left to blame but stress. Stress. They could all agree on that.

'Have you been stressed lately, Nicole?'

What was the correct answer to that? Haven't we all been stressed lately? Is that what we would name the metamorphosis I was going through? Was I to keep my mouth shut, surrender to my aches and adapt to this faulty version of myself? It's not like I didn't try. Following medical advice, I stopped eating gluten, dairy, yeast, flour, red meat, garlic, onions and peas; I'd started taking cold showers and walking five thousand steps a day; my diet had become taste-free, and I had kept a diary to help 'identify my triggers'; I had taken vitamins, supplements, anti-inflammatories, antibiotics and steroids; and I had changed my wardrobe to feel more comfortable trapped inside this new body. But nothing had changed, and nothing was clear.

I was tired. And so were they. I was angry. And so were they. I could see it in the ever-changing colours of eyes above masks. I could see that they – the doctors – felt the same. And that, in the context of being in the middle of a pandemic, whatever it was that I was suffering from was not deemed deadly enough to take another ounce of their energy, especially if I did not plan to pay my dues by bringing another child into this apocalyptic world.

That last appointment with Dr Maeve ended with her giving me one of those 'Oh, well. I guess that's all for now' looks and handing me new prescriptions for all the medication I had to take. 'Rest, Nicole. Rest,' she said as she led me to the door.

My legs tingled when I got outside the clinic. The bus stop was quite far, so I sat in the front garden on a bench in the middle of a circular path marked by trees. I stretched my legs up and down, hoping to relieve the numbness. New patients came and went as that morning in July turned windy. I pulled a denim jacket from my backpack and covered my chest.

On this side of the world, when my teeth clattered, my spine shivered, and the sound escaping from my mouth was BRRRR ... was it me feeling cold or calling home? At some point, slumped on that bench, I wondered if the lodged pain, the retained liquid, the dampness in me, was my body saying: go back. Go back to the place where you took your first breath. Where the sun always shines and the rain is not polite. Go back to the landscape that formed you. To the geology of your bones. The meteorology you can predict. The language you can speak without thinking. Go back to your people. The answer is there.

Daydreaming of Brazil, I watched weak shafts of light attempt to warm me as the cherry blossom petals fell exactly where my body ached. That's when I knew I had to cross the Atlantic again.

These Precious Days

The kid in seat 22C kicked my seat as I tried to read *These Precious Days* by Ann Patchett. Covering my ears with noise-cancelling headphones and leaning over the food tray on the seat before me, I scanned the table of contents. One of the essays was called 'There Are No Children Here'. I started there.

My visit to Brazil had four phases. The first I spent with Dad, his third wife, Isabel, and Grandma in São Paulo. After Grandpa died, Grandma's health gradually declined until she started falling in her house, and each fall brought a fracture that made it harder for her to recover. One day, seven years after burying her husband, she called my father and said, I'm ready to sell this house and move to one of those places where old people die.

I remember Dad calling me and confessing a mixture of relief and guilt as he had just paid for a month's trial period so she could see what it was like to live in a retirement home before getting rid of all she had built in eighty-five years of life. He wished he could care for her, but he and Isabel worked all day. Grandma being alone in their place was no better than being alone in her house. So Dad looked for the best retirement homes in town, found one that offered food, shelter, art and music classes, and added her to a waiting list. Six months later, she entered the home with one suitcase. Then the pandemic started and she was stuck there. When I arrived, one and a half years had passed since she had last seen her house and personal belongings.

Fortunately, during my visit, the harshest restrictions in her home had been lifted. She still wasn't allowed to leave, but she could receive visits and now we could bring her items from the outside. I called her in the morning to say I was in São Paulo, wished to see her and asked if she wanted anything from her house. She asked me to bring the photo albums. Relatives were not allowed inside, so I sat on a string chair by the gate, on the pavement, and she sat in a wheelchair inside. We both had masks and gloves on. Between the gate bars, she held my hand. I wanted to hug her the way we had always hugged when I lived at her house, tight embraces that lasted longer than the hugs we gave anyone else. But we couldn't. Every time I visited her, we picked a different photo album to look at. With my legs crossed on the chair parallel to the gate, I flipped the pages, holding the album up so she could see herself, her husband, children and grandchildren frozen in time.

On my last visit, I gave a package to the nurse so she could pass it over to Grandma. She unwrapped it carefully, saying what she always said when she got a present, that we shouldn't have spent money on her. Then she read aloud the words on the journal's cover: 'Grandma, tell me your story'. She may have only studied to the fifth grade, but she loved writing letters and was brilliant at expressing her feelings with metaphors and astounding detail. When I saw that journal in a gift shop, I thought it was the perfect way to keep her mind active while learning new things about her. She was ecstatic. Reading each of the prompts printed on the pages, she launched into anecdotes about her earlier years. She was going to write it all down, she said. And I couldn't wait to read it.

When I told her I had to go, she said, 'Send my love to *your husband* and give him a child soon, as children are the glue of a relationship.' She couldn't remember that she had said that before, nor that I was no longer married because she had been diagnosed with the early stages of Alzheimer's. And I had forgotten that because I didn't want to think about it. But now that she mixed up her grandchildren's names and forgot about my previous visits, it was impossible not to.

I spent the time I had left in São Paulo with Dad and Isabel, mainly in the evenings, as they couldn't take time off from work. We ate together, watched movies and caught up on the latest in each other's lives. They were happy together, and Dad was pleased about a recent promotion to a supervisory position that granted him financial stability. The only thing that saddened him was talking about Grandma in the care home.

Yara picked me up at Brasília Airport. Davi wasn't there because he had moved with his girlfriend and son to Fortaleza. 'He too wanted to live close to the sea,' Mom said as she pressed my masked face between her hands and kissed my forehead. Tácio was behind her, and I could barely hide my shock at his appearance. His hair had gone completely grey, and he had lost so much weight that I could feel his collarbone as he hugged me.

On the way to their house, they commented between themselves about how I had gained weight, calling me *she* as if I wasn't there. I had gone back to being the invisible kid in the back seat. Parking in front of the house where I had visited them the last time, but now, without the heavily built man holding a gun, Mom showed me to Milena's room upstairs. Milena was no longer living there.

Watching Tácio drag his feet as if lifting them was impossible on his way to the living room, I asked, 'What happened?'

'Covid. Twice,' she said, sitting on the bed I would sleep on for the next few days. And if I thought I was tired, I thought again as I looked at the dark circles around her eyes and tried to get used to a military-style haircut I had never seen her try before. 'Do you like my hair?' she asked, blinking and placing her hand under her chin.

'It looks convenient. I'm sure it helps with the heat,' I said, unable to come up with anything better. She said nothing. 'Did you feel like changing or ...?' I tried again.

'I had no choice. It was falling in patches like I was shedding. The house was covered in hair. So I chopped it. It stopped getting in the way when I had to move Tácio out of bed.'

'My god, Mom. I knew it was bad, but this bad? You never told me.'

'Why would I? The borders were closed, and even if they weren't, I'd never want you to risk getting this virus in a country governed by a maniac who didn't buy the vaccines for his people.'

I reached for her hand.

'Don't worry. The worst is over. We have vaccines and Tácio is getting better,' she said, wiping away a tear. Sliding my body toward her, I held her torso, caressed her head, and told her I was sorry I hadn't been there through all of this. I was sorry. So very sorry. I must have told her a dozen times. This time I extended my visit and stayed twice as long as I'd planned with her.

After twelve days in Brasília spent mostly doing house chores or watching TV crime series with Yara as Tácio rested, I flew to a small town in the state of Minas Gerais, where Gabriela, her husband, Fernando, and their two children, Rafael and Pedro, had moved after they got married. Their countryside home was a dream; every window had a view of the mountains. I was given the Spider-Man room and could sense Rafael wasn't very pleased. He would hide behind Gabi as I tried to talk to him or walk away and talk to Alexa instead.

'Aleeexa, tell me a story.'

'Aleeexa, make the sound of a shark.'

But he would say it while looking at me sideways, so I'd reciprocate by keeping my eyes on him as I helped Gabi make lunch. Having seen behind the curtains of a virtual assistant's show, I knew a few tricks, which I shared by whispering voice commands for easter eggs and some lesser-known fun features. By dinner time, we had played several rounds of *Mad Libs* and *Kids Quiz!* All but Pedro, who spent most of his time contact napping or attached to Gabi's breast.

Coming in for a quick weekend visit to her new home, I had zero expectations that Gabi and I would get to spend any time alone. I knew how busy she was running a child psychology clinic, raising a three-year-old and a ten-month-old, and trying to keep her marriage alive, so when, on Sunday afternoon, only sixteen hours before I was due to get on a bus and continue my pilgrimage elsewhere, she revealed her plans for a little getaway, I was thrilled!

Rafael had allowed me into his toy box, and we were playing with Woody and Buzz Lightyear when Gabi opened the bedroom door and said, 'All right, buddy. Mommy will go out with Aunty Nic for a bit, and you'll stay here with Daddy.' Rafael looked down and crossed his arms. I stood up slowly, expecting a tantrum to start. But Gabi didn't take his bait. 'When you finish playing, please put your toys back into the box.' Rafael didn't respond. Squatting to meet his gaze at eye level, she put her hands on his little legs and said gently but assertively, 'Aunty Nic came from far away to see us, and she spent a lot of time playing with you; now Mommy is going to show her our town. Daddy will stay here, and you can do something together. I'll be back very soon, okay?' He nodded. She kissed him on the cheek as Fernando poked his head through the door, saying, 'You ladies have fun. The boys will be just fine. We can order food later so no one has to cook.' Gabi kissed Fernando and took the car keys from his hand.

The first time we stopped, Gabi said, '*This* is the best bakery in town, so we will get whatever you want here, and then go to our final destination.' A large smile crossed my face as we walked inside, ordered sweets I hadn't eaten in ages and two large hot chocolates, then went back to the car. Going to bakeries has always been our thing. Every time we've met since I left Brasília to live in São Paulo at seven-teen, we had our catch-ups in some bakery. The second time we stopped, she parked her red Peugeot in front of a phar-macy and waved to an older woman behind the counter as we walked down an alleyway that led to a coffee plantation. I glanced at her with a confused expression. 'I'll explain; just keep walking.' After five minutes by foot on uneven terrain, we reached an open field by a large pond. Gabi took out a long beach towel from her floral satchel bag, spread it on the dry mud and lay down. Propping herself up on both elbows and biting on a chocolate truffle, she said, 'So, this is my happy place.'

'It's beautiful.'

'Yeah. And quiet.'

'Very quiet. Do you come here often?'

'Almost every day.'

'Really?'

'Well, almost every day in the past three months or so. Before that, it was impossible.'

'Because of the kids?'

'Because of everything. And because of how I was dealing with everything.' She paused, ate the other half of the truffle, then continued. 'Having to breastfeed and spend the nights awake again almost drove me mad. I wanted more help from Fernando, but whenever he took on anything, I wanted it to be done my way. I started treating him like a third child, dis-trusting his ability to do the smallest thing for me, the house or the kids. Then I'd shout at him for not doing his part. She paused again. 'The whole thing was so fucked up. Until a few weeks ago, I didn't think we'd make it.'

'Jesus, Gabi. How are things now?'

'On the mend. I think this place saved our marriage. And my sanity.'

'I'm sorry. It sounds very tough,' I said, turning towards her. 'We've been Zooming all this time. You didn't think you could talk to me about this?'

'No,' she said, staring into the pond with her small brown eyes.

'I see. Do you know why you didn't think you could talk to me about it?'

She reached for the bag of sweets, picked the coconut one, and placed it next to my hand. 'Still your favourite?' Then she picked another truffle and ate it without answering my question.

'It is. Thanks. Is it because of my book?' I asked.

'The book? No! Why would it be the book?'

'Because it's about not having children?'

'It's not because of the book, honey. But it was because you don't have children, yes.'

'So you don't think I can understand your struggle because I don't have children?'

'I . . . ' she hesitated. 'I know you can understand. But you can't feel it.'

Feeling a punch in my stomach, I locked my arms under my legs, wanting to shrink myself. I wanted to turn into a ball of grass, roll over into the pond and submerge so I'd not hear those words. I also wanted to know how Gabi felt, so I waited a bit.

'It was easier to talk about the hell I was in with someone who had been there too. We can never be sure where other mothers are emotionally in their journey because nobody really talks about it, so it's all a guessing game. But they are mothers, and, even though some of them were strangers, I felt I could only talk to them at the time,' she said.

'Right,' I said as my voice cracked. 'At the time. Did things change?' I asked.

'I changed. After I got pregnant with Pedro, I changed my mind about a second child. Rafael had transformed my world for the better, and although you know I had always wanted two kids, I didn't think I could do it again after surviving those first years. I was content with what I had. But Fernando had gone the other way, from wanting one to two kids. And somewhere in between changing pills and keeping track of Rafael, we got careless and ... bang. When I texted you that I was pregnant again, your reply was "And how are you feeling?" I hadn't told many people yet, but you were the only person who didn't congratulate me, scream excitedly or turn your attention to the baby. You asked about me. You asked how *I* was. And you didn't assume, like everybody else, that I was happy. You let me tell you how I felt. And I did. I remember telling you I was miserable, and you never made me feel bad about that. I was so grateful for that. So much so that we spoke a lot while I was pregnant, but once Pedro was born and my days turned upside down again, I forgot that and gravitated towards the people who could understand the disruption of having a newborn ...'

'That makes sense,' I said, feeling my throat less tight.

'So I realised that there will be times when we all need support from different people. And all of them are important to help us make it through.'

'I longed to talk to women without children when I thought I was going mad too.'

'There you go. And I bet it helped. And, still, here we are again,' she said.

'Indeed. Batman and Robin.'

'By the way, Batman. Only you know I come here,' she said with naughty eyes above her freckles.

'No way!'

'Way.'

'Not even Fernando?'

'Especially Fernando. Now, enough about me. Your turn.'

Drinking the cooled hot chocolate, I told her about my writing setbacks and health relapses. She listened attentively and held my puffy hand. The next morning, Gabi came in and wheeled my suitcase outside Rafael's bedroom. He followed her and asked, 'Will she come back?'

'Why don't you ask her?'

'You can stay in my room again if you come back,' he said timidly.

'I'd love that. Thank you, Rafael.' I asked if I could have a big goodbye hug. He indulged me.

On the way to the bus station, Gabi asked, 'Do you think it's a coincidence that your body aches where it does?'

'Sorry, what?' I asked distractedly, zooming in on an offline map of the town I was going to next.

'Do you think it's a coincidence that your pain is in your right ovary and your right hand?' she rephrased.

'I don't know. What do you think?'

'I don't think it's a coincidence.'

The Sun House

My last stop in Brazil was a place I had wanted to visit for a long time.

Fourteen years separate the day I met Hilda Hilst on the page from the day I rang the bell of her house. The stream of consciousness and fractured reality she used to write about the body, female sexual liberation, passion, mysticism and madness had pulled me strongly to her life and books, and she became one of the authors without children whose works I read the most.

From the gate, I followed the path of imperial palm trees leading to the ample living room. After imagining it for so long, I was finally there – in rapture over how intrinsic to her mind the place felt. Sitting on a black armchair, I sought to take everything in: the style and arrangement of the furniture, the portraits and masks hanging on the terracotta walls, the wooden goblets and mythic figures above the fireplace. I could almost see her. And I could feel her everywhere.

In 1964, Hilda had given up on a career as a lawyer, moved away from a glamorous social life in São Paulo and moved to Campinas, where she supervised the construction of her dream house built on a piece of land belonging to her mother.

Under a fig tree in the garden, she watched the bricks turn into walls until the place was ready to host her genius, friends and dogs. Hilda named the house Casa do Sol (Sun House) and lived there until she was seventy-three, leaving behind volumes of poetry and prose. Today, the house is a retreat for writers, a shelter for dogs and a home for her best friend.

On my first night there, I was buzzing with an anomalous combination of lethargy and creative energy. I strolled around and peeked into several rooms without any rush, as if I were in a museum. I considered writing for a bit but remembered I had deliberately left my computer in Dublin. Instead of going to bed, I lay down on the hammock stretched across one of the ten arcs that formed the courtyard and watched the darkness turn red and then orange until yellow and warmth engulfed me.

Hours later, when cranky pigeons woke me up, I yawned as I made my way to the bedroom where I had left my things earlier. As I turned to close the door, a black dog with inquisitive eyes stood there. I left the door open and went to sleep. When I woke mid-morning, she was on the crocheted rug beside the bed. She would follow me wherever I went for the rest of my stay.

Sharing a pot of fresh coffee in a kitchen with the most windows I had ever seen, I asked my hostess if I could help with anything. She said I could water the plants and pointed at the garden hose outside and the section of the vast land she had planned to water that day. Then she returned to her painting studio, a room across from mine, where she remained until dusk.

When I finished watering the plants, I was breathless. The

heat radiated from the red earth, and sweat dripped down the back of my neck. I tried to tie my hair up, but my fingers would not bend. So I sat on one of the stone seats under the fig tree and examined my roundness – the bloat in my belly covered by a light loose-fitting muslin dress and my sausage fingers trapped in compressed gloves. There was no denying it. My brokenness was visible then and had been for months in the form of a stiff claw, always cupping the lower part of my belly where my ovaries sat.

I thought about Gabi's question. Did I think the places where my body ached were a coincidence? No. It was hard to miss the symbolism in it. But the interpretations could be many. Did I feel I had to choose between writing and having children? No. Many women had brought children and books to life, and several had written about that topic: being a writer and a mother (Alice Walker, Anne Enright, Doris Lessing, Natalia Ginzburg and Rachel Cusk, to name a few).

Did I make myself sick by exploring the 'alien notion' that women could find happiness and purpose outside mother-hood? No. I could not believe such nonsense. What was it then? Why did I feel so heavy and so sick? What weight had I been carrying that had me swollen into a full moon like the pregnant doll I had traded when I was little?

As I sat where Hilda had sat, watching her future taking shape, it dawned on me that I was indeed the sponge my mother had said I was when she read my palm all those years ago. I had internalised the scepticism I had encountered in others about my certainty of a desired life without children. I had not changed my mind, but I had lived consumed by other people's concerns that I would change my mind or regret my choice. Being deemed too young to know what I wanted in my late twenties, I had followed her advice and kept the door open. I knew she meant well when she told me to give it time until I was certain, to let life happen to me. And that served me well for a while. It stopped me from spiralling. It gave me room to breathe and time to redirect my life. The thing was, ten years had passed, and still, there had never been any doubt.

When, about a year into my marriage, I felt that pivotal question, *Do I want to become a mother?* pinch my brain, and the answer was negative, I had the urge to understand why – which I did by looking back at moments that had moulded me into a woman who did not wish to reproduce up to that point. I had also dealt with my difficulty in seeing how I'd live without children if I were to continue making that choice by seeking out women who would not become mothers and listening to their stories. In hindsight, I could see that it wasn't me doubting myself; I wanted to know myself better and find out if a happy life without children was possible. By mistaking curiosity for doubt, I entered a realm of unknowing while knowing. A limbo state in which I trapped myself for too long.

Since then, I had thrown that question like a boomerang into the air a thousand times, and even though each time a resounding 'noooo' returned to me, I had continued to strain myself, never letting go of the question or allowing my mind to rest. This pretence of taking time to think was not something I needed; it was something others insisted upon to make sense of my lack of wanting a child. But that part of me would not change with time. I knew that now at the edge of forty.

That day around noon, sitting under the

two-hundred-year-old tree around which Hilda had built her fortress, I felt a vibration so strong coming from within that I could swear this certainty would kill me if it were to stay inside of me any longer. It was there, in that sacred spot, that I understood I would have to break the dam and let it all spill over. My leaky gut, tumid knees, sausage fingers and watery ovarian cysts would have to flood out of my body and onto the page for me to stop sinking into my consciousness.

Before leaving, I walked around the house looking for Gigi, the black dog that had become my companion since I arrived, and found her sitting next to a mantelpiece resembling an altar. Above it, there was a square clock with gold pointers and something other than numbers was on its face. I moved closer and squinted as I read the shimmering letters:

It's later than you think.

The Nest

When I rang my doorbell in Dublin, I did so with a heightened sense of clarity and urgency.

Ben opened the door and I gave him a long 'I missed you' kiss. The next day was a Sunday, and I woke up with him fussing in bed. Not ready to get up yet, I disappeared under the blanket, trying to shield my eyes from the light from the half-closed curtains. Soon afterwards, I heard Ben entering the ensuite bathroom and the water pouring from the shower. He returned smelling like bamboo-extract shower gel.

'Big spoon or breakfast?' he asked.

'Already with the hard questions?' I uncovered my head slowly.

'I can bring it here.'

'Yes, please?' I said, half-opening my eyes. Half was all I could do, as it felt like I had carried a sandbag from Brazil inside my eye sockets.

'Brekkie on its way,' he said, disappearing into the hallway.

Watching him walk half-wrapped in a towel and wearing koala slippers made me smile. I reached for my phone and noticed the navy blue leather-bound notebook I had given him when he moved to London on his bedside table. The bookmark ribbon was two-thirds into the pages. I grabbed it and read it from the start.

I don't know how long it took for him to return, but I had lost track of time remembering our story through the poems I had continued writing in that same notebook over the years. I thought about how passionate and fun our time together was and how the apartment we called home was the only place I had never wished to leave.

For as long as I could remember, I had left places. My mother's many houses and my grandmother's house in Brazil, the home I had built with Erik in Sweden, the apartment I had shared with Erik in Ireland, and the apartment I had shared with Ben in England. But the apartment I had bought with Ben was different. And that was because I could see my future self there. That was my place. My nest. And Ben was my person.

'Orange juice and scrambled eggs, madam,' he said in his standard cheerful morning mood. 'Thank you,' I said, gulping the juice and placing the tray on the bedside table as he watched me with a puzzled face.

'Listen, I've been thinking . . . and we should get married.'

He stared at me, unsure he had heard the words right.

'Wait. Huh? Nic, are you proposing to me?'

'Yes,' I said with a twinge in the pit of my stomach.

He took another second to read my expression.

'Let's do it!' he said, beaming.

'Yeah?'

'Yes! Let's get married!'

'Okay. Let's get married!' I said, clapping, then stopping because it was ridiculous. We burst into laughter.

'Should I get you a ring or something?' he asked.

'No. I don't want a ring.'

'Are you sure?'

'Positive.'

'That's easy enough.'

'I suppose it is. By the way, I hope it's not too late, but—'

'Already trying to get away, are you?'

'No, silly. Just letting you know I made up my mind about the kid.'

'Oh?'

'I'm not going to have a child. That's it. I've decided,' I said.

'That's good because I've been considering getting a vasectomy.' A vasectomy? I had not seen that coming! He continued, 'I don't want kids either, so I'd rather just get this over with.'

'Are you sure?'

'Yep. We get married, I get snipped, and we are all set.'

'Sounds good to me!'

'You know what, Nic?' he said, climbing over me.

'Tell me.'

'You and I are going to grow old together.'

Copper leaves gathered on our balcony as the October temperature dropped and the air dampened. The mosquito bites reminding me I had been to Brazil were gone, but the precious days spent with family and friends lingered and lifted me. I could wash my hair thoroughly and tie my shoelaces again, and I wanted to hold on to that positive feeling. Having seen Grandma's and Tácios's mental and physical health decline so abruptly, I felt I too was running out of time and had wasted enough days and energy.

I thought about Ann Patchett's essay and how she had designed her whole life so that she could do this one thing, which was to write; about an interview in which Amy Tan declared that what's in her that she wanted to pass on was already in her books; about Hilda Hilst, who had given up on a comfortable career as a lawyer to become a full-time writer; and about Molly's memoir, in which despite domestic and financial troubles, she describes allowing no deviation from her master plan to become a poet. All of them had placed writing, not babies, at the centre of their lives. And that would become my centre too.

Later that year, I handed in my notice at work. Again. No more snoozing. No more safety nets.

2022

Mother Tongue

If the previous January had sent me to hospital, this January sent me into a continual state of scribbling – I could write longhand or type for a couple of hours without feeling pain. I was sleeping whole nights and going for longer walks in the park, and I had stopped taking medications.

In that year of rumination bought with my savings, I would do three things: write, keep a vow of frugality and pray for no family emergencies. After that, I'd go back to freelancing as a translator. But not yet. Besides writing, there was a wedding waiting to happen.

In the first week of February, Ben and I invited twenty-two people, hoping they would join us the following year to celebrate our union. It would be a simple do: a short ceremony late in the morning and lunch on a vintage bus that would take us to the Wicklow Mountains – where we had fallen in love. We hoped to book the registry office, accommodation, transportation and buffet early to secure decent prices and forget about it all for the rest of the year.

By late March, everybody but Mom had confirmed they were coming. I was growing increasingly anxious, so I texted her again. 'Is everything okay? Did Tácio get worse?' She had replied to my previous messages, but her answers would fluctuate between 'We're coming, fifi' and 'He's having a bad week, I'm not sure we'll be able to make it'. And I'd reply, 'Okay. I hope he gets better soon. Let's wait a bit longer, then.'

When April came, Molly and I agreed on dates for me to send her new chapters and to have feedback calls during the rest of the spring and summer months. So I started outlining the last third of the book, but I noticed I was doing so in the living room, dining room, and even on the chilly balcony. Everywhere but in the room I had set for myself to write. What was that about? I went out for my daily walk and came back home with the conclusion that it was – surprise, surprise – about my mother. Not knowing if she would attend my wedding kept nagging at me and pulling me out of the dimension I was trying to enter.

My May messages had a bridezilla tone. 'It's just that I have to buy your plane tickets and book the hotel rooms, so please tell me by ...' I knew Tácio was getting better. He had had some setbacks but was also planning on returning to politics by discussing a new candidacy on his social media, so I thought he couldn't be that sick anymore.

'Did you think about the dress yet?' she replied, deflecting my question.

'Yes. I have it already.'

'You do?!'

'Yes. It's not new. I saw it in a vintage clothing shop a while ago and bought it.'

'What colour is it?'

'Creamy, off-white, ivory? Not sure what to call it. But it's not very bridal.'

'Please tell me it's not beige. You have to stop wearing beige; you already are beige!' she said jokingly, but I knew she meant it.

'There's nothing wrong with beige, Mom,' I said, swallowing my pride.

'Are you going to add some other colours? In the accessories, maybe?'

'Uh-huh.'

'Which colour?'

'I'm thinking of blue shoes and a wool belted coat I already have. Also blue.'

'Beautiful! And some brighter lipstick? You should wear bright lipstick with your complexion.'

'I haven't thought about the lipstick I'll wear yet. Have you decided if you're coming?'

'Unless Tácio gets worse, we will be there in March.'

'March? The wedding is in February, Mom!'

March, although I had sent the invite by mail, by email and discussed dates for her to arrive. *We*, always *we*, meaning *her* and *him*. And *her* opinions coming at me like darts – that hurt. Never like arrows that pointed toward things I was supposed to see. Something snapped in me like that night I woke up in pain. Except that this time, the pain was elsewhere. My heart beat fast as I typed a reply, zigzagging in the kitchen. Then I deleted what I had typed, sat on one of the dining-room chairs and recorded an audio message. I wanted her to listen to me.

In the message, I told her she had to stop. She had to stop pretending she and Tácio were an entity. She had to stop giving her opinion about my weight, hair, wedding dress, lipstick, sense of humour and decision to live abroad. She was my mother, and I loved her, but she had to stop. I wanted to share things about my life with her, but I often didn't because I had to dodge her opinions about everything about me. I had thoughts about her too, which I had managed to keep to myself. Maybe she could do the same? How long did she think we had? I was almost forty, she was nearly sixty, and we had seen each other less than once a year for the past fourteen years. Our time was running out! We were running out of milestones. On my side, there would be no giving birth or breastfeeding, no first steps or first days at school for us to talk about. There would be a wedding. That was that. That was the day I wanted to share with her. I *wanted* her to be there holding my hand, helping me zip up the beige dress regardless of what she thought of it. I had made that clear for months now. But, if she was not coming, all I was asking was for her not to do what she had done before, when I got a divorce and explicitly told her I needed her to be by my side, and she didn't tell me until the last minute she was not coming. All I was asking was for her to tell me if she was not going to attend my wedding so that I could process it in advance, let go of it, and enjoy that special day without the shock of her absence ruining everything.

My hands trembled as I sent the message, but my voice was firm. The words came out of my mouth and I sent it. For the first time in thirty-nine years, I had told her how I felt. And if what I had said was too much for her, then she could walk away. But I was tired of making myself smaller than her, adapting to her, muting myself to her or running away so as not to hurt her.

I turned my phone off for the rest of the day.

The next morning, I dreaded the thought of touching my phone, and it wasn't easy to stop thinking about it, but I forced myself to do so. I had breakfast around 9 a.m. and headed to the Rose Garden, where I was building the habit of reading the pages I had written the day before. I turned my phone on again after I read the pages and made notes on their margins. And when I did, I found a voice note from Mom sent two hours after I had sent her mine. I pressed *Play*. Her tone was comforting like when she read my palm in Sweden.

'My daughter, I'm sorry I made you feel this way. I wish I had been a better mother to you. But my life was very tough, and I had to be as tough to make it here. This is no excuse; it's just the truth. You might not believe this, but I always knew I'd have you and I wanted you. I've always wanted a daughter. Still, when you came along, I was not ready. I was a kid. I knew nothing, nothing at all. I only knew that I'd do anything to protect you from going through what I did. I know I was hard on you, Nicole. Too hard, too often. I know. I was scared to fail you and not give you enough opportunities. I knew no other way to raise someone. Nobody teaches us these things. I'm sorry. I am. But you are the light in my life. I love you. I love you so much. I just don't know how to say it. And when I try to say it, it always seems to come out the wrong way.' She paused, and I heard a muffled sob for a few seconds. Then she took a deep breath and continued: 'I will be there for your wedding in February. No matter what happens here. I will be there with or without Tácio, I promise. You can buy the tickets.'

My whole body shook on that park bench as I listened to her message on repeat. I must have spent another hour there, just sitting with the feeling of having been capsized by a wave I had not seen coming. When my breathing stabilised and my eyes dried, I walked the two kilometres back. And what I brought home that day was this peace. A peace so strong, like nothing I had felt before.

Forest of Mirrors

On the summer solstice of 2022, I returned to my writing room. This time for good.

From the desk in the corner that turns gold later in the day, I glanced at the family photos on the cork memo board, the portraits of my muses on the wall, the books on the shelves and the transcripts on my desk. I had reached the point of longest light and shortest darkness in my life.

There was no trace of doubt, loneliness or sadness left. And that's because, one way or another, they were all present: the women who whispered wisdom as the motherhood question hammered in my head. The women who took me by the hand and guided me along the pitch-dark path. The women who shone flashlights at my feet. The women who watched over me as I sat there, inside my temple, for another season.

And when I finished typing the last page of this book, I heard myself say:

It's the uterus that is empty.
Not you.
Not your life.

Resources

A list of sources of information about having no children by choice or circumstance, as well as literary works by or featuring women without children as protagonists. Within each category, the resources are listed in order of importance to my work:

Books

Paradise, Piece by Piece by Molly Peacock

Motherhood by Sheila Heti

The Baby Matrix: Why Freeing Our Minds From Outmoded Thinking About Parenthood & Reproduction Will Create a Better World by Laura Carroll

Families of Two: Interviews with Happily Married Couples Without Children by Choice by Laura Carroll

Beyond Motherhood: Choosing a Life Without Children by Jeanne Safer

Childfree by Choice: The Movement Redefining Family and Creating a New Age of Independence by Amy Blackstone

Childfree Across the Disciplines: Academic and Activist Perspectives on Not Choosing Children edited by Davinia Thornley

Bearing Life: Women's Writings on Childlessness edited by Rochelle Ratner

Reconceiving Women: Separating Motherhood from Female Identity by Mardy S. Ireland

Living the Life Unexpected: How to Find Hope, Meaning and a Fulfilling Future without Children by Jody Day

Decline and Prosper!: Changing Global Birth Rates and the Advantages of Fewer Children by Vegard Skirbekk

Hannah Arendt: For Love of the World by Elisabeth Young-Bruehl

The Sovereignty of Good by Iris Murdoch

The Female Eunuch by Germaine Greer

Harpy: A Manifesto for Childfree Women by Caroline Magennis

The Mother of All Questions by Rebecca Solnit

Seven Steeples by Sara Baume

A House of My Own: Stories from My Life by Sandra Cisneros

Convenience Store Woman by Sayaka Murata

Girl, Woman, Other by Bernardine Evaristo

These Precious Days by Ann Patchett

Upstream by Mary Oliver

The Carrying by Ada Limón

Notes to Self: Essays by Emilie Pine

Olive by Emma Gannon

Instead: Navigating the Adventures of a Childfree Life by Maria Coffey

The Facts of Life by Paula Knight

The NoMo Book Club: instagram.com/thenomobookclub/

Podcasts and radio shows

New Legacy Radio on Voice America: https://newlegacyinstitute.com/about-new-legacy-radio/

Population Balance: https://www.populationbalance.org/podcast

Are Kids for Me?: https://www.arekidsforme.ie/podcast

We're Not Kidding: https://podcasters.spotify.com/pod/show/anna-marie-olson

The Stories of Childfree African American Women: https:// podcasters.spotify.com/pod/show/nobibsburpsbottles/
The End of the Line: https://www.theendoftheline.co.uk/
Other than Motherhood: https://podcasts.apple.com/ae/ podcast/other-than-motherhood/id1698137209
Childless, a radio documentary: https://soundcloud.com/ hilfen/sets/childless
Kids or Childfree: https://www.kidsorchildfree.com/podcast

Documentaries

My So-Called Selfish Life by Therese Shechter: https:// myselfishlife.com/
To Kid or Not to Kid by Maxine Trump: https://www. tokidornottokid.com/

Events

Storyhouse Childless Chester: https://www.storyhouse.com/ seasons/storyhouse-childless/
Childfree Virtual Convention: https://www.instagram.com/ childfreeconvention/
World Childless Week: https://worldchildlessweek.net/
Childless Collective Summit: https://childlesscollective.com/

Communities

Childfree on Reddit: https://www.reddit.com/r/childfree/
We are Childfree: https://wearechildfree.com/
Gateway Elderwomen: https://gateway-women.com/ gateway-elderwomen/

Organisations

New Legacy Institute: https://newlegacyinstitute.com/
Ageing Without Children (AWOC): https://www.awwoc.org/
Childfree History Museum: https://childfreehistory.com/

Notes

1. UN World Population Prospects (2022), https://www.un.org/development/desa/pd/sites/www.un.org.development.desa.pd/files/wpp2022_summary_of_results.pdf
2. The Global Economy, Fertility Rate Country Rankings (2021), https://www.theglobaleconomy.com/rankings/Fertility_rate/
3. Office for National Statistics, Childbearing for women born in England and Wales (2020), https://www.ons.gov.uk/peoplepopulationandcommunity/birthsdeathsandmarriages/conceptionandfertilityrates/bulletins/childbearingforwomenbornindifferentyearsenglandandwales/2020
4. Vegard Skirbekk, *Decline and Prosper* (Palgrave Macmillan, 2022)
5. Ibid.
6. Tomáš Sobotka, 'World's Highest Childlessness Levels in East Asia', 2021, https://www.ined.fr/en/publications/editions/population-and-societies/world-s-highest-childlessness-levels-in-east-asia/#:~:text=In%20Japan%2C%20Hong%20Kong%2C%20and,married%20women%20remaining%20without%20children
7. Anna Brown, 'Growing share of childless adults in U.S. don't expect to ever have children', Pew Research Center, 2021, https://www.pewresearch.org/short-reads/2021/11/19/growing-share-of-childless-adults-in-u-s-dont-expect-to-ever-have-children/
8. New Legacy Institute: Social Justice Advocacy for People Without Children, https://newlegacyinstitute.com/
9. In the process of sharing their story with me, some women realised they weren't yet ready to share it with the world. Other stories didn't make the cut simply for lack of space. And so, although this book features the stories of fourteen women, at least a dozen more are present in the form of insights and anecdotes told throughout the book.
10. Jamie Grierson, 'Two hundred UK women can take legal action over Essure contraceptive device', Guardian, 5 September 2023, https://www.theguardian.com/society/2023/sep/05/two-hundred-uk-women-legal-action-essure-contraceptive-device.

11. Rhodesia is the former name of a large territory in central-southern Africa, divided into Northern Rhodesia (now Zambia) and Southern Rhodesia (now Zimbabwe). As Candice was born when the region was still called Rhodesia, she refers to her nationality as Rhodesian.

12. The Festival of Choice (2014–2017) aimed to raise awareness of threats to reproductive rights and the plight of those in countries around the world who do not have access to safe and legal abortion.

13. Laura Carroll, *The Baby Matrix* (2012), p. 11.

14. Doreen Akiyo Yamoah, 'Being childfree is not an "interesting debate"', Doreen Akiyo Yamoah, 17 September 2014, https://doreenakiyomoah.com/2014/09/17/being-childfree-is-not-an-interesting-debate/

15. Nalina Eggert, 'Female politicians and babies: a lose-lose situation?' BBC News, 2 August 2017, https://www.bbc.com/news/world-40800687

16. Rachel Thompson, 'People think this infographic about "childless" female politicians is sexist', Mashable, 5 September 2016, https://mashable.com/article/sunday-times-sturgeon-sexism

17. Libby Brooks, '*Sunday Times* criticised for portrayal of female politicians without children', *Guardian*, 4 September 2016, https://www.theguardian.com/politics/2016/sep/04/sunday-times-criticised-portrayal-of-female-politicians-without-children-nicola-sturgeon

18. *The Baby Matrix*, p. 41.

19. Afua Hirsch, 'Why should Theresa May have to answer questions about her childlessness?' *Guardian*, 12 May 2017, https://www.theguardian.com/commentisfree/2017/may/12/theresa-may-children-politics-women-gender

20. Patrick Martin, 'Don't have kids? Neither do some of the world's most powerful leaders', *Washington Post*, 25 May 2017, https://www.washingtonpost.com/news/worldviews/wp/2017/05/25/dont-have-kids-neither-do-some-of-the-worlds-most-powerful-leaders/

21. M. Pulimeno, P. Piscitelli and S. Colazzo, 'Children's literature to promote students' global development and wellbeing', *Health Promot Perspect*, 2020 Jan 28;10(1):13–23, https://www.ncbi.nlm.nih.gov/pmc/articles/PMC7036210/

22. '*Torschlusspanik*', 17 October 2023, https://www.instagram.com/p/Cyg0AjsMmsy/

23. Kris Snibbe, '"Shadow pandemic" of domestic violence', *Harvard Gazette*, 29 June 2022, https://news.harvard.edu/gazette/story/2022/06/shadow-pandemic-of-domestic-violence/

24. A. Rebecca Rozelle-Stone and Benjamin P. Davis, 'Simone Weil', *The Stanford Encyclopedia of Philosophy* (Summer 2023 Edition), Edward N. Zalta and Uri Nodelman (eds.), https://plato.stanford.edu/archives/sum2023/entries/simone-weil/

25. Dominique Goldschmitt, 'What's It Like Being Childfree at

Work?', SHRM, 8 June 2022, https://www.shrm.org/topics-tools/
news/managing-smart/--whats-like-childfree-work--2022-study-
26. Zoe Williams, 'Tax the childless! Encourage "our own"
to breed! What an asinine, inhumane way to tackle
a population crisis', *Guardian*, 4 July 2018, https://
www.theguardian.com/commentisfree/2022/jul/04/
population-crisis-britain-paul-morland
27. Adam Lashinsky, 'Why do we listen to tech moguls like
Elon Musk?', *Washington Post*, 17 July 2023, https://
www.washingtonpost.com/opinions/2023/07/17/
elon-musk-technology-leaders-influence

Acknowledgements

My deepest gratitude to:

The dozens of women without children who shared their stories with me – thanks for waiting and not losing faith in this book.

Hannah Schofield at LBA Books for opening the door to a dream and being the fiercest agent out there.

Sharmaine Lovegrove for believing in this book's ethos and lifting the manuscript to its best version; Joelle, Eleanor, Millie, Emily, Charlotte, Emma, Elaine and the entire team at Dialogue Books, who make magic happen behind the curtains.

The beta readers who survived the vomit draft: Francisco, Amy, Ali, Renata, Fabiana, Emma, Magnus, Itai, Julia, Rita, Eliso, Irina, Shona and Ricardo.

The musketeers: Adriana, Dea, Jo and Luciane, for a lifetime of friendship.

The local crew: Lisa, Sharon, Silvia and Sarah, for your continuous support in the form of coffee and cake walks and loving messages in our WhatsApp group.

The unofficial editors: Sarah, Holly and Jane, for fixing and forgiving my non-native attempts to make sense on the page and not shouting at me when I send long voice notes.

Lara O'Brien: for helping me sift through hundreds of pages and shape the interviews into nuggets in which the women who told me their stories recognized themselves.

Christine Erickson: for the most encouraging texts, the data research that made it into the introduction and the crucial work you do with the New Legacy Institute.

Molly Peacock: for showing me what the life of a writer without children can look like and mentoring me into it with such grace and generosity. Oh, yeah, and for that cantaloupe soup!

Mieke for celebrating each of my literary milestones with a loving phone call.

My parents, grandparents and step-parents for giving me so much for so long. I love you and owe you everything.

Freek, for being the best thing that has ever happened to me. I wouldn't be as happy outside the writing room if it weren't for you. I would also not be as healthy (thank you for feeding me and reminding me to take breaks). My tachycardic heart is irretrievably yours.

About the Author

Nicole Louie is a writer and translator based in Ireland. A former content strategist and creative writer for virtual assistants, she holds a BA in advertising and postgraduate diplomas in literature and translation. When not writing, she is reading about the lives of women without children. Her essays about not having children have appeared in *Oh Reader* and *Childfree Magazine*, and her curated collections of books, movies and podcasts about women who are not mothers by choice, circumstance or ambivalence can be found on Twitter and Instagram: @bynicolelouie. *Others Like Me: The Lives of Women without Children* is her first book.

Bringing a book from manuscript to what you are reading is a team effort.

Dialogue Books would like to thank everyone who helped to publish *Others Like Me* in the UK.

Editorial
Sharmaine Lovegrove
Joelle Owusu-Sekyere
Eleanor Gaffney

Contracts
Megan Phillips
Bryony Hall
Amy Patrick
Anne Goddard

Sales
Caitriona Row
Dominic Smith
Frances Doyle
Hannah Methuen
Lucy Hine
Toluwalope Ayo-Ajala

Design
Charlotte Stroomer

Production
Narges Nojoumi

Publicity
Millie Seaward

Marketing
Emily Moran

Operations
Kellie Barnfield
Millie Gibson
Sameera Patel
Sanjeev Braich

Finance
Andrew Smith
Ellie Barry

Audio
Binita Naik

Copy-Editor
David Bamford

Proofreader
Saxon Bullock